Don't Panic!
It's Only NetWare

Becky Campbell
Mickey Applebaum

New Riders Publishing, Indianapolis, Indiana

Don't Panic! It's Only NetWare

By Becky Campbell

Published by:
New Riders Publishing
201 West 103rd Street
Indianapolis, IN 46290 USA

Printed in the United States of America 1 2 3 4 5 6 7 8 9 0

Library of Congress Cataloging-in-Publication Data Available Upon Request

Publisher
Lloyd J. Short

Associate Publisher
Tim Huddleston

Acquisitions Manager
Cheri Robinson

Acquisitions Editor
Rob Tidrow

Managing Editor
Matthew Morrill

Marketing Manager
Greg Bushyeager

Product Director
Steve Weiss

Senior Editor
Nancy E. Sixsmith

Production Coordinator
Lisa Wagner

Production Editor
Steve Weiss

Editors
Patrice Hartmann, John Kane,
Rob Lawson, Greg Robertson,
Nancy Sixsmith, Lisa Wilson,
Phil Worthington

Technical Editor
Kelly Sonderegger

Book Design and Production
Lisa Daugherty
Rich Evers
Stephanie McComb
Roger Morgan
Juli Pavey
Angela Pozdol
Alyssa Yesh

Proofreaders
Ayrika Bryant
Mitzi Foster Gianakos
Sean Medlock
Linda Quigley
Ryan Rader
Tonya Simpson
Dennis Wesner

Indexers
John Sleeva
Jennifer Eberhardt

Acquisitions Coordinator
Stacey Beheler

Editorial Assistant
Karen Opal

Publishing Assistant
Melissa Lynch

About the Author

Becky J. Campbell is a reviews editor at LAN Magazine. Becky has worked in computers and technical stuff for the last 11 years, the past 6 of which have been spent designing and implementing Local Area Networks, specializing in NetWare. She has served on the Board of Directors of NetWare Users International (NUI) as Operations Chair. It was under her pushy leadership that the NUI publication, *The NetWare Connection*, began. Becky is also a Systems Operator (SysOp) on CompuServe, in the LAN Magazine forum. She has worked with and trained a number of NetWare Administrators over the years.

Mickey Applebaum has been working with computer systems of one kind or another for over 15 years. He has been specifically working with Novell's NetWare and network design/development for 10 years, starting with Novell's NetWare 4.57 product and moving through all versions of NetWare including the latest releases of NetWare 2.2, 3.12, and 4.01. Mickey has also been a NetWire SysOp for 3.5 years, posting on average over 600 messages per week. Mickey currently works for Uinta Business Systems of Salt Lake City, the largest Novell Platinum reseller in Utah.

Dedication

Becky: This book is dedicated to William J. DeBus, Ph.D., who gave me the opportunity.

Mickey: This book is dedicated to Linda R. Schlomann. Without your belief in me, and your continuous support, I would never have believed I could do this computer stuff. I still love you.

Acknowledgments

Both: Becky and Mickey would like to acknowledge:

Steve Weiss, at New Riders Publishing, for his extraordinary hard work and heroic efforts to make this book happen.

Cheri Robinson, Tim Huddleston, Lloyd J. Short and the other really fine folks at New Riders Publishing, all of whom provided their expertise and help on this project.

Kelly Sonderegger, for his technical expertise (straight from Novell) as technical editor.

In addition, Becky would like to acknowledge:

Mickey Applebaum for providing his incredible expertise and good humor to the project, and without whose efforts this book would not have happened on time.

A big thanks to Bruce Hallberg for donating his computer and support to the cause and for writing the chapter on Menus. He also reviewed several chapters before they went out the door.

A special thanks to Ross M. Greenberg, one of this country's leading experts on computer security and viruses, for loaning his security and virus knowledge so generously.

Jamie Sanders, Mickey Applebaum, Don Crawford, and all the other NetWire SysOps who made my first experiences on NetWire so pleasant and patiently answered all my questions.

Joe and Marybeth Higuera, and Conni Gallo, for providing their support.

The fine folks and regulars in Section 8 for keeping me amused, as usual.

Starbucks Coffee, for providing such excellent beverages that keep me going.

And Mickey would like to acknowledge:

Becky Campbell for allowing me the opportunity, and for listening to all the stories of the strange and weird.

Steve Crandall, Team Leader for Novell's NetWire Support Group for putting up with the time I took off the 'Wire to write my parts of this book and for dealing with me in the long run.

All the other folks at Novell's NetWire Support Team. Go Team! (hehehe)

Don Crawford, NetWire SysOp, for providing support and suggestions.

Novell, Storage Dimensions, ProComp, ASP Computer Products, Intel, Morton Management, Computer Tyme, Infinite Technology and all the other manufacturers who support, and have supported me through the use of NetWire over the years.

And all the NERDS and NERDETTES who hang out on NetWire.

Trademark Acknowledgments

New Riders Publishing has made every attempt to supply trademark information about company names, products, and services mentioned in this book. Any trademarks indicated below were derived from various sources. New Riders Publishing cannot attest to the accuracy of this information.

Macintosh is a registered trademark and Macintosh Quadra is a trademark of Apple Computer, Inc.

Unix is a registered trademark of Unix System Laboratories, Inc.

Trademarks of other products mentioned in this book are held by the companies producing them.

Warning and Disclaimer

This book is designed to provide information about the Internet. Every effort has been made to make this book as complete and as accurate as possible, but no warranty or fitness is implied.

The information is provided on an "as is" basis. The author and New Riders Publishing shall have neither liability nor responsibility to any person or entity with respect to any loss or damages arising from the information contained in this book or from the use of the disks or programs that may accompany it.

Contents at a Glance

Table of Contents

Introduction

In the following chapters, you'll find key terms to look for in this box.

This makes it easier to get all this NetWare and networking jargon down. This introduction, mercifully, has no jargon.

Don't Panic! It's Only NetWare
(Or Why You Are Reading This)

As more companies and institutions look for ways to maximize their re-sources, many of them look to PC-based networks. Networks can help increase productivity and efficiently establish and maintain communication among the people who use them.

Out of all the network operating systems available today, Novell's NetWare has about a 65 percent share of the market. Its nearest competitor has a percentage of the market numbering only in the low teens, and the rest of the network operating systems have even smaller chunks of market share. Obviously, Novell is doing something right (besides marketing), and most experts agree that Novell's operating system has a lot to offer, including its excellent security features and flexibility.

What does all this have to do with you? Simple. You volunteered to be the network administrator. Or, someone volunteered you. Or whatever. At least your network uses NetWare. This book explains how to understand network-ing and how to set up and manage a network using your own brains and Novell's NetWare versions 3.11 or 3.12. It also includes a few tips and tricks along the way so that you can avoid making the same mistakes that are made by most beginning NetWare administrators.

Serious Business

The very fact that you are bothering to read this at all suggests that you take your job seriously—at least seriously enough to give learning about NetWare a chance. Heck, we don't know if you're an eager volunteer, or a job delegator, or if you are being dragged kicking and screaming into the throes of network management. At this point it probably doesn't matter anyway.

The point is, running a network of any size is a serious job—you'll have a lot to learn. Which brings us to another topic: the style of writing in this book. Neither New Riders Publishing nor the authors feel that a somewhat more casual style of writing than the usual business-oriented approach takes away from the seriousness of the topic. (And make no mistake—we do take it seriously.) A slightly casual style, and even a bit of humor here and there, just might help keep you awake while reading it, though.

Why I Wrote This

I was quite happy when New Riders approached me to write this book, because I sure wish I'd had a book like it when I started networking in 1987. Back in the olden days (when we shoveled coal into our steam-powered PCs) there were plenty of books about the theory of networking—the down-and-dirty bits and bytes stuff—but almost nothing about what I really needed to know: the basics of what a network is, what a network administrator should do, and how administering a network should be done.

Since there wasn't very much information of the type I needed at that time, I pretty much worked in a black hole: by myself, with only the NetWare documentation to help me figure out things. After a couple of years, I discovered that there were user groups for NetWare users all around the country—except where I lived. I was so relieved at the thought of getting help from, and talking to, other people doing what I was doing and dealing with the same problems that I was, that I founded the Denver Area NetWare Users' Group. A year later I was elected to the Board of Directors of NetWare Users International (NUI), on which I served for about six months. (NUI is explained and discussed in Chapter 14, "Help at Hand.")

In the course of being involved with user groups I ended up talking to a lot of people all over the country. From that, and from my own experiences, I found out a few things:

➜ Few people can be an expert at *all* aspects of NetWare. I've learned a lot over the years and designed and implemented about a half-dozen networks myself, but I am not an expert at *all* aspects of NetWare. That is why there are some chapters in this book written by Mickey Applebaum, one of the best NetWare experts in the country.

➜ Although my technical background (along with the expertise of the group I worked with) had saved our group from making a lot of mistakes, the mistakes we made (and sometimes came close to making) were the same ones made by nearly everyone else I talked to!

➜ Running a network and company politics are not (unfortunately) mutually exclusive. No matter how apolitical you are—or may wish to remain—networks involve people, and the successful administrator must integrate some people- and company-handling skills into performing this job.

I welcomed the opportunity to share my own experiences, as well as the experiences of others I talked to in the course of my travels, in the hopes of helping at least a few people avoid some of the same headaches and pitfalls.

So, don't think you're alone in starting down the bewildering path of NetWare administration—you're not. All who have gone before you have been where you are at right now. We want to share our experiences with you so that you don't have to learn it all the hard way.

What's In It for You

If you read this book from cover to cover, you'll learn everything you need to understand the basics of networking and how to use NetWare on your network. Later, you can access each chapter as you need to in order to review. And if you already have a general knowledge of networking down, you can skip straight to the NetWare stuff. There, you'll learn quickly and thoroughly just how NetWare works and how you can use it.

This book is written as a lean, mean reference book, without all the extra stuff that bogs down other "introductory level" books. At the start of each chapter there's a list of networking and NetWare terms to watch for as you read the chapter so that you'll learn these terms fast. At the end of each chapter there's a short-and-sweet section that reviews each main point you should have learned from that chapter. In between, you'll find succinct, informative discussions on the core of NetWare knowledge.

If, after you read this book, you want to learn more, by all means get some networking theory under your belt and dive into the exciting world of NetWare *internals* (the guts of the operating system and how it works). The more you learn, the more valuable and successful you'll be. But if you are worried about having to turn into some type of computer nerd who walks around spouting three-letter acronyms, don't be. I have trained and talked to many administrative assistants who learned what they needed to know, were very good at network administration, and just didn't care to take this networking business any further.

If you want to learn some practical tips and tricks and avoid a few common pitfalls, then this book is for you.

How This Book is Organized

This book is laid out pretty logically for an introductory level-affair—each new element of material builds on what was presented before it. That way, you can read this book straight through (more or less) the first time to get a good grounding in NetWare, and later to review. Here's what you get.

Part One, Networking 101

Chapter 1, "Egads! I'm Going To Be a What?" and Chapter 2, "How Does a Net Work?" explain a bit about what networks are and what you can expect your duties as the network administrator to be. They start out with some basic networking information and begin to build on that.

Chapter 3, "Have You Got a Plan Yet?" is about planning a network. Even if your network is already in place, it still is recommended reading. A periodic review of what you have and what you are doing on your network is a good thing. A fresh viewpoint always helps—take a look.

Part Two, NetWare and Networking Unraveled

Chapter 4, "NOS Hardware," is an overview of the type of hardware you will need if you are building your network from scratch, and Chapter 5, "NOS Software," deals with the software. Once again, even if you already have a network in place, these chapters might be worth a peek and can help in planning future purchases.

Chapter 6, "Security," deals with the security issues you need to be aware of—and deal with—on your network. If something goes wrong, there usually is a lot of finger-pointing—make sure it's not at you.

Chapter 7, "Disk and Directory Management," shows how disk and directory management is different for a network than it is on your own personal PC; you need to become acquainted with this topic. Hey, nobody said that networking was *glamorous*!

Part Three, Where Every NetWare Guru Starts

Chapter 8, "Printing," is a subject you will soon become acquainted with. Once again, this topic isn't going to make the best-seller list, but computers aren't of much use if you can't print out the results.

Chapter 9, "Login Scripts," might sound boring at first, but pay attention, because you might find yourself having a bit of fun here. Let your creativity loose on your co-workers!

If the users in your office are not, well, the most computer literate folks, then you won't want to miss Chapter 10, "Menus," so that you can find out how to set up networking menus to help them muddle through their tasks.

Part Four, Now THIS Is Managing a NetWare LAN!

Chapter 11, "Disaster Planning and Tape Backups," is the most important one you will read in this book, after Chapter 3. You will find out what to do when disaster strikes. And make no mistake—it's not a matter of *if*, but *when*. Make like a scout and Be Prepared!

Chapter 12, "Regular Duties," talks about some chores you will need to incorporate into your schedule. Some are daily, weekly, monthly, or just when the mood strikes—or duty calls.

"The network is down!" "My workstation won't connect!" Ahhhh, the soothing sound of happy network users. Learn how to troubleshoot some common problems you are likely to run into in Chapter 13, "Troubleshooting." Guns are not recommended equipment.

Part Five, Zen Secrets, E-mail, and Installing Apps

The secret to becoming a successful network administrator is revealed at last in Chapter 14, "Help at Hand." You don't have to know everything—just learn where the answers can be had. Learn about the myriad resources that are available to you in this chapter—at low or no cost.

You will find that electronic mail is the most beloved application on your network. Chapter 15, "E-mail and Other Applications," talks about different aspects of this important lifesaver and how to deal with them.

Chapter 16, "Actually Installing Applications," talks about installing applications on your network. Learning patience, grasshopper, is one of the first steps.

Addenda Was NetWare

The Glossary is a collection of all those annoying TLAs (three-letter acronyms) and nerdy networking terms that you, too, can use to amaze your friends and be the life of the party!

Appendix A and Appendix B deal with installing a workstation and generating IPX drivers, respectively (and respectably). These are not required activities for network administrators, but would be helpful skills if you want to learn them. These are not intended to be substitutes for the Novell documentation. Appendix C has a bit of information that you might want to know about NetWare/network cabling and wiring. This will be especially useful if you are beginning to purchase and install a network for the first time.

Typing Conventions

Luckily, this does not refer to a gathering of keyboard mavens, but rather the different type styles you will see in this book. It will help guide you through determining what it is you are supposed to type, what it is you are supposed to read, and what your computer screen might display.

➜   **Bold**. If the book tells you to type something (such as a command or some text), the actual words you must type appear in **bold**. Here's an example:

Type **I CAN'T BELIEVE I'M GETTING INTO THIS!** and press the Enter key.

➡ **Italic**. When a new term or phrase is introduced, it appears in *italic*. Italic type also is used when stressing a point because it is *important that you pay attention to that particular point.*

➡ **Special type**. Sometimes DOS or NetWare may show you a message. When this book shows you one of those messages, it appears in a special typeface, like this:

```
Don't Panic! It's Only NetWare!
```

Other times you'll need to enter lines of programming information. This book also shows this special input in a special typeface, like this:

```
COMSPEC <d>:\<path>\<filename.ext>
```

➡ **Hot keys**. Luckily, these won't burn your fingers, but sometimes you can take a shortcut on Novell menus by typing a shortcut key, or just one letter of the menu item. Shortcut keys for menus appear in color and are underlined, as in this example:

Select <u>S</u>upervisor Options, and then choose <u>U</u>sers.

Asides

Along with the exciting text in this book, you will see little asides to help you on your guided tour of NetWare. Look for these interesting and useful items as you read:

A Note lets you know a particularly valuable or important piece of information. Even though this entire book is bursting with valuable and important information, the notes are especially outstanding.

Tips are scattered throughout the book to give you a "heads-up": you need to pay special attention here. For instance, a tip might be to bet $5 on Shadowfax in the fifth race. Or not. Lots of the tips are things you won't find anyplace else, including in the Novell documentation.

A Warning means that if you don't pay special attention here, your network will crash and Western Civilization as we know it is in danger. Stop and read the warning carefully.

You will be reading some live network stories that are included to underscore a point that is being made. These are real, true, live stories of things that have happened to me directly or have been told to me first-hand by the people who experienced them. I definitely suggest you pay attention to them—they just might be valuable to you and help you avoid costly mistakes.

Other Things You Should Take Into Consideration as You Work

The folks at New Riders want you to know the following:

The staff of New Riders Publishing is committed to bringing you the very best in computer reference material. Each New Riders book is the result of months of work by the author and staff who research and refine the information contained within its covers.

As a part of this commitment to you, New Riders invites your input. Please let us know if you enjoy this book, if you have trouble with the information and examples presented, if you have a suggestion for the next edition, or if it was worth it to ride herd on yet another procrastinating author.

If you have a question or comment about any New Riders book, please write to NRP at the following address. We will respond to as many readers as we can. Your name, address, or phone number will never become a part of a mailing list or be used for any purpose other than to help us continue to bring you the best books possible.

New Riders Publishing
Attn: Associate Publisher
201 West 103rd Street
Indianapolis, IN 46290
FAX: 317-581-4670

If you prefer, you can contact the product director for this book via CompuServe Information Service at 70031,2231.

Legal Stuff

The legal folks, having to justify their salaries, have demanded that this bit of information be inserted here (just kidding, guys—honest!):

Please note that the New Riders staff cannot serve as a technical resource for NetWare or NetWare-related questions, including hardware- or software-related problems. Refer to the documentation that accompanies your hardware or software package for help with specific problems.

And Now for Something I Want to Say

Thank you very much for selecting *Don't Panic! It's Only NetWare!* A lot of people have worked very hard to bring this book to you, and we hope that you enjoy reading it as much as we enjoyed producing it.

I sincerely hope it meets its purpose of teaching you what you need to know and what you need to be aware of as you take up your NetWare administration duties. I welcome your questions, comments, suggestions, remarks, and jokes, so feel free to write to me directly. My CompuServe addresses are 71154,626 and 70702,3522. I hope to hear from you soon!

PART ONE

"So, Bizatz tells me you find networking a fascinating business!"

Joe froze... he suddenly knew the jig was up. He'd been fingered as a potential network administrator.

Life would never be the same...

Egads! I'm Going to Be a What?

(Or, Things You Should Know Before You Begin)

You may be reading this book against your will. In other words, you might be among the computer users who, through no choice of their own, have been chosen to become network administrators. We know who you are. You're pretty good with computers, your office or department needs to set up a network, and before you know it, bada-bing! You've been volunteered. To lead the whole parade. No, to organize it, lead it, and keep it going perpetually. Hang in there.

Of course, you could also be a networking novice, eager to learn new and fascinating aspects of information systems management. If so, welcome aboard. But don't snicker at the folks in the paragraph above. We're all here to learn, as quickly and painlessly as possible.

And actually, once you're well into this adventure, you might find that being a network administrator isn't as bad as you thought—you might even have fun with the job. Stick with us, and we'll show you how.

To get you up and running as a network administrator as quickly as possible, this chapter covers some important topics that you should know before you begin, including the following:

➜   What a network really is and its purpose in life

➜   Why a network administrator should not be a gossip columnist

➜   How networks can change the way you work and why shoe stores don't like them

➜   Why you should add a "P" before the "LAN"

What Is a Network?

You probably already know what a network is. Try taking this little quiz:

A network is:

A.   A very efficient fishing method requiring four people and a pelican.

B.   Safety equipment for the Flying Wallendas.

C.   Two or more computers hooked together so that they can share programs and data.

D.   None of the above.

If you answered A or B, you can really use this book. If you answered C, you are well on your way to becoming an expert network administrator. If you answered D, you should probably go back to sleep.

A network administrator's job is more than just baby-sitting computers. A network administrator is responsible for making sure data backups are performed, authorized users can access the system, and applications run smoothly over the network.

NOTE
A user is not a drug addict, it's a person who uses a local area network (LAN).

A network administrator's job is the type of job that you can either spend the minimum amount of time performing, or make it grow into a possible new career. What you make of the job is really up to you.

Getting Your Fair Share (network detail—but not too much)

A network's purpose in life is to make sharing as easy as possible. With a network, we can share application programs, data, printers, and all sorts of other equipment.

NOTE

In network lingo, the hardware and software that can be shared are usually referred to as resources. This includes, among other things, printers, modems, disk drives, and software (both applications and data).

The central focus of a network is the fileserver. A *fileserver* is a PC (personal computer) equipped with a large, family-sized hard disk drive and a lot of memory. In addition, it usually is the fastest machine in the office. The fileserver for a Novell 3.11 network is not used by anyone to perform daily work; that's why it's referred to as a *dedicated fileserver*. It's dedicated to just one very important job.

PCs are attached so that they can communicate with the fileserver and share its resources. Those PCs are referred to as *workstations*. These workstations are the PCs that sit on employees' desks. A PC that is not hooked up to a network is called a *stand-alone PC*.

A workstation usually is attached to a fileserver with some type of wire or cable but can also be connected through radio waves (these are called wireless networks). Wireless networks, however, aren't very common yet because the technology is just beginning to mature.

NOTE

In computer lingo, mature technology means that the gadget, gizmo, or whatchamacallit has been around long enough and the following things begin to happen:

continues

→   *most manufacturers use the same basic type of
      hardware and software so that their different devices
      can "talk" to one another*

→   *the price starts falling (remember when a VCR was
      over $1,000?)*

To attach to a network, a special board is put in the fileserver and the
workstation PCs. These special boards are called *network interface cards*,
which usually is shortened to *NICs*. The wire or cable is connected to the
back of the NIC so that the PCs can communicate with each other. A non-
artist's rendering of a simple network is shown in figure 1.1. You probably
have seen this type of drawing before—it seems like no book on networks
has ever been published without one.

Figure 1.1

*Surprise! A simple
network.*

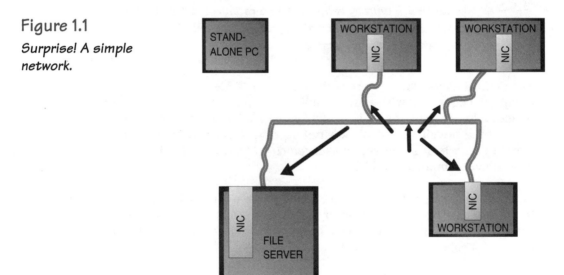

Without an operating system, all the PCs, NICs, and wire would be pretty
useless. Actually, they wouldn't even be pretty—just useless. An *operating
system* (or OS for short) is what makes the hardware talk to the applications
that you run on your computer. The workstations can run many different
types of operating systems, but the most commonly used operating systems
are DOS and OS/2. The fileserver has to run its own special operating system, which is the *network operating system*, or NOS. In this case, it's Novell
NetWare version 3.11 or 3.12.

NOTE

Novell has published many versions of NetWare over the years. The current versions are NetWare 2.2, 3.12, and 4.01. NetWare 3.12 is brand-new and is essentially a cleaned-up version of the extremely popular version 3.11. Between them, NetWare 3.12 and 3.11 are by far the most popular versions of NetWare in use. They offer an excellent balance between performance, ease of use, and affordability. That's why we decided to focus this book on NetWare 3.11 and 3.12.

NetWare 4.01 is intended for large networks with several file-servers. It is definitely not for beginners. In fact, your LAN may never need the advanced features that NetWare 4.01 provides.

NetWare 2.2 is the last version of NetWare that will run on a server that has an 80286 microprocessor (like an IBM AT). It's harder to maintain than version 3.12/3.11. The only good reason to use version 2.2 is if your budget won't allow you to buy a server based on an 80386 or an 80486. However, the extremely affordable nature of newer PCs puts a NetWare 3.12 server within the reach of almost any organization.

NOTE

DOS stands for Disk Operating System. It's not pretty because it's a character-based operating system. That means it doesn't have any pretty pictures or colors to make it look nice and make it easier to use. If you want to jazz up DOS, you need to run Windows on it. Windows is a graphical user interface, or GUI (pronounced gooey).

DOS comes in many different flavors. You can run MS-DOS from the Microsoft Corporation, Novell DOS from Novell, IBM-DOS from IBM, Compaq-DOS from Compaq Computer Corporation, or Crazy Bob's DOS—it doesn't really matter because they all function about the same. NetWare really doesn't care which brand of DOS you use.

NOTE

Windows is not an operating system; it is referred to as an environment. DOS is the underlying operating system that Windows runs on, but Windows is what you really see and work with. (This changes with Windows NT, which really is an operating system. But we digress.)

When you are running PCs on a network, you need a few more pieces of software to make all the software and hardware talk to each other. Both the fileserver and the workstations must have a device driver for the NIC. A *driver* is a special piece of software that makes the hardware function properly with the program being used.

NOTE

A device driver is needed for all types of hardware—printers, mice, and NICs. But the device driver has to be matched up carefully with the manufacturer's particular version of hardware along with the version of software being used. If the wrong device driver software is used, the device either will not work at all or won't work correctly.

The last items you need are a couple of other software programs for the workstations. We'll lump them all together for now, but the major one intercepts some of the DOS commands and converts them to NetWare commands before it sends them to the fileserver. The names of the programs depend on the version of NetWare you're using:

➜   In NetWare 3.12 and 4.0, the workstation software is called a DOS *requester* since it enables the workstation to request network services. The new requesters can also be used with older versions of NetWare such as 2.2 and 3.11.

➜   In earlier NetWare versions this group of programs was referred to as the NetWare Shell because they act as a protective shell between the workstation OS and the NOS. Novell no longer recommends that you use the NetWare Shell technology, primarily because it won't work with NetWare 4.0. Also, some future programs might require the new requesters.

Now, review the collection of hardware and software that has been discussed so far. Better yet, take a look at figure 1.2.

Figure 1.2

The main stuff that
makes up a network.

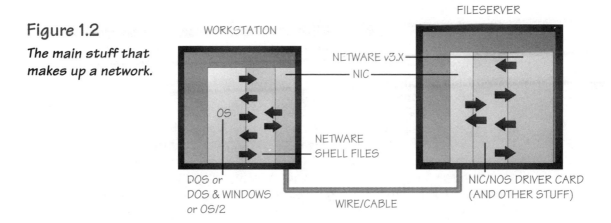

Sharing Hardware Resources

One reason PC-based networks became so popular was that when PCs were
invented, hardware such as hard disks and printers could be very expensive.
Although the price of all types of hardware has declined considerably since
those early, expensive days, none of it is as cheap as say, a pad and pencil. It
just doesn't make sense for every computer in a company to be equipped
with all the hardware ever needed to perform any type of task.

Take a look at a good laser printer, for example. Different types of work
require different amounts of printing, but few people can keep a printer busy
all day long. And because printers don't need coffee or lunch breaks (their
union doesn't require it), someone else might as well be using the printer if
you aren't. Even though the street price of a personal laser printer starts at
about $600, providing a laser printer for every person in the office could still
get pretty expensive.

Sharing Application Resources

Another reason PC-based networks are so popular is that they make it
possible for companies to buy fewer copies of application software even if
everyone in the company needs to use the same programs now and then.
Putting software applications on a network serves the following two purposes:

→   You'll use smaller (or no) hard disks to store the applications

→   You'll need fewer copies of the software

When you buy software, you actually buy a license to use it on a specific PC. Installing copies of the software on several PCs is a no-no unless you purchase a copy for each PC. But what if all of the PCs don't need to use the software all of the time? Isn't it pretty costly to need all those copies to provide for occasional use? You bet it is!

For this reason, some vendors offer a network version of their software. A *network version* of a software package means that you can buy one copy and load it on the fileserver, allowing several workstations to run it at the same time. Network versions are priced higher than individual copies, but still are less expensive than buying several copies. Even though you have ten users on your LAN, you may only need a five-user license to cover your users' needs.

If your favorite software package is not offered in a network version, you still can run it on a network without violating the licensing agreement. To do this, buy as many copies of the software as you might need at any one time. Load one copy onto the network and store the others. Then buy a network monitoring utility to monitor the number of workstations running the software at any one time. Set up the monitoring utility to allow only a number of workstations to run the software at one time. If, for example, you have five legal copies, allow only five workstations to run the software at the same time. This way, a sixth person cannot run the software from his workstation until someone else is done using it.

Sharing Data Resources

Many people working in the same office or company not only need to use the same programs, but they also need to use the same data from those programs. The data might be anything such as a database, agreement, form, or a letter (or a form letter). By storing most (or all) of the data on the fileserver, everyone can share it.

Of course, you wouldn't want the whole company to see the payroll files, for instance, but that information can be made accessible to the people who need it. Access rights are part of the security available on a network and are discussed a little more in the next section.

The ability to access the same data from all the workstations in a department or company is the reason shoe companies don't like networks. No one has to put the information on a floppy disk and walk the disk over to the person who needs it. Not only do you save wear and tear on your shoes, but you can save a lot of time getting information.

NOTE

Loading data on a floppy disk and passing the disk to the person who needs it is called running a sneakernet.

This really came from when users had to put on their shoes and walk a disk over to whoever needed it. If you think that sounds crazy, imagine the logical alternatives: wingtipnet, open-toe pumpnet, pennyloafernet... you get the picture.

What Does a Network Administrator Administrate?

The network administrator needs to perform a variety of tasks. These tasks vary depending on the size of the company and how the network is used, but most administrators do the tasks listed here. It might seem a little intimidating at first (okay, a *lot* intimidating) but above all, new network administrators need to remember that no one is born knowing everything there is to know about computers, and especially networks.

TIP

Don't try to learn everything about NetWare all at once. You can acquire your networking knowledge gradually from this book or other books. Chances are astronomically high that a lot of other people have had the same questions that you have or have run into some of the same problems that you will. Read Chapter 14, "Help at Hand," to find out where you can learn from other people and their experiences.

Back Up the Fileserver

Because so much information is stored on the fileserver, it can be costly if any of this data is accidentally erased or lost due to an equipment failure. Regularly archiving network files on tape is essential insurance for any LAN and is a key responsibility for any LAN administrator. Quickly restoring that information is an important part of an administrator's job.

Secure the Data on the Fileserver

Not everyone in the office should be able to view or access everyone else's data. The administrator, however, does need to have access to everything so that "rights" permissions can be set for those who use the system. The network administrator can view everyone's data, but should use this power discreetly. The administrator should only peek at data if absolutely necessary, and above all, he should never tell others what he has seen (whether by accident or on purpose).

Load and Monitor Applications

If everyone were allowed to load applications on the fileserver, there could be lots of problems. The software licensing agreements might be violated and applications might be set up incorrectly. Besides that, installing applications on a LAN requires skills at least as good as those you're getting from this book. Before long, the mere thought of allowing just anybody to add applications to your server will be enough to kick off your heartburn.

Add Workstations (optional)

As new employees are added, or new equipment replaces old, workstations need to be added or replaced on a network. As the LAN administrator, you will come to be regarded as one of the PC gurus of your office. Everyone will come to you when they need an option card installed or a bolt tightened. So it's very helpful, if not essential, for you to feel comfortable with a screwdriver (the hardware—the drink is optional) so that the NIC can be installed and the wire hooked up correctly.

Add and Delete Users

As new employees join the company or department and old employees leave, the network administrator must add and delete authorized users to and from the network. Deleting users is easy—just find the user's name in a list and hit the Delete key. Adding users gets more involved. Besides just adding names to a list, it also means making sure that users can access the right information and can't access things they shouldn't.

Make Adjustments to the NOS

NetWare is a complex piece of software, and the programmers who wrote it are not perfect. As new bugs are discovered, Novell often offers patches to the operating system that the network administrator needs to load to the NOS. A *patch* is a great way to fix one problem without replacing the entire NOS. In addition, because not everyone needs all the options that Novell offers, each company can pick and choose certain pieces that will complement the basic NOS software. The network administrator needs to understand some basic NetWare concepts so that they can properly use some of these options.

NOTE

The primary difference between NetWare 3.12 and 3.11 is that 3.12 includes all of the patches that were introduced over the years for 3.11. It is no longer necessary to manually install patches when you install a new server. (Of course, patches for 3.12 are probably on the way.)

Another type of adjustment the administrator needs to be able to make is to reallocate resources on the fileserver. This can mean anything from adjusting the way the disk space is used, to adding or deleting a printer service.

Make Adjustments to the Fileserver Hardware (optional)

Sometimes the fileserver hardware needs to expand or change. A network administrator who can add an NIC, hook up a printer, or even add a disk drive can be a real asset. But don't worry if you aren't comfortable with these kinds of tasks right now. These tasks can be learned, or can be contracted out.

Help Network Users

As users of the network encounter problems or questions, they tend to ask the network administrator to help them out. It is important that the network administrator is a friendly, understanding source for helping other users. Not everyone in the company can or should become network experts.

Sometimes users will ask the administrator about applications rather than the network. Taking the time to become knowledgeable about the applications, as well as taking the time to help users, is another matter and should be considered as a separate function. Some companies have resources to allocate, others do not. This matter is discussed more in Chapter 13, "Troubleshooting."

As you can see, the network administrator's position is an important one. Someone who is knowledgeable about computers, willing to learn about networks, and interacts well with others is the most likely candidate to make an excellent network administrator.

Why Are We Using Novell NetWare?

NetWare is the most popular network operating system on the planet for local area networks (LANs). The people who make their living determining such things don't agree on the exact number of users (if they agreed, they probably couldn't charge as much, right?), but they estimate that about 60 to 80 percent of LANs run NetWare.

The Advantage of Big Market Share to Customers

Because Novell has the lion's share of the market, it means big advantages to users of NetWare. Some of those advantages include the following:

➜   Lots of software is made to run on NetWare. That means more choices for the users.

➜   Lots of hardware is designed to run on NetWare. Because NetWare is so popular, manufacturers (and software vendors) tend to make stuff for NetWare before they make stuff for Brand X when they have to make choices.

➜   Lots of knowledgeable people can help you out in designing and running your network.

Reliability

NetWare was first introduced in 1982. Even though NetWare 3.12 and 3.11 haven't been around for quite that long, they have been around long enough to become reliable, dependable products. Some of the same programmers who wrote the first version of NetWare designed and wrote NetWare 3.11 and 3.12. They have a *lot* of experience.

Performance

Performance of any type of computer product is difficult to really measure with any accuracy. Why? Because performance depends on the particular usage of the product, the other products being used in conjunction with that product, and the types of tasks being performed. That's why you should never completely believe tests that supposedly benchmark performance. That said, most people agree that NetWare is one of the top NOS performers available today.

Security

NetWare is tops in offering all sorts of security features. In addition to controlling who can access what files, you can determine what times of the day users try to log in. You can also set NetWare to detect intruders by allowing only a limited number of password attempts and a specific period of time to attempt entering a password. These types of features lock out people who try to break into networks.

NOTE

Some people get concerned when they find out that NetWare doesn't have a C2 rating. (That's a rating one of the government agencies gives to really secure software.) As a matter of fact, that type of rating is misleading. After a C2 rating is attained, it means that the code cannot be changed, even to fix bugs, let alone to be improved upon (such as adding new features). The security features in NetWare actually exceed the requirements of a C2 rating; it's just not official.

So? What's the Point?

The network administrator should never lose sight of the real purpose of the network. Some administrators get so caught up in the fun and excitement of running the network, improving the network, and tuning the network, that they forget why the network was installed in the first place. Remember that *the network is a tool*.

Whether you are designing and planning your first network, or running one that has been around for awhile, it is important that the administrator keep focused on the primary business of the company or organization. If the administrator doesn't know why the company is in business, then she won't understand how to make the network fit into the "big picture."

Work Flow

To find out how to use the network to its maximum potential, you should ask the following questions:

➜   How does the company or business make money? Most organizations are in business to make money (although there are exceptions). Whether your organization bills for products or for services, never lose sight of the reason for its existence.

➜   How can the network help the business process? If your organization sells a product, you can look for ways to get the product to market faster. If your organization sells services, you can look for ways to maximize billable time.

Requirements Required

After you've figured out why the organization exists and how the network might help make the work flow a little smoother and faster, it's time to get down to details. This is referred to as *requirements analysis*. As the term implies, you analyze your requirements. As you go through this process, you often find that the original requirements were stated poorly (or even incorrectly). The end product selection is much better if first you figure out the exact task to be accomplished and how to accomplish it.

Figuring out the exact task to be accomplished can save an organization a lot of money in purchasing the correct software and hardware the first time.

Because many products offer similar functionality, it is important to take a careful look at the features of each product and prioritize the features that are important to your particular task or application.

Figuring out how to accomplish the task saves the network administrator about five million wasted hours of adjusting, readjusting, and readjusting again the way your network is set up. By planning the way the work flows, you can plan your disk space and directory usage properly the first time, making only minor adjustments (if any) as needed.

Proper requirements analysis is a topic that cannot be stressed enough. Even if your network has been in place for a long time, periodic reevaluations are worthwhile. Obviously, requirements analysis is not a job for the network administrator alone. Requirements analysis should be done as a team with the network administrator and upper level management.

Vendors and Consultants

Some organizations place their complete trust in network vendors or consultants. Selecting the right vendor or consultant is a very important decision. A bad one can cost you lots of money, but a good one is a real asset.

Buyer Beware

A consultant or vendor should be chosen with the same type of care that you use to select any other product or service. Just because someone is friendly, knows a lot of buzzwords, or has some type of certification, doesn't mean he or she is a good network consultant or vendor. LAN administration is no different than any other profession—there are good consultants and there are bad ones. Even if you don't know much about networks, here are a few tips to help you make the right selection:

➡ **Planning.** A good consultant will refuse to sell you anything (services or products) until he sits down with you for a preliminary planning session. He should ask you about your business and your requirements. Expertise costs money—plan to pay for this time.

➡ **Existing equipment.** A good consultant understands that you don't want to throw away all your old stuff and start out with brand new, shiny PCs. If she wants to sell you new equipment, you should ask why and how it will help you accomplish your tasks. It also is important to understand that some equipment might require a big time or money investment to work well with a network.

→ **Experience and references.** How long has the consultant been consulting? How many networks has he designed and implemented? Obviously, the higher both numbers, the better; don't settle for less than about three years experience and about a half dozen networks. Ask for a half dozen references and find out how long each reference has been a customer. Check them all out.

→ **Certifications.** Novell requires that vendors and dealers take certain courses before they can sell Novell products. The courses and designations vary by product. Call Novell at 1-800-453-1267 to find out if your dealer or consultant is certified on the right products.

TIP

Never completely rely on certifications. Novell courses have some value, but the education division is there to make money. Experience and a trail of satisfied customers count for a lot in the networking biz.

→ **Good communications.** Don't ever hire a consultant and then walk away. Make time to get periodic reports and discuss how the work is progressing. Interim meetings provide an opportunity for adjustments to be made along the way.

→ **Payment.** A reputable consultant understands that final payment will not be made until all the hardware and software is actually installed and working in your environment.

A New Business Partner

After you have carefully selected a vendor and consultant, work to make them a part of your business. Cultivate and nurture this relationship carefully. A good vendor or consultant can be invaluable to you. Usually, a good vendor or consultant will:

→ **Provide evaluation software and hardware before you make purchasing decisions.** A vendor will only do that type of loaning if she knows you will be making consistent purchases from her.

➜ **Provide advance information about new products.** Vendors have good relationships with manufacturers. Utilize that relationship to your advantage. This is especially helpful if you work for a large company and have a very long procurement process.

➜ **Provide backup assistance and products.** If you have an unexpected hardware failure and you find yourself without a spare part, a vendor will work with you to get the equipment in as fast as possible.

NOTE

A good vendor or consultant can be an invaluable asset in helping you to have a successful network. Be sure to pay your vendor or consultant on time.

Chapter 1, Short and Sweet

This chapter gave a brief overview of networking and a network administrator's job, as follows:

1. A network's purpose in life is to share resources. Computer resources include, but are not limited to:

    ➜ disk space

    ➜ application programs

    ➜ data (the result of doing something with an application program)

    ➜ modems

    ➜ printers

2. In order for computers to start networking, they need to be equipped with Network Interface Cards (NICs), cable, device drivers, and, of course, a Network Operating System (NOS).

3. In a Novell network, the computer that handles all this sharing is the fileserver. The computers that are attached to the fileserver are the workstations. The fileserver is not used for everyday work; it is a *dedicated* fileserver.

4. A computer needs an *operating system* (OS) to act as an interpreter between the software applications and the hardware.

5. PC-based workstations attached to a Novell network can use either the OS/2 or DOS operating systems. To add pretty pictures to a DOS workstation, you need to add Microsoft's Windows. Windows is an environment, not an operating system. You can also hook up Macintosh- or Unix-based computers to a Novell NetWare fileserver. Novell markets a version of Unix, called UnixWare, that is neatly integrated with NetWare fileservers.

6. Utilizing a network offers certain costs savings. Some applications come in a network pack (sort of like a six-pack) and can save money over buying the same number of individual copies of programs. Also, fewer printers, modems, and other hardware are required when they can be easily shared by everyone.

7. Besides saving real dollars, a network can help save time. The same data can be used by many people without them having to manually pass around information on a disk (a *sneakernet*).

8. Some of the network administrator's duties include: making backups of the fileserver; making sure the data is secure; loading and monitoring applications; adding and deleting users; making adjustments to the NOS; and helping network users.

9. Some of the optional network administrator duties include: adding more workstations to the network and making hardware adjustments to the fileserver. Don't worry if you are not comfortable doing those kinds of things.

10. Novell's NetWare is a pretty good choice for an operating system. Since it has such a big share of the market, some of the advantages of running it include available expertise, and choices of programs and compatible hardware. It got to be the King of the Network Mountain because it offers reliability, security, and performance.

11. The network administrator should not lose sight of the fact that the network is in place to help the company be more profitable.

12. Be extremely picky when selecting a network vendor or consultant. You don't have to be a computer wizard to practice common sense and check references. Once the selection is made, make that vendor or consultant a sort of business partner—a good one will be invaluable to you.

How Does a Net Work?

(And What's This Strange Language?)

Chapter 2

Key Terms to Look for:

→ Distributed process-ing network (DPN)

→ Central processing-network (CPN)

→ application program

→ drive mapping

→ mainframe or mini-computer

→ dumb terminals

→ modularity

→ client-server network

→ peer-to-peer network

→ networking protocols

→ Ethernet

→ nodes

→ CSMA/CD

→ Token Ring

→ ARCnet

→ bus configuration

→ de jure/de facto standards

→ six month rule

→ Novell certified

The good news is that you don't have to be a rocket scientist to understand a few basic concepts of how networks work. The other good news is that this chapter covers the following:

→ Distributed and central processing

→ Client-server and peer-to-peer net-works

→ Explanations of Ethernet, Token Ring, and ARCnet

→ How to avoid a few pitfalls with NetWare

→ Some of the buzzwords of network terminology and what they mean

The other good news is that this chapter introduces you to a lot of new networking terms; each of these terms is broken down and dissected so that it will not be confusing by the time you finish reading this chapter. Luckily, dissecting these terms is not smelly, ugly, or nearly as disgusting as dissect-ing a frog (blech). If all dissection were this easy, there'd be darn few frogs left in the world.

Distributed versus Central Processing

Before we discuss what distributed and central processing are, let's break down these terms:

→   *Processing.* Everyone is familiar with food processors; you put in some raw ingredients, turn it on, and the food processor shakes up and munges together the ingredients, spitting out the results. Computer processing is not much different, but instead of dealing with things like bananas and eggs, the microprocessors deal with instructions, numbers, and letters. The raw materials (numbers and letters) are munged according to the instructions (programs), and the results are spit out.

→   *Central.* With central heating or air conditioning, the air is either heated or cooled at one place where all the pipes meet. The pipes then carry the heated or cooled air throughout the building. A central processing computer is one in which all the processing is done on only one computer and the information is then sent out to the machine that made the request.

→   *Distributed.* A clothing distributor is a business that sends clothes to lots of stores, which then sell them. Every store shares in the work of selling the clothes. With distributed processing computers, each machine does its share of processing; it's not done at one central place.

Distributed Processing

PC-based networks are *distributed processing networks.* At first glance, it might appear that they are central processing networks because the focus of a PC-based network is the fileserver. But look at the term "fileserver" for a moment. Note the two words "file" and "server." That's exactly what it does— it serves up files. Each workstation does the actual work of processing the files. On a Novell network, no application programs are actually run at the fileserver.

NOTE

An application program is one that is "applied" to solve problems. Word processors, spreadsheets, and communications programs are all examples of application programs, or "applications" for short. Well, okay, "application" isn't very short; some people refer to them as "apps."

Computer applications are stored in executable files. A file is just a chunk of information that is stored on a computer's hard drive. Think of a file in a file cabinet and you'll get the idea: each file contains a specific set of information and each file is identified with a name.

Executable files contain instructions that tell the computer to do something. A word processor executable file contains the instructions that turn your PC into a word processor. You can easily identify executable files on a PC. Their names will end either with .EXE (for "executable") or .COM (for "command").

Files that contain information are collectively called data files. Word processing documents, address lists, spreadsheet data, are all examples of data files.

When you are using a stand-alone PC, all of your data and application files are stored on your PC, either on floppy disks or on your hard disk drive. When you hook up your PC to a network, however, you can also access files on the fileserver.

Your local files will be stored on disk drives with names like A:, B:, or C:. When you are connected to a network, the fileserver will look to you just like another local drive. After you connect, you may find that you have a new drive named F:. No, you haven't just added a new hard drive. F: is the drive letter for the server's storage. In NetWare terminology, drive F: has been *mapped* to the server's hard drive. Any applications or data files on the server are now available to you on drive F:.

Yes, application programs and data files can live on the fileserver, but when a workstation wants to run the application or examine the data, the contents of the appropriate files are shipped out over the network cable to the workstation PC and run or processed there. The diagram in figure 2.1 depicts distributed processing.

Figure 2.1
*A distributed
processing network.*

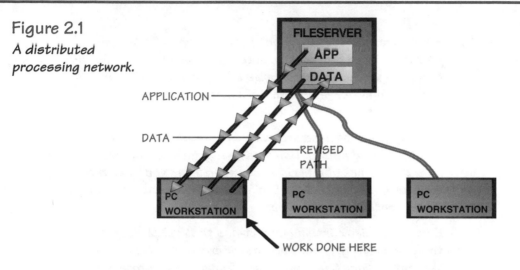

Keep in mind that it's only a *copy* of the application or the data that is
shipped to the workstation, which means that the files are available to other
users on the network. All network users can share applications. More
importantly, they can share data. Everyone can access the same telephone
number database, for example.

Central Processing

To get a better handle on what a distributed processing network is, let's take
a look at a central processing network. A *central processing network* is
different from a distributed processing network in two major areas:

1. The central computer is more powerful than a PC-class machine.
   Really big central computers can support thousands of users and
   trillions of bytes of file storage.

NOTE
*The biggest central computers are generally called main-
frames. Together with disk drives, tape drives, communication
devices, central processors, printers, and so forth, they can
fill a huge room.*

*Smaller central computers are frequently called minicomput-
ers or minis. At one time, it was possible to draw a pretty
clear line between them. Minis were a whole lot smaller!*

However, manufacturers who started making minis have made their systems more powerful so that they often compete against mainframes. And mainframe manufacturers have evolved to offer smaller, more cost-competitive systems.

Therefore, it is very difficult to draw the line between what is a mini and a mainframe. Often the name just depends on what the manufacturer chooses to call it. If a manufacturer wants to identify a system as seriously huge, they'll call it a mainframe. If the system is supposed to be powerful but more affordable, it will be called a mini.

2.   The workstations attached to a central processing network are either "dumb terminals" or PCs that have special hardware and software added so that they act like "dumb terminals." A dumb terminal is usually just a keyboard and screen hooked into a central computer located elsewhere. This is opposed to a smart terminal, which contains processing circuits that interact with a host computer. The smart terminal can carry out its own computing operations; the dumb one can't.

A PC that is configured as a dumb terminal (using terminal emulation software and hardware) has lost its smarts. However, terminal emulation means that you don't have to have both a PC and a terminal cluttering up your desk.

A diagram of a central-processing network is shown in figure 2.2.

Although many companies use PCs as terminals for their mainframes and minicomputers, it is important to note that although these PCs are acting as terminals to the mainframe or minicomputer, they are not helping those central computers do any of the processing. All of the thinking is taking place in the central processor. If the central computer goes down, the terminals go dead.

A distributed-processing network is quite a bit different. The terminals are replaced with PCs which, of course, are independent computers. They can process things just fine. Your PC doesn't need a network to run a word processor.

Figure 2.2

A central-processing network.

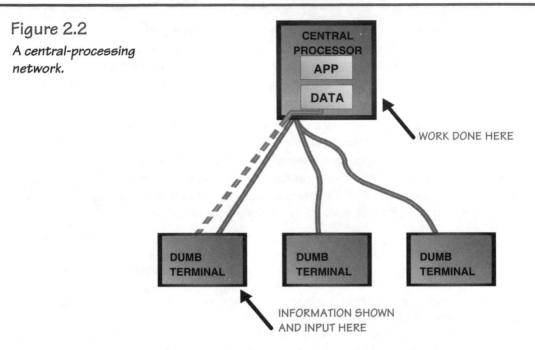

All PCs need a network for is to share services with other PCs. You've seen that the fileserver provides file services, enabling many users' PCs to share the same files. The server also can provide print services, allowing the PCs to share printers on the network. Other things that might be shared are modems, electronic mail, and fax systems. If there's a computer device, someone somewhere is looking for a way to share it on a LAN.

So, a central processor does everything that's done on a network. A fileserver does only part of the work. Most of the application processing and data manipulation is distributed on the PCs that share the network. The fileserver on a distributed network can be smaller than a central processor and support the same numbers of users. In fact, the fileserver itself can be a PC.

So Why Is This the Way To Go?

Although each type of network has its strengths and is appropriate for different applications, one of the main reasons that PC-based distributed processing networks became so popular was that the price was (and for the most part still is) usually lower than most mainframe or minicomputers. Another reason is that owners of PC-based networks can select the vendor with the best product and the best prices. Mainframe and mini based solutions are typically one-vendor solutions with few choices about products and, most important, prices.

Yet another reason for LAN popularity is modularity. Adding and deleting components according to need is typically more flexible on a LAN than on a mainframe or minicomputer.

Client-Server versus Peer-to-Peer

Now that we know we are working on a distributed processing network, we need to find out whether it's a client-server or peer-to-peer network. Let's look at those terms:

→ **Client.** Any customer is generally referred to as a client. A client is one who is waited on and receives services.

Workstations on LANs are frequently called clients because they receive services from the network.

→ **Server.** A server is someone or something that serves the client. A server delivers some type of services or product.

Fileservers, print servers, modem servers, and so on are called servers because they provide services to client workstations.

→ **Peer.** In this case, we are not referring to English royalty, but rather equals. A peer is someone or something having skills or capabilities equal to someone or something else.

A peer workstation on a LAN can be both a client and a server. It might function as a print server by sharing its printer with other peers that it regards as clients.

Or, a peer workstation might be a client and regard another workstation as a fileserver. The fileserver workstation shares files on its local C: drive with other workstations.

So, the same workstation might be a client using another workstation as a print server, while at the same time it is acting as a fileserver for other workstations.

If all PCs on the network can function both as a server and as a client, the PCs are regarded as peers.

Client-Server Networks

By these definitions, we can see that a *client-server network* is one in which one computer serves up the information (mmmm.... isn't that file delicious?) and another computer acts as the client, receiving that information or service and performing some type of action on it.

A Novell network is a client-server network. One computer, the fileserver (surprisingly enough), acts as the server, and the workstations are clients. The workstations don't talk to each other, only to the server. Figure 2.3 shows a client-server network configuration.

Figure 2.3

A typical client-server network configuration.

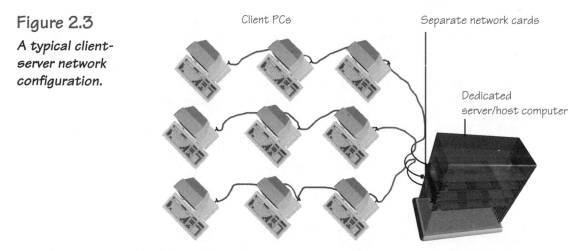

Client PCs

Separate network cards

Dedicated server/host computer

Peer-to-Peer Networks

Some networks are peer-to-peer networks and a computer can act as a client, as a server, *or as both*. In other words, the computers can talk to each other directly and aren't limited to talking to the server only (see fig. 2.4). NetWare Lite is a peer-to-peer network. Other popular brands of peer-to-peer networks are Artisoft's LANtastic Network and Microsoft's Windows for Workgroups.

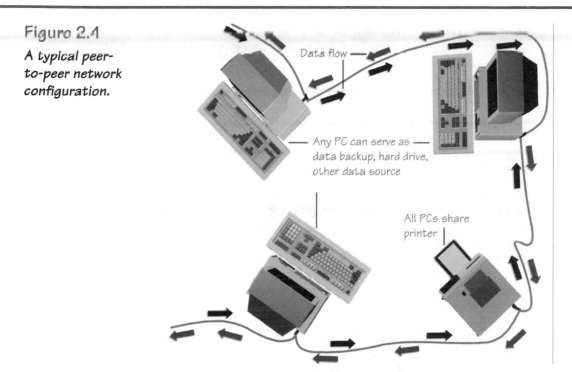

Figure 2.4

A typical peer-to-peer network configuration.

Data flow

Any PC can serve as data backup, hard drive, other data source

All PCs share printer

Peer-to-peer networks are considered ideal for small offices and departments, say 2 to 12 computers. However, they are also useful in larger settings where users need to share files or devices on an informal basis. Groups of people who work together in a cohesive but informal fashion are frequently called "workgroups." Peer-to-peer networking is well suited to the needs of such workgroups, and peer-to-peer computing is often referred to as "workgroup computing."

How To Choose

There is a time and a place for client-server networks and a time and place for peer-to-peer networks. Peer-to-peer networks are considered advantageous in that they don't require a dedicated fileserver that cannot also be used by someone as a workstation. The big disadvantage is that it can be difficult to get a good handle on who has access to what information.

In offices where file security is a sensitive issue, a client-server network has a definite advantage because only one person, the supervisor, can grant file permissions. In small offices where file access isn't an issue, but sharing a $2,000 laser printer is, a peer-to-peer network is ideal.

The nice thing about a NetWare network is that you can mix and match. In other words, you can hook up most peer-to-peer networks to the NetWare 3.11 network so that those people on the peer-to-peer network can have the best of both worlds.

Ethernet, Token Ring, ARCnet, and NetWare

Here are a few really exciting words to add to your vocabulary: Token Ring, Ethernet, and ARCnet. Before you go hopping around the office in ecstasy, let's view these terms from your point of view. The big question is: Will knowing the meaning of these terms help you appreciably in understanding NetWare and how to administer your system? The answer is no, not especially. But we'll discuss them briefly anyway so that you won't be in the dark when you hear them mentioned.

All of these are networking *protocols*. We hear the word "protocol" most often in terms of the form of communication with heads of state and royalty. Actually, that isn't too far off the mark in how it applies to computers, either. It would be very bad form to go visit the Queen of England and bow at the same time she reached out her hand to shake hands with you. So then you reach out to shake hands just as she is bowing and you poke her right in the eye. In other words, you weren't shown the proper protocol for communicating with her, not even a proper greeting!

Computers aren't very sophisticated in that they have to be told down to the very last detail how to do certain things, including greeting each other properly. As you can imagine, getting down to the exact details of how they communicate could be pretty tiresome. But there are some people who do specialize in that area, and if you want to see a good shouting match and a few bulging foreheads, ask a couple of nerds which protocol is better for a network and step back to a safe zone.

Ethernet

Ethernet is the most commonly used protocol for network communications. Current estimates are that about 20 million Ethernet network nodes exist in the world. The term Ethernet is derived from *luminiferous ether*, through which electromagnetic radiation was once thought to propagate.

NOTE

Anything on a network is a node, whether it is a server, a client, or a peer.

Ethernet works like this: You give the workstation some type of command to tell the fileserver. Your workstation cups its hand to its ear and says, "Anyone there?" If your workstation doesn't detect anyone else using the network, it goes ahead and sends the command or information to the fileserver.

But what if two or more workstations listen at the same time, don't hear any other traffic, and then go ahead and send things? Yikes! They would collide and all the bits would be jumbled together, the way two cars on the highway collide when they try to occupy the same piece of road at the same time. What happens is that the workstations then wait for a random amount of time and resend the information. Because the times are random, chances are very low that they all will retry at the same time. (See fig. 2.5.)

Figure 2.5

A typical Ethernet configuration.

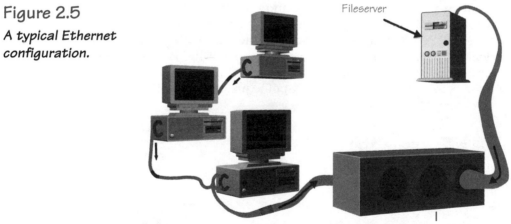

At first, this might sound like it would take a long time for your workstation to listen, transmit, and then have to wait and retransmit if it detects a collision. But the whole process doesn't take long at all. As a matter of fact, it takes a lot less time to do all this than it takes to say "CSMA/CD." Times on LANs are measured in milliseconds. LANs are fast!

CSMA/CD stands for Carrier Sense Multiple Access/Collision Detection, and that's what Ethernet uses. You use CSMA/CD every time you are in a meeting, and it's easy to understand what CSMA/CD means by examining the process of communicating in a group of people.

1. Carrier Sense—Everyone listens to the conversation looking for a quiet time when they can talk.

2. Multiple Access—Anyone can talk any time they detect silence.

3. Collision Detection—If two people start talking at once, they shut up and try again.

So, although various participants might interrupt each other (their conversations collide), they politely resolve their conflicts and communication resumes. Some collisions are normal on an Ethernet, but they usually don't become a problem.

Token Ring

Remember the relay races you ran when you were a kid? Whoever had the baton was the one who ran. Token Ring is similar in that a token (baton) is passed around the wire. If a workstation wants to make a request or issue a command to the fileserver, it waits until the token comes along and then hangs on to the token while it transmits the information. The workstation releases the token when it has finished transmitting. The token makes its way around the ring, stopping and asking each workstation whether it has a message to transmit. This is a very polite protocol. (See fig. 2.6.)

Figure 2.6

A typical Token Ring configuration and how the "ring" works.

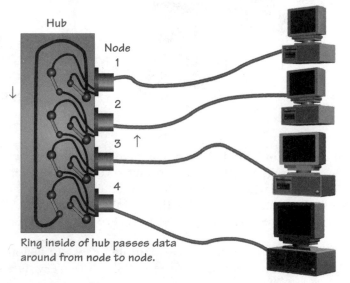

Ring inside of hub passes data around from node to node.

Again, it takes a lot longer to say "Token Ring" than it does for this to actually work on your network.

ARCnet

ARCnet (for Attached Resource Computer NETwork) is a token-passing scheme also. Introduced in 1977, it was the first commercially available LAN. ARCnet's advantages generally outweigh its disadvantages for smaller networks: it's inexpensive, easy to use, and hard to crash. On the down side, it's rather slow compared to some of its tonier competitors.

ARCnet works basically like this: instead of the wiring running in a circle or ring, like Token Ring, the wiring can be arranged in what is called a *bus* configuration. A bus means that the wiring can be laid out so that the two ends of the wire do not connect. Figure 2.7 shows a variation, the star-bus-configuration. Note that the data still travels from "stop" to "stop."

Figure 2.7

A typical ARCnet bus configuration.

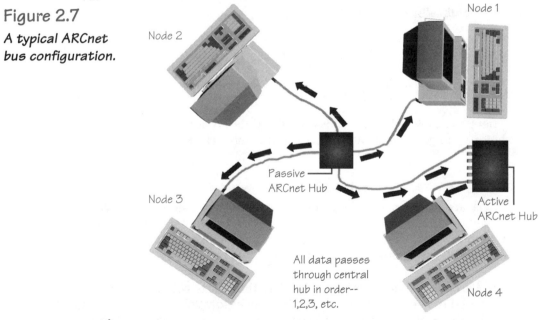

Node 1

Node 2

Passive ARCnet Hub

Node 3

Active ARCnet Hub

All data passes through central hub in order-- 1,2,3, etc.

Node 4

NOTE

The general consensus seems to be that the term "bus configuration" came from an analogy to, well, a city bus line. A signal moves along its electronically wired path, stopping at intervals to pick up or drop off data, just as a bus moves along its route, picking up or dropping off passengers.

Despite the fact that ARCnet is so widely used worldwide, it is not a *de jure*, or officially recognized and adopted, standard. Nevertheless, its commonsense appeal to many small LAN administrators has made it a *de facto* standard.

Mix and Match

The best protocol to use depends on a number of factors, including, but not limited to, other computers that you might want to talk to, the type of applications you are using and the type of traffic they generate, and so on. But the fact of the matter is that they all work well, and if you want, you can mix and match.

That's right, NetWare doesn't care which protocol you use and you could use all three right in the same fileserver. Or, you can have three fileservers all using different protocols hooked up to each other. All you do is slap the right kind of network card into the fileserver, load the right driver, hook up the wiring, and away you go.

Some Miscellaneous Information about NetWare

There are a few odds and ends about NetWare that you should be aware of before you get too deeply involved in the network world.

2.x versus 3.x versus 4.x

There are some basic differences in the different versions of NetWare that you should be aware of. First of all, the *x*s in the numbers are not algebraic variables, but denote additional numbers that make up the version numbers of the NetWare software.

NetWare 2.*x* and any version of NetWare that starts with the number 2 is designed to run on a PC with an 80286 processor. You don't *have* to run NetWare 2.*x* on an 80286 processor; it can be run on a 386 or 486, but NetWare 2.*x* only uses the 80286 processor instruction set.

NOTE

The processor is the "brain" of the computer. Although there are many good clone processors, Intel is the company that originated the 80x86 series of processors. The original IBM AT computer was based on the 80286 processor. That series of processors is usually referred to in the shortened term, where the leading "80" is left off the name, and the remainder of the number is used, as in the '286 (often referred to as a "brain-dead" processor), the 386, and 486. There is no processor called the 586, for the simple reason that Intel found out you cannot copyright a number. Intel named it the "Pentium" instead.

Because there are severe memory constraints in the 286 processor, Novell offers NetWare 3.*x*, the current version of which is 3.12. Although you can't run NetWare 3.12 on a 286 processor, you can run it on a 486 processor, but it uses the 386 instruction set. Incidentally, NetWare version 3.12 is primarily a cleaned-up version of version 3.11, Novell's most popular operating system version. 3.12 has some new features, and it's easier to install because all of the fixes (patches) required for 3.11 are built-in, but the two versions are pretty similar.

By the naming conventions just discussed, you would think that NetWare 4.01 requires a 486 processor. It doesn't. It only requires a 386 processor, but there are significant feature differences. Those feature differences are mainly useful in very large networks, usually two or more networks hooked together. If your users will be sharing two or more servers, you might find it advantageous to use NetWare 4.01.

Versionitis

Because NetWare is a network operating system and is designed to coordinate information from many different computers and run many different programs, it's a pretty complicated piece of software. It should come as no surprise that although Novell performs extensive testing on each version of NetWare it releases, a lot of different companies use it in many different ways. It follows that some "bugs" are not found until the new version is released on an unsuspecting world.

NOTE

The term bug, meaning a problem in the software, has an interesting beginning. Back in the olden days, when computers worked with vacuum tubes and relays and switches, work came to a screeching halt one day. After investigating, the problem was found to be a moth that had gotten caught and was causing a relay switch to stay open. Nowadays, of course, it means that there is a mistake somewhere in the program code. Stories persist that the moth is still preserved, wrapped in tape and attached to a page of the archived system logs (yet another reminder of the utility of keeping comprehensive network system logs).

A bug in a program can be anything from a minor annoyance to a wrong answer to a *crash*, where the system locks up completely and for (potentially) hours at a time.

Software companies use version numbers as follows: A brand new number before the period indicates a major revision of some type in the software. In the case of NetWare 2.*x* and 3.*x*, it involved rewriting the software. The numbers after the period indicate that a new release of the software has been made, but the new release consists of a few minor new features plus bug fixes. That's why many computer professionals have what is called a "six month rule."

The "six month rule" states that no hardware or software is to be purchased unless it has been on the market for a minimum of six months, or the next revision has been released. In the case of NetWare, the current release of the 3 series is 3.12, which is virtually identical to version 3.11. Since version 3.11 has been on the market for longer than six months, both 3.11 and 3.12 can be considered "safe" by anyone's standards. That doesn't mean they are bug free, only that the major bugs have been found and fixes have been made or are available.

TIP

Bugs happen in any software, but they're particularly bad news when they happen to network operating systems because the bugs affect many users.

To stay on top of bugs, be sure you have a CompuServe account and that you periodically check the NetWire forum

for updates on bugs and fixes. Even if you haven't been bitten
by a particular bug yet, consider putting the fix in. Think of it
as insect repellent.

In other words, it is generally advisable never to purchase software that has a "0" at the end of the version number (as in 3.0). With NetWare, like any other software, it's probably advisable to wait until at least a one has been added. 4.01 is probably OK, but you shouldn't jump too quickly to convert your network over to version 4.0. This applies to the add-ons that go with NetWare, also. Any "dot-oh" product is "bleeding edge" technology.

NOTE

Incidentally, an odd thing has been happening to version
numbers lately. The brand—spanking—new product Windows NT
has the version number 3.1! Don't be fooled. The first version
of any new product is always a "dot-oh."

Novell Certified: The True Story

A lot of companies advertise that their products are "Novell Certified." At first glance, this seems to be a ringing endorsement of some type and appears to be a safe purchase. That is not necessarily the case. When you see this label in connection with a computer that is advertised as either a workstation or fileserver, be extra careful.

For a computer to be certified by Novell, it is tested by Novell for compatibility with a NetWare network. The thing is, it might have needed a few adjustments to work with a Novell network. The "adjustment" can be anything from a device driver (usually easily obtained from the manufacturer) to a different chip. And sometimes the manufacturer doesn't include the different chip as standard equipment.

There are two ways to find out whether there are any caveats concerning using a particular piece of computer equipment with NetWare. The first is to check on NetWire. Refer to Chapter 14 for more information on NetWire. The other way is to call Novell at 1-800-453-1267.

Shareware and Networks

Shareware is a unique breed of software that you are encouraged to try *before* you buy. If you "try before you buy" with commercial software (including Novell), you're in violation of the licensing agreement and subject to severe fines and legal action; in other words, you're in big trouble.

Shareware is typically written by enterprising individuals in their spare time. Because they aren't a big commercial enterprise, they have little to no advertising budget and generally limited resources. The only way for them to sell their software is to let you try it and then hope that you like it so much that you pay them for it.

Therefore, shareware is software on the honor system. You can install it and use it with no obligation. After a defined time period (usually 20 to 30 days), you need to make an executive decision. If you don't like it, erase it from your hard disk and that's it. If you like it and plan to continue using it, then you send the author the amount of money requested. Shareware prices start at around five bucks and go up from there.

Shareware Shortfalls

Although there is some really good shareware out in the world, it's best to think twice before installing shareware on the fileserver and using a shareware program for something like the menu system or some other type of daily-use product.

The reason for this caution is that shareware is typically written by one person. Suppose that person gets hit by a truck or decides to stop writing software altogether? It's not the money that's a big concern here, but rather the program itself. If it is something that's highly visible to everyone on the network, switching to another program may have a big effect on many people.

It is generally advisable to consider commercial products from established companies as a first choice. They are more likely to keep up with the latest and greatest changes in Novell as well as workstation operating systems and be more responsive to customer needs. One person working at home after a "regular" job might not have the resources and contacts to keep his or her software current with the commercial vendors' products.

It doesn't hurt to use a nifty utility here and there; it's just not always advisable to make a shareware program an indispensable part of your network strategy.

Chapter 2, Short and Sweet

This chapter covered some important concepts:

1. Distributed processing is what a Novell 3.12/3.11 network is all about. Each workstation can perform its own "work" and does not rely on the processor in the fileserver to process information.

2. Central processing networks are networks in which not only all the file handling and file requesting is done at the fileserver, but also the application processing occurs in the fileserver as well. A PC is not required to hook up to a central processing network; a "dumb terminal" does the trick nicely.

3. Novell NetWare 3.12/3.11 is a client-server network, wherein the file server "serves" up the files and programs and services all requests to the workstations, or "clients." The clients do not talk to each other, only to the fileserver.

4. A peer-to-peer network is one in which the workstations talk to each other, and any one of them can be the fileserver. These types of networks are ideal—not to mention cheaper—for smaller groups.

5. The three major types of protocols that can be used on a NetWare network are Ethernet, Token Ring, and ARCnet. A protocol is the bits-and-bytes method of communication that is used over the network. Each type has its own merit.

6. The Ethernet protocol stops, listens, and transmits. If there are any collisions, it retransmits after a random amount of time. The method of managing transmissions in Ethernet is called CSMA/CD, or Carrier Sense Multiple Access/Collision Detection.

7. The Token Ring protocol passes a little token around the wire. If a workstation has something it wants to transmit it waits until it receives the token, transmits its message, and releases the token when it's finished. Since only one token exists at a given time, only one workstation can transmit and collisions cannot occur.

8. ARCnet is similar to Token Ring in that it uses a token to coordinate access to the fileserver.

9.   You can mix and match protocols on a NetWare network, because NetWare is very flexible and really couldn't care less which protocol you use.

10. NetWare 2.*x* only runs on an 80286 processor, whereas NetWare 3.*x* and 4.*x* run on 80386 processors and above.

11. It's usually a very good idea to follow the "six-month rule" and wait six months after software has been released or wait for a release that does not have a zero at the end before making a purchase. You'll have to take fewer Maalox and aspirin tablets that way.

12. It's best to think twice before using a shareware program on your fileserver as a main program or utility. Remember that what you gain in money saved you generally give up in product support and overall reliability.

Chapter 3

Key Terms to Look for:

➡ fileserver
➡ working area
➡ directory
➡ file name
➡ supervisor
➡ sneakernet
➡ K.I.S.S.
➡ RAM
➡ tape backups
➡ log books

Have You Got a Plan Yet?

(Or, Stuff That's So Important It Deserves a Separate Chapter)

A successful network is one that provides a productive environment for the users of the system.

How do you accomplish the installation of a successful network? There's only one way: planning. Okay, planning doesn't sound very glamorous, and if you get right down do it, it's just plain hard work. But a well-planned network is marked by the problems that you *don't* have.

The truth is that you don't need to be a network expert to be able to sit down and understand a few basic concepts of how a network works so that you can figure out what you want to do with it. What you *do* need is the discipline to sit down with the others in your office and plan out this whole network business. In this chapter, you learn:

➡ The basic questions you need to ask to get you started in planning your network

➡ How to avoid really costly mistakes in setting up your network

➡ What kinds of changes you can *really* expect a network to make in the way you work

Planning, Planning, Planning

Consider the following Network Story:

A person from another department in the company where I was working came to me one day and asked me to install their Novell network. "Do you have your work flow planned?" I asked.

"No," came the response.

"Do you know what applications you are going to run on it?"

"Well, no. We're going to figure that out later."

"Do you know which people should have access to which files?"

"Well, no, but we know we can share files more easily, so we submitted a schedule for some work that was based on getting the network up and running as soon as possible."

"When can we schedule a planning session so that we can settle these issues?"

"I don't see how we can fit any more meetings in right now. Our project's just starting up and everyone's schedules are completely filled."

"You do realize that the network isn't going to do you any good until you know the answers to those questions, don't you?"

"Well, look, we don't have time for that now, we just need to get NetWare installed and get it running."

Not one to refuse budget money, I complied with the request to install NetWare. They were all hung up on the mechanics of doing it and wouldn't listen when I said that the mechanics of installation were the least of their problems.

You've got to plan before you install, but would my networking neophytes listen?

It didn't take long to successfully install the NOS (network operating system), and as soon as I finished, I turned to the group representative and asked how the users should be set up. "Well, I don't really know", she said, "I don't really understand how all that works, but show me how to run NetWare." *Obviously, there wasn't much to show her, but I did the best I could at the time. I checked in a couple of months later to see whether they had any questions or needed any help. The fileserver was sitting in a corner of the room, unused. "We just don't have the time; we're behind schedule on that project," I was told.*

The moral of the story: The mechanics of actually installing NetWare are a breeze. If you don't take the time to plan exactly what it is you are going to do with a network, however, you might as well not bother with one.

There are three types of analysis that you need to do for a successful network:

1. Analyze your current work flow.
2. Plan your anticipated work flow.
3. Plan your installation.

What may seem like a tough job at first isn't really that bad if you break it down into smaller steps.

Current Work Flow

The first thing to do is to sit down and draw a flow chart of how the work in your office proceeds now. This is a good time to review procedures and eliminate unnecessary steps. The next thing to do is to translate that work flow into how the work will proceed on a network.

A Good Candidate for Network Streamlining

As an example, take the case of a mythical law firm, Lucky Litigators.

Like most law firms, each client is assigned a client number for billing and filing purposes. Work generally proceeds as follows:

1. The attorneys prepare a document by marking up a similar agreement done for a different client.

2. The secretary copies the old document to a new document name and makes the indicated changes. After printing the revised document, the secretary returns it to the lawyer.

3. The secretaries pass around floppy disks to share their documents with each other. Each disk represents all the documents for one particular client.

4. The attorney makes changes to the printed document (surprise!) and returns it to the secretary for changes.

5. The document bounces back and forth between attorney and secretary several times. The process is finally stopped (and the secretary's sanity is barely saved) only because the client shows up and wants the document.

6. The signed document finally goes to rest in the permanent client file.

These steps are repeated endlessly by all the attorneys and their support staff. Now let's make a flow chart of this process, like the one shown in figure 3.1.

Right now, the secretary is working from a stand-alone PC. One thing that doesn't show up clearly in the work flow diagram is the fact that the attorney or the secretary must go rummaging around in the file room to find the document that is being used as a template for the new work. And face it, that's a pretty inefficient way to run a business.

A Networking Solution

After completing analysis of the current work flow, you and the users need to sit down and figure out how this work can proceed smoothly on a network. You do not need to modify the basic procedure here at all.

Instead of a disk representing each client number, how about designating an area on the fileserver for final client documents?

Figure 3.1

Work flow at Lucky Litigators.

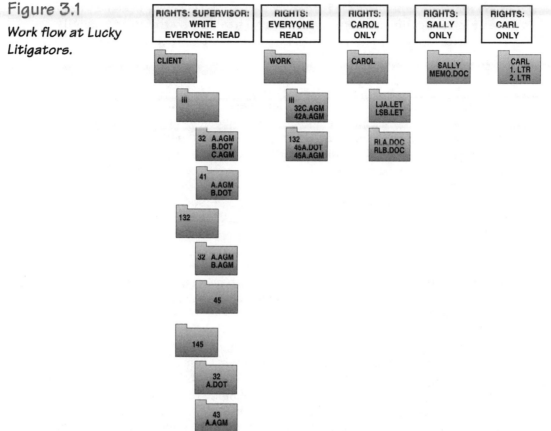

Then determine who needs to access these documents and what kind of access they need. Broadly speaking, you can define two categories of access privileges:

➡ *Read-only* access gives users the ability to examine the contents of files but not to modify them. This is useful for document templates, for documents that are stable and should not be modified, or for documents that may be examined by all but should be altered by few.

➡ *Read-write* access allows users to modify the files. Obviously at least the appropriate secretaries need read-write access in order to create new documents.

If the main document area is read-only, then each secretary needs a *working area* for the documents being modified and finalized by the attorneys. All secretaries can then write, or save, the documents to their personal working area.

Hmmmm... at first it might make sense to provide each secretary with a personal directory for this work, but let's carry that through another step. What if a secretary is sick and someone else needs to finish the document? No one wants to have someone else mucking around with their personal files. So let's make a "client-file working area" on the fileserver's hard disk that everyone has access to.

We still want to provide each secretary with a personal directory, but that will be for work that doesn't have to be shared, such as the attorneys' letters and memos.

Somewhere along the line, you should address the subject of conventions for naming the document files. In DOS, you only have eight characters to work with (eleven if you don't want a standard file name extension like .DOC), and that can be pretty restrictive.

Each submatter may have two or three agreements designated with the same submatter number. (Submatter is just what our law office friends call related files.) How do we differentiate the documents? Well, how about if we append an alphabetic designation to the file name or use an alphabetic designation as a prefix? That should do it. Now it's time to draw a chart showing how the fileserver will be set up and how the work will flow on the server (see fig. 3.2).

Note that NetWare has a special name for the system administrator: *supervisor*. In the case of Lucky Litigators, when a document has been signed by the client (or otherwise wrestled from the attorney grasping at the red revision-marking pen), the supervisor copies the document from the working area, in this case the WORK directory, to the CLIENT directory. Don't forget, we don't want anyone else to be able to write to the directory where the final documents are kept, so that they aren't accidentally erased or otherwise messed up.

If you don't want to rely on the supervisor to do this file copying, it is possible to define directories so that users can store files in them but cannot modify or delete the files once they are stored. Nor can they copy a new file over an old file with the same name without assistance from the supervisor.

You might call these directories save-only, but users can also read any file in a save-only directory.

Figure 3.2

Work flow at the Lucky Litigators Law Firm on a fileserver.

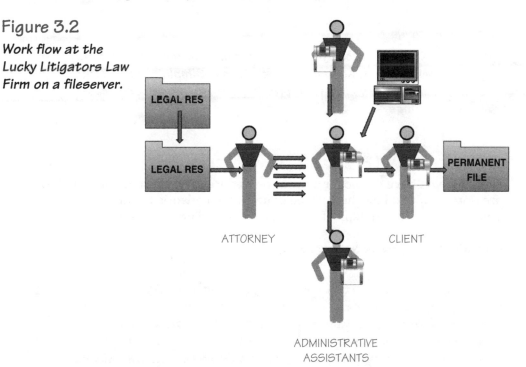

As you can see in figure 3.2, we have not significantly modified anything from the original work flow; we've merely eliminated the "sneakernet." Now, everyone's files are stored in a central location that is accessible to all. Trading files on floppies is a thing of the past.

Keep in mind that this is only an example of how the Lucky Lits can set up its network fileserver for producing client documents. The law firm not only needs to go through this process for client documents, but for other things that are done on the stand-alone computers as well. Some examples:

→   How are the lawyers tracking their time for billing purposes?

→   What about the firm's accounting system?

→   Would it be useful to have a central phone and address index?

You need to sit down and figure out the best way to make working on a network operate most effeciently and productively for your unique situation.

TIP

Remember when you are setting up your fileserver to KISS. No, not me. KISS stands for Keep It Simple, Stupid. KISS should be your watchword. Don't try to overly complicate things.

New Work Flow (A Brave New World)

Now that you have gone over all your procedures and charted out how they are done now and how they can be done on the network, it's time to use your imagination and think of what else you could do with a network.

Consider the following Network Story:

When we planned our first network, we sat down and calculated the disk space we would need for the work that everyone would share our client database. Then we doubled that amount and purchased the disk size accordingly. What we should have done was doubled that amount again, because what we didn't account for was that as soon as the network was set up and in place, everyone started thinking about the things we could do—both new applications and changing existing procedures—with the network. Within a year we had to triple the size of our disk storage space.

Yup. This is an extremely common mistake that is made where new networks are installed. And although adding disk storage space isn't a catastrophe, it's usually cheaper, and certainly easier, to do it when beginning to set up a new network.

Another Network-Related Solution or Two

So, in the case of the Lucky Litigators, let's look at an additional procedure (besides the actual file and document management) that could be performed differently because of the network. How about timekeeping? Right now, it's done as follows:

1. Attorneys and secretaries keep track of their billable time by noting the times on a form.

2. The daily form is turned in to the bookkeeper, who hires someone to input the time for the law firm.

3. The program generates a report that is handed back to each attorney and secretary, who make sure that their time was entered correctly.

4. After every attorney and secretary checks his or her time from the reports, statements are generated and sent to the clients.

Well, this is certainly a labor-intensive process, isn't it? How about if we shake things up at the law firm a little bit and install a network timekeeping program? Why then, everyone could <gasp> enter their billable time directly into the system! That would eliminate the need for someone to enter everyone's time! They could check their own billable time for the month and then give the okay for the statements to be prepared! Wow! In this case, we need to allow additional disk space for a networkable timekeeping system.

And how about completely new applications that could be run on a network? Why, just think if an electronic mail (e-mail) system were installed! The attorneys could send messages to each other and their secretaries while they were talking on the phone, without wasting time to catch someone when they were free. (Are attorneys ever free? No, and they're not cheap, either.)

How about a network scheduling program? Members of the firm could schedule conferences, conference rooms, and all sorts of things, freeing up time and making the most of their resources.

These ideas are just the tip of the iceberg. But it's a really good idea for everyone concerned to have a bit of a brainstorming session to come up with ideas and wish lists.

Don't Make Those Pennies Squeak

In addition to underestimating disk space, a common mistake that people make when installing a network is trying to cut corners on all sorts of things—wiring, computers, tape backups—all of which can cost vast amounts of money to correct. It is *always* cheaper to spend money on the good stuff in the beginning rather than trying to correct a problem later. In addition to the cost of the equipment itself, tremendous amounts of time are wasted on troubleshooting.

Consider the following story:

> A large manufacturing firm installed a network at its plant and main offices. They decided to install cable that was OK for their present network, but left no room for performance improvement. Soon, however, company management decided that document imaging was a key technology in their business and that they should jump on the bandwagon. Document imaging produces a lot of network traffic. Oops, the cable they installed couldn't support higher speeds! To make imaging work, they would have to rewire the entire office complex with wiring that would have only cost a few cents a foot extra the first time around.

Consider the costs to the company here, including the cost of the wire both times, the cost of the labor of the firm hired to install the wire both times, and the cost of reducing the company's competitiveness while they waited to implement a key technology. Was it worth saving five cents a foot the first time the cable was installed?

Just in case you don't get the point yet, consider another story:

> A large firm was considering two different brands of computers to use as fileservers. The choice was between a Compaq and Brand Z. To get the Compaq set up and running as a fileserver was a "no brainer." To get Brand Z up and running required sending away to the Brand Z company for a new chip, waiting several weeks, receiving the chip, installing it, and then installing NetWare. When that didn't work, they had to contact Brand Z company and obtain a few special drivers and another chip.
>
> Although the Brand Z computer was a few hundred dollars cheaper, how much did it cost in labor, lost production time, troubleshooting, and more labor to get Brand Z up and running? Quite a bit more than the difference in the initial purchase price of the original machines.

No, you don't have to buy the most expensive equipment available to get a good network. It does pay to ask real live people whether they are happy with the equipment they have purchased, what sorts of problems they have had, and how much time, trouble, and money have been poured into making them right. See Chapter 14, "Help at Hand," to find out good sources of checking with real live people about their successes and failures.

Selecting Software

It may seem obvious, but it's worth stating that you should select the software to fit the task, not the task to fit the software. Too many people hear about a program from a friend and then decide to use it for their tasks simply based on that friend's endorsement. Once again, this can turn out to be a costly mistake.

Here are a few tips on selecting a software package that fits the task:

1. Write down just what the end product should be; for example, a report(s) of some kind, a database of customer names and information that you want to use in many types of applications, or whatever.

2. Now start working backwards. Are there any interim reports you will need? Will you need to have several people access the information? Do you anticipate a lot of changes to the information? How about volume?

3. Working with the information in items 1 and 2, make a wish list of the features that are important to you. Don't forget to include things like costs of the original program as well as technical support costs, and so on. Now, give each feature a "weight." You might use a scale of 1 to 10 for weights. "Works with our existing document files" is probably a 10. "Flexibility of reports" might be a 7. "Includes a Thesaurus" might be a 2.

4. Take your list to your dealer or consultant and find out the top three programs that fit your criteria the closest. Look for reviews of those types of products in trade magazines at the library, or make inquiries on CompuServe Information Service (see Chapter 14 for more information about CompuServe).

5. Arrange for a demonstration of the program, or better yet, arrange for an evaluation copy so that you can install and work with it yourself.

WARNING

Never make a decision to purchase software or hardware based solely on a review in a computer publication. Reviews are a good starting place, but remember that their results will often differ from your own due to many different factors: the equipment they used, the type of tests they ran, the data they used, and so on. In some cases, these differences can be significant. Also keep in mind that the software or hardware sent to publications by the manufacturers are sometimes twiddled with so that the reviews will tip the scale in the manufacturers' favor.

6. In the end, you'll likely have to figure out your own optimum balance of options to weigh. How stable are the early versions of the software's release? Are there special prices available on upgrades? How reliable and accessible is software support from the company that sells it? How critical is a particular brand to your company's operations? The watchword is still *planning*. The more thought you put in ahead of time, the less likely you are to be unpleasantly surprised in the long run.

Selecting Hardware

NOTE

In the interests of introducing the reader to the basic concept of pre-LAN planning, this chapter briefly covers the areas you'll need to consider. For more in-depth discussion, however, you should refer to Chapter 4, "NOS Hardware;" Chapter 7, "Disk and Directory Management;" and Chapter 11, "Disaster Planning and Tape Backups."

After you have selected the software that you need to use, it's time to select the hardware. Start by looking at the memory and processor requirements of the software you have selected. Generally speaking, don't go with the minimum requirement. Technically, Windows will run on a 16 megahertz 386SX, but life's too short for that. If in doubt, talk to users and find out what is an adequate configuration.

For workstations, it's necessary not only to look at the current tasks being performed but to try to anticipate future needs. Don't be stingy, but don't wildly overbuy here. If the people in your office are never going to perform any task except for relatively small word processing jobs, it is clearly not necessary to purchase machines with 32M of RAM.

On the other hand, while getting more RAM upfront is easy, upgrading CPUs and increasing speed later on can be a bit of a pain; therefore, if you see a realistic need for increased Meg (megabytes) in the near future, save yourself the trouble and get ready for it now.

Backup Systems

When selecting a tape backup unit, buying more than you need is usually a pretty good idea. The reason is that you want to be able to make unattended backups, and if you outgrow your backup system very soon, the options are:

1. Make unattended backups of critical data every other night.

2. Back up during the day (this slows down the system for everyone and some files cannot be backed up when they are in use).

3. Purchase a whole new back-up unit (expensive).

Be sure the software you select is designed to work with NetWare! There's hidden stuff on a server (called the Bindery) that some software can't back up. Ideally, the software should be tested and certified by Novell for NetWare compatibility.

Then pick a tape drive that works with the software. The drive you select is less important than its capacity. Ideally, you should be able to back up the entire server with one tape. Otherwise, unattended backups at three in the morning aren't very practical. Tape backup units are available with capacities up to about 8 gigabytes, and multi-tape changers are available if your backup requirements are huge.

NOTE

Don't be too attracted by the new, inexpensive tape backup systems that are intended for use on personal computers. $300 probably isn't enough to spend, but good tape backup units can be had for as little as $700 if you don't need a lot of capacity. Get an industrial-strength tape backup unit and be sure your dealer will get it repaired promptly if it fails.

TIP
Finally, before you put any users on line, back up your server, erase all the server files, and try to restore it. I can't tell you how many times users have tried to restore files after a disaster only to find out that they couldn't.

Monitors

The fileserver really doesn't need a color monitor with a high-resolution screen. This is one place where cheap is smart. Probably the only one, though. When purchasing monitors for workstations, it is best to make side-by-side comparisons, just like you do when purchasing a television.

WARNING
(Okay, so we're repeating ourselves here. Better to heed this warning twice than to pay again a higher price, no?) Never make a decision to purchase software or hardware based solely on a review in a computer publication. Reviews are a good starting place, but remember that their results will often differ from your own due to many different factors: the equipment they used, the type of tests they ran, the data they used, and so on. In some cases, these differences can be significant. Also keep in mind that the software or hardware sent to publications by the manufacturers are sometimes twiddled with so that the reviews will tip the scale in the manufacturers' favor.

Together at Last

Before attempting to install any hardware or software, make sure that you follow these simple rules:

1. Check the documentation, making sure that you have the necessary hardware and software resources you need.

2. Allocate plenty of time for the task.

3. Allocate plenty of time for testing before springing the new software or hardware on an unsuspecting office.

4. If something doesn't work, never change more than one thing at a time.

5. Describe all the changes you have made in a log book; then, if the same problem arises or a new configuration goes awry, you can get back to where you started.

If you are planning a new network installation and have decided on several new network versions of programs to run on the network, do not even think about trying to get them all installed and running at one time. Plan to install one at a time, making sure it works with everyone's workstation before moving on to the next program. Allowing a schedule of one program every two weeks or so is probably a good idea, depending on the program and how many people use it.

Network Expectations versus Realities

Many people read newspapers and magazine articles and see those magic words "LAN" and "PC" and think that a network will be a cure-all for whatever ails the company. Unfortunately, this is not the case, and it'll occasionally fall into your hands to delicately remind management of this fact.

On the other hand, people in a company often feel threatened when told that a network is going to be installed. They don't understand it, don't know what to expect, and feel like they are being left out of critical company direction planning. Further, the spectre of Big Brother, watching over everyone's shoulders as they go about their business, is a powerful one. Therefore, it'll also fall into your hands to address employee concerns about this—frankly and with a sympathetic point of view.

As mentioned in the previous section, a network is a tool. Just how successfully the tool works in your organization depends on how much up-front planning and requirements analysis the company does. It also depends on how well the network is accepted by the people who will use it.

Getting the Users Involved

The best way to ensure that the network is successful and meets needs is to have at least one or two planning sessions with *everyone* in the company or department involved. They don't have to know anything about computers to become involved. The important thing here is that they *are* involved.

Here are the things that you should discuss:

1. **Expectations.** Find out what everyone's expectations are. Get them to be specific. This will help focus on items that can and cannot be accomplished with the network.

2. **Wish lists.** This is a good time to make up the wish list of tasks that can be performed on the network. Even though you may not be able to integrate every employee want and desire into the LAN, you can at least address them and get a handle on what others will look for in their LAN.

3. **Concerns.** Find out what everyone's concerns are. Maybe they will be worried about losing valuable time while installation is proceeding. Or cost, or whatever.

4. **Policies.** What will be your policies for security, for example. How often will users be expected to change their passwords. What is your company's policy on privacy? Will managers be examining users' electronic mail and files? All such concerns should be addressed in a policies and procedures manual so that users know what to expect.

If you won't be installing the network yourself, it is best to invite to the meeting the dealer or consultant who will be installing and supporting the network. That person will be able to get a much better idea of what the network needs to accomplish to make sure that they have a satisfied client. They can help select the software and hardware to meet the requirements defined in this meeting.

This type of meeting will help eliminate any surprises after the installation of the software and hardware is complete.

Keeping the Users Involved

A second meeting is a good idea. That meeting should focus on addressing any leftover expectations, concerns, or wish list items that have not already been addressed. Another good idea is to firm up software selections and new procedures that will be implemented.

Open communication between all involved can really help to allay fears and problems that a new network installation may cause. Consider this communication an integral part of the planning process.

Chapter 3, Short and Sweet

The key points covered in this chapter were:

1. Chart current procedures and work flow so that they can be properly translated into a workable network structure.

2. Chart the way the work will flow on the network, planning the directories and the overall access that will be granted to the directories and files as you proceed.

3. Brainstorm new procedures for current applications and totally new uses that the network will enable everyone to use.

4. Don't buy hardware or software based on best price. "Best price" products will cost everyone in the office lost work time, not to mention added replacement costs.

5. Never buy products until firm requirements have been defined. Start the process by asking what problem will be solved or what job is to be accomplished.

6. Never buy products based solely on publication reviews or word of mouth. Just as you don't have to be a mechanic to be a good consumer when purchasing a car, you don't have to be a computer wizard when purchasing computer stuff. Just be a good consumer—ask around and do your own test driving when you can. Seeing is believing.

7. Schedule your complete software and hardware installation over a reasonable period of time. Remember that patience pays.

8. Involve everyone in the office with the network before making or finalizing any decisions; everyone can contribute good ideas. A surprise-free network is a blessing.

Above all, KISS! (Keep It Simple, Stupid!)

PART TWO

NetWare and Networking Unraveled

Joe considers the bailiwick that has been thrust upon him, and momentarily weighs the benefits of slashing his wrists...

NOS Hardware

(Or, Things You Should Know Before You Buy, Borrow, or Lease)

Chapter 4

Key Terms to Look for:

→ redundancy

→ cannibalizing

→ disk duplexing

→ split seek

→ disk mirroring

→ IRQ (interrupt request)

→ Direct Memory Access

→ shared memory

→ base I/O memory

→ bus mastering

→ hexadecimal

→ mirror image backup

→ file-by-file backup

→ incremental backup

→ off-site storage

→ UPS (uninterruptible power supply)

→ file corruption

→ brownouts

→ spikes

What does the well-dressed LAN wear this year? This chapter discusses all the components that you will need for a well-outfitted LAN and explains some things you need to know about each component. This chapter will cover:

→ How not to worry about IHO (Instant Hardware Obsolescence)

→ What makes a server different from a workstation, and why it's important

→ Understanding Network Interface Cards (NICs)

→ Why wiring is critical

→ All about backing up and the best equipment for doing so

→ Why UPS has other meanings besides United Parcel Service (hint: this hardware could save you your job)

→ Things to consider when selecting network printers

➜   Modems, faxes, and things that go beep in the night

➜   Giving a look to monitors

LAN Equipment Life Span

No matter what equipment you select for your LAN, it will be technologically outdated practically the day after it is purchased. Tomorrow there will always be something smaller, faster, and more powerful, so don't expect to stay ahead of the technology curve. Don't let the fact that you cannot stay on top of the latest technology give you heartburn; no one else can, either.

A three-to-five year useful life span is generally the goal in making computer purchases. The right decisions depend on a number of factors, including the type of applications you are running now, the type of applications you anticipate running in the future, the number of users on the network, the type of information involved, and so on.

The trick is to purchase above current needs, but not so far above that you do not need the horsepower for five years (or ever). At the same time, do not purchase just to meet current needs. And never, ever purchase far below them, so that the equipment must be replaced within three years. The following sections explain the factors that you need to consider.

Servers and Workstations

The fileserver is generally going to be the most powerful computer in the office. Even though the fileserver computer is not actually running application programs (the workstations do that), it is working hard to service everyone's requests in fetching and storing the programs and data they ask for. Ideally, the fileserver will be powerful enough to respond to requests as fast as if the user was working off the local workstation hard drive.

Special-Purpose Fileservers

Some companies have worked hard designing computers whose sole purpose in life is to be fileservers. Sometimes you will hear them called "superservers" to differentiate them from more conventional PCs that are powerful enough to be good servers. Superservers can be really fine machines and optimized to the max, but they do have a few drawbacks.

The first thing to consider is that many of these machines cannot be used as a general purpose PC. Consider what will happen in a few years when it is bogged down by all the new users on the LAN, it's running too slow, and it's time for a new fileserver. In most companies, fileservers get recycled as workstations and workstations get recycled as gateways and gateways get recycled to the trash or your favorite charity. In this case, the fileserver could only go right to the trash or serve as anchor on someone's sailboat.

Some superserver companies, as well as PC makers, do offer upgradable machines, but who knows what's going to happen in a few years and maybe you won't feel comfortable staying with that vendor for a variety of reasons. In most cases, I recommend against the special purpose fileservers because they cannot serve extra duty as workstations, and spare parts cannot generally be cannibalized from a general-purpose PC. As a general rule, the additional performance does not outweigh these drawbacks.

Before you discount a special-purpose fileserver, consider the case of an oil company I know about in Canada. This company puts an extremely heavy load on its fileservers to wring every possible ounce of performance out of them, and the fact that the machines will be on the trash heap in a few years doesn't faze the company at all. The extra performance the company gets for its applications, usage, and type of business is well worth the drawbacks that I have mentioned here. Perspective is everything.

Redundancy

Once the LAN is up and running and everyone relies on it to function smoothly to get their work done, people tend to get upset if the network fails for some reason. Well, okay, some people actually scream, but we'll deal with those pesky users in Chapter 14. Your job is to get the network back up and running as quickly as possible first and then figure out what went wrong.

The fastest way to fix something is to replace it as quickly as possible with a duplicate component. In several cases, NetWare will change over to the duplicate automatically, without missing a heartbeat. Redundant components aren't just an idle investment; they are insurance against that inevitable day when a component fails. And components always fail at the most inconvenient time. Murphy says so!

The best redundant component is a complete replacement fileserver. Nice, but expensive. If you can't get a second fileserver in your budget, however, don't give up. There are other options that protect the most important thing on your network: the data on your fileserver.

Backup Fileserver

Let's start with the obvious. In a perfect world, ideally the best thing to do is to order a computer that is a duplicate of the fileserver machine, but perhaps with less disk space. This machine can be put to use as the network administrator's workstation, even if it does have a bit more horsepower than necessary for ordinary workstation tasks.

When the server computer fails there are three immediate courses of action available:

1. Restore the NOS and critical information onto the duplicate machine from the backup tapes you have made regularly (there's more on doing backups later in this chapter). Your network can be back up and running within a couple of hours and the fileserver machine can be worked on without everyone breathing down your neck.

2. If the hard drive(s) or disk controller is not the failed part(s) on the fileserver, swap the server's drives with the ones in the workstation machine and troubleshoot the fileserver computer at your leisure. No restoring from backups is necessary with this option.

3. Cannibalize the required part from the workstation computer (if possible) and repair or replace the failed server part without disrupting the network further.

The best duplicate server is one that is used strictly for that purpose. If you have a spare server, you can cut downtime to a minimum. Each morning when you come in, restore last night's backup tapes to the duplicate server. Now, if your main server fails, just pull its plug and fire up the duplicate. Ten minutes of downtime should be about the maximum you'll experience with this plan.

TIP

What happens if you can't afford even a minute of downtime or a byte of lost data? If your LAN is that important, you can probably convince your company to get NetWare with System Fault Tolerance III (SFT III). This level of fault tolerance wires

two servers in parallel so that they exactly mirror each other. If the primary server fails for any reason, the backup server takes over without a hiccup. Expensive, but if your LAN is tracking stock trades, medical patient data, or other such critical data, SFT III is probably worth it.

Disk Duplexing

Unless you go for SFT III (big bucks!), a duplicate server won't protect you against lost data. If your hard drive crashes, every file in use will probably be corrupted. Several things can cause a hard drive to fail: mechanical failure of the hard drive itself, blown circuits in the disk controller card, or just a bad hard drive data cable.

Suppose, however, that a second disk drive could be hooked up as a mirror image of the primary drive? Then, if the primary fails, the secondary can take over. You can leave the server up while you order a replacement disk drive and then replace it after hours. Your users will never know you had problems.

There are two ways to do this: duplexing (the deluxe route) and mirroring (the economy plan).

Disk duplexing requires both two disk controllers and two disk drives in the fileserver. Figure 4.1 illustrates this simple but effective form of redundancy.

The information on disk drive #1 is exactly mirrored on disk drive #2. With disk duplexing, all the disk-related bases are covered. Your server will continue to function through any single failure of a disk drive, disk controller, or cable. The network never misses a beat.

Besides the nice warm fuzzies of knowing your disk and controller are duplicated, disk duplexing also provides a boost to performance in the fileserver. What happens is that when information is requested, one disk can be getting information while the other disk is busy writing. If both disks are idle, they can cooperate with each other in getting the information.

Figure 4.1

Disk duplexing.

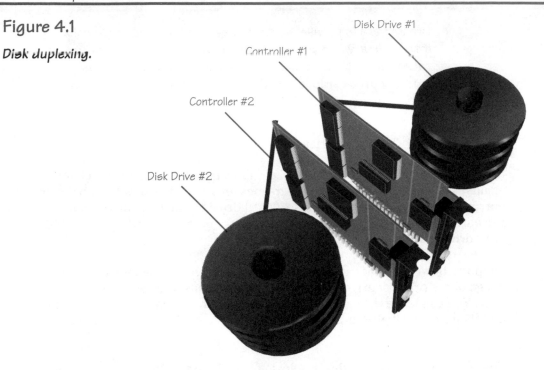

Disk Drive #1

Controller #1

Controller #2

Disk Drive #2

NOTE

When you use disk duplexing and the two disks are sharing the chore of reading the information that has been requested, the correct terminology is split seek*. At first this might sound like you have a schizophrenic system to deal with, but NetWare has been written so that whichever disk drive can fetch the information fastest does so. Or, NetWare will figure out which drive can get which part of the information fastest and both of the drives fetch different parts of the information.*

The only catch to disk duplexing is that if you happen to use two different sizes of disk drives (not recommended), then the difference in disk space is wasted space. The capacity of the smaller of the two drives is what is mirrored. In other words, if you have one disk drive with 200M of space and the other one with 225M of space, and you decide to duplex the disks, 25M of disk space on the 225M drive will never be used.

Disk Mirroring

Disk mirroring is another way to provide redundancy on the system, but with only one disk drive controller. This is a good option to use if the cost of an additional disk controller just stretches your budget too tight or there is no more room in the fileserver for another board. Figure 4.2 shows what disk mirroring is all about.

Figure 4.2

Disk mirroring.

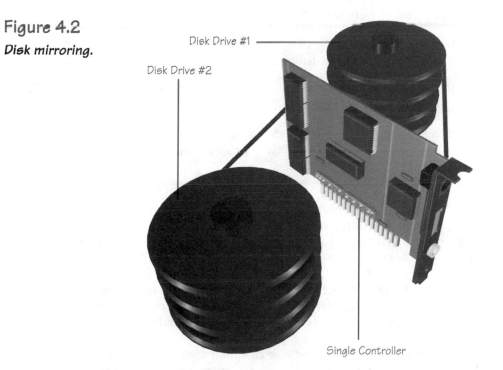

Disk Drive #1

Disk Drive #2

Single Controller

Since disk mirroring only involves one disk controller, writing information can be a little bit slower, because there is only one controller to write to both disk drives. Reading is still liable to be faster than with one disk. If one disk is busy writing, the other disk can be busy reading information and getting ready to send it over the network.

Disk mirroring is pickier than disk duplexing because it does require that both disks be the exact same type and size. But once again, if one disk fails, the other one is right there ready to keep the network going full speed.

Like Brands

Purchasing all the same brand of computers for the fileserver and workstation is often a good idea. Some of the reasons for doing so would be:

➔   The person or consulting company that supports your installation will not have to learn the idiosyncrasies of several different brands of computers. Come to think of it, *you* won't either.

➔   Owning several models of the same brand of computer will allow for juggling the hardware around easily in a pinch.

➔   If purchased at the same time, negotiating for volume discounts is (usually) easily accomplished.

➔   Troubleshooting is much easier: swapping parts between like models of computers helps to establish a baseline on what is working and what isn't.

I've seen LANs in which the workstations ranged from monochrome monitor IBM ATs, through five different brands of 386 PCs , three different 486 models, and a dozen Macs. Some of the manufacturers of the PCs in this goulash hadn't been in business for years! Every new PC that went on the LAN was an adventure. I am firmly convinced that the hidden support costs far outweigh the value of such old PCs. Now if I could just convince management. If you have to work with such an equipment mix, my sympathies. If you're lucky enough to be starting from scratch, remember to KISS.

A note of caution though. Just because one manufacturer offers several models does not mean that disk drives or memory or other parts are interchangeable between the different models.

Network Interface Cards (NICs)

NIC prices are relatively cheap. However, along with disk drives and disk controllers, NICs are also one of the biggest sources of bottlenecks in network performance. The best thing to do is to get ultra-super-duper NICs for the fileserver, since those NICs are the ones that work the hardest.

Faster Highways and Mixing Traffic in the Fileserver

If your fileserver will have more than about fifty workstations working from it, or if a few of the workstations will be putting a really heavy load on the fileserver, it's a good idea to consider putting two or more NICs in the fileserver. This is like building a four-lane superhighway, rather than expecting rush-hour traffic to make do with a two-lane country road.

If you have some workstations that are running Token Ring and some workstations that are running Ethernet and some that are running ARCnet, or a combination of these, you can mix and match these protocols in the fileserver by installing the correct NICs.

NetWare doesn't care if you mix and match the types of NICs or if you have two or more of the same type of NIC. As long as you load the correct device drivers, NetWare supports them all.

NICs are a prime source of performance bottlenecks on a network and splitting the traffic by hooking up some workstations to one NIC and another group of workstations to yet another NIC can help the performance of the network.

Having multiple NICs is a good reason for not skimping on the cost of a fileserver. Make sure you'll have plenty of empty slots after you install your disk controllers, video card, and other interface cards. Plan ahead.

Server NICs

The bus in a PC is the row of slots on the main circuit board in which you install accessory cards. If you bought a PC expressly to use as a server, your dealer probably recommended that you get one with an EISA or a Microchannel bus.

I'm not going to bore you with the technical characteristics of these busses. Suffice it to say that both EISA and Microchannel are much better performers than the ISA bus you probably have in your PC. That's good, because your server is going to be busy.

The primary way you tell buses apart is by the pin configurations of where the cards plug into the bus. Figure 4.3 shows the pin configurations for the three buses mentioned in the previous paragraph.

Figure 4.3

Pin configurations for various PC expansion cards.

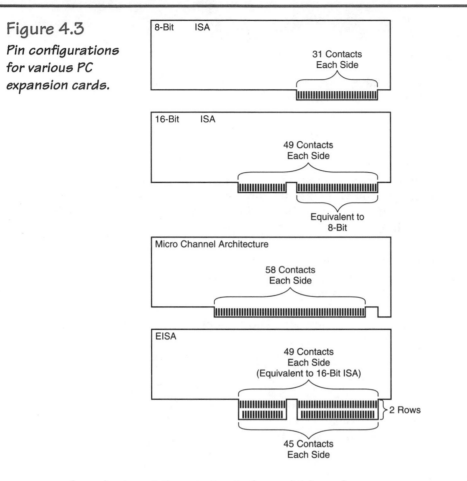

In order to get the most out of your high-performance server, make sure that you get high performance NICs to go in it. If you have an EISA server, make sure you use EISA NICs, not the ISA cards that the dealer is selling you for your workstations. Both will work, but only EISA cards will maximize your server's performance.

Newer, cheaper, better NICs are appearing daily. The competition among manufacturers is fierce! The dealer who sells you your server is your best source of information on suitable server NICs.

Workstation NICs

Whereas ultra-super-duper NICs for the workstation would be nice, they don't do quite the same amount of work that a fileserver NIC does and so they don't have to be quite as fast. Also, if the workstation is an older machine like an AT-class machine, or has a slower clock speed (like 16Mhz or less), a fast NIC is really a waste of money, even if it's cheap.

TIP

You only have one server, but you may have hundreds of workstations. To simplify your support, select one brand and model of workstation NIC for all your PCs, even if a new one comes out that is cheaper, faster, or whatever. Next year, when Novell brings out a new version of workstation software, and you have to visit every PC in the company to install the upgrade, having one NIC model on all machines will make your job a lot easier.

Backup NICs

Since NICs are relatively inexpensive, and far more likely to fail than other types of computer components, it's a very good idea to keep an extra two or three on hand for workstations. An extra NIC for the fileserver is a good idea also.

NIC Conflicts

Setting up an NIC is probably one of the more confusing aspects of networks unless you eat terms like DMA, Interrupt, Base I/O Memory Address and Network Address for breakfast. But don't let those terms give you indigestion just yet. (These and myriad other terms are explained in the glossary, by the way.)

The truth is that I know a lot of people who can set up an NIC for installation in a workstation or fileserver as neatly as you please without really knowing what these terms mean. So read the following explanations (and see fig. 4.4) but don't get heartburn if you don't understand them thoroughly.

Interrupt Requests

The Central Processing Unit (CPU) inside of the computer is the "brains" of the operation. It goes merrily chugging away until it is interrupted by one of the components on the computer like the hard disk or keyboard, or floppy drive or NIC (or any number of other devices). When one of those devices wants some attention, it interrupts the processor and says "Hey! You, over there! I need to talk to you!" This is called an *interrupt request*, or *IRQ*. The CPU stops what it's doing and saves its place, much like putting a bookmark in a book and laying it aside. Then the CPU looks to see what interrupted it. The CPU can tell what the device was that caused the interruption, because each device has been assigned an IRQ number.

Figure 4.4

A prototypical NIC (here with Microchannel architecture).

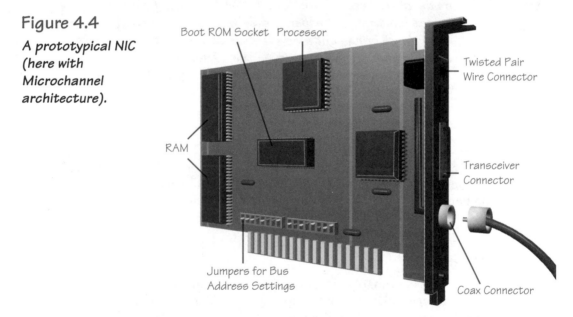

Boot ROM Socket   Processor

Twisted Pair Wire Connector

RAM

Transceiver Connector

Jumpers for Bus Address Settings

Coax Connector

NOTE

Two devices can use the same IRQ or Interrupt Request number if and only if they do not try to talk at the same time. You can, for instance, assign IRQ 3 to the NIC only if you never attempt to use the COM2 port (for a modem, for instance) at the same time you want to be actively connected to the network (COM2 uses IRQ 3).

The only important rule you need to know about interrupts is that each card in the PC must be assigned its own interrupt. Why and how interrupts work is a nerdy detail.

Concerns about interrupt conflicts do not apply to Microchannel and EISA machines if the NIC device driver properly supports shared interrupts.

There are several devices in PC-based computers that have been assigned interrupt numbers that cannot be changed and should never try to be used by anything else. The assigned interrupts vary by computer class (i.e., XT, AT, MCA), but the documentation that comes with both NetWare and the NIC will help you to select the proper interrupt.

Table 4.1 lists the interrupts for an IBM AT. Most PCs that were built after the AT use these same interrupts. Notice that the majority of available interrupts are numbered 10 or greater. Not all NICs can use these interrupts, but it's a good idea to buy ones that do. Especially in the server!

Table 4.1
Interrupts on an IBM AT

IRQ	STANDARD USE
2	Cascade to IRQ 9
3	COM2
4	COM1
5	LPT2
6	Disk controller (hard and floppy)
7	LPT1
8	Real-time clock
9	Available
10	Available
11	Available

continues

Table 4.1
Continued

IRQ	STANDARD USE
12	Available
13	Coprocessor
14	Hard disk controller
15	Available

TIP

In the interest of KISS (Keep It Simple, Stupid, remember?), it's a very good idea to have all your NICs use the same settings. In order to set this up, check out the machine that has the most interface cards in it and select an IRQ that isn't being used in that machine and then follow suit with the rest of the computers in your office.

Memory

Once the NIC has the attention of the CPU, it needs to transfer the data from or into the computer's memory. It can perform the memory transfer in one of several different ways, but the important thing is that the area in memory that is used does not overlap with other devices in the computer. If there is memory overlap, the NIC will either not function at all and a proper connection to the network cannot be made, or the connection will be made but may be unreliable.

Addresses

Every piece of the memory in a computer has a unique address. This is no different than your house or office address. Every address in your city has to be unique so that you can receive your mail and direct people to the right houses and offices.

Probably the most confusing thing about setting an NIC card is that the addresses and sometimes the IRQ numbers are not shown in our regular decimal numbering system. The numbering system most commonly used is hexadecimal, which is usually shortened to "hex."

The decimal system that we use for everyday living is base 10, and uses the digits 0 through 9. Computers only really understand on or off, so the binary numbering system is used to talk with computers at the most basic machine level. Binary is a base 2 numbering system and uses the digits 0 and 1.

Before this begins to sound like a math class, the point of this discussion is that hex is a base 16 numbering system. But if we only have the digits 0 through 9, how do we represent the rest of the numbers in a base 16 numbering system? With letters. That's right, the letters 'A' through 'F' represent the digits 10 through 15. (A numbering system always starts with the digit 0.)

NOTE
You can actually have some fun with the hex numbering system and spell out words with the "numbers" 'A' through 'F'. If you need to assign a node address, you can be creative and assign it "ACE" or "FED" or "BAD," or use a combination of letters and numbers. Don't forget that what are words to us are valid numbers to the computer.

In the hexadecimal numbering system the number 20 is notation for the decimal number 32. Sometimes you will see hex numbers preceded by an "x" or followed by an "h" or the word "hex."

Don't let the hexadecimal notation and usage throw you for a loop. Every discipline has its own unique way of measuring or numbering things and using certain notations.

Types of Addresses

You may run into three types of addresses when installing NICs. Remember, it's not important that you understand what these memory types are all about. You just need to be sure that no two cards are set to the same address.

→   I/O Addresses are usually shown as three-digit hexadecimal numbers, such as 300h, 330h, or 2F8. They always end with a 0 or an 8. Every NIC will have an I/O address, and it is very common for NICs to be shipped already wired for an address of 300h. Since this address is common, be sure another card in the PC isn't using it.

Each address represents a range of memory. If one card is using an address of 300, another can't use 301. It's a good idea to have each card's address end in 0. That ensures that no two cards can possibly overlap.

→   Shared memory addresses are usually shown as four or five digit hexadecimal numbers. Examples are C0000, C8000, D0000, and D8000. Each card using shared memory requires a *range* of memory, so you can't set a card for C0000 and another for C0001. Ordinarily, if one card is set for C0000, the next card will need to be set for C4000 or C8000 to prevent conflicts. Few modern NICs use shared memory addresses.

→   DMA (direct memory access) is seldom used with modern NICs. If your NICs use DMA, a DMA number must be assigned, usually in the range of 2 through 5. No two devices can share the same DMA number.

TIP

Finding out all the interrupts, I/O addresses, shared memory addresses, and DMA channels being used in a PC can require a lot of detective work. Unless, that is, you purchase a program that snoops around and digs out the numbers for you. Microsoft Windows includes such a program, called MSD. An extremely capable program of this type is called QA Plus. Others are available as well. These are excellent diagnostic and testing programs, and one should be in your administrator's toolkit.

Getting Wired In

Wiring is one of the more costly elements of a network. Oh sure, at first glance it looks to be one of the cheaper hardware items on a network, at anywhere from less than a dollar to a few dollars a foot. But it's not the cost of the wire itself, it's the cost of the labor to install it that's expensive. Don't even think about trying to save money by installing wire yourself or by using cheap wiring. Almost every network expert agrees that wiring is a job for professionals.

The reason that you need a professional installer for wiring is that wire is sensitive to interference like fluorescent lights and other types of electrical and magnetic fields. Another reason is that wiring connections really have to be very good in order to work. Network wire and connections are not very forgiving and need to be properly installed to work.

As long as you are incurring the expense of professional installers, you might as well get the latest and greatest in wire.

Wire is definitely an area where you will need to consult a professional.

TIP

Wiring is the one aspect of hardware that you want to purchase for beyond the three-to-five year hardware life-span discussed at the beginning of this chapter. The longer the better; try to shoot for a ten-year or longer life span in wiring.

The most common cable used for new installations is called unshielded twisted pair (UTP). If you are installing UTP, insist on Category 5 cable. This stuff will serve your needs for years. New technologies let Category 5 cable support as much as ten times the speed of current network types such as Ethernet or Token Ring. That gives you plenty of room for growth.

Tape Backup

Backing up the fileserver is one of the top priorities for a network administrator. As a matter of fact, backups on any computer should be a priority for all users, but they usually aren't. Until a critical file or whole directory is accidently erased. People who have lost information are usually the best backer-uppers.

Because many files on a network cannot be backed up unless the file is closed, i.e., no one is using it, most backups are performed at night. Many tape backup units come with software that enables the network administrator to set up unattended backups. If yours doesn't, there are some utilities that allow you to make unattended backups. Check Chapter 14, "Help at Hand," for sources.

You will probably be adding disk space to your LAN faster than you expected, and it's best to get a tape backup unit that has at least two or three times the capacity of the current fileserver drive size so that unattended backups can still be made for some time to come. All tape backup units are not created equal, and I strongly recommend that you make inquiries at your local user group or better yet in NetWire (see Chapter 14, "Help at Hand") for brand name selections. Since you are making backups because you will very likely have to restore information at some time in the future, check the restore features carefully.

When checking out tape backup features, do the following:

➔   Make sure that the backup will continue if an open file is encountered on the network.

➔   Make sure the backup can continue, and most certainly the restore process, if a bad spot is encountered on the tape.

➔   Make sure that the backup and restore software is flexible enough so that you can selectively backup just one file instead of an entire directory.

➔   Make sure that you can make the backup onto two tapes, if needed. That is, when one tape is full, the software should prompt you to insert another tape, if necessary.

➔   Make sure your backup software and hardware are tested and certified by Novell for compatibility with your version of NetWare.

Backup Types

There are three types of backups that can be made:

1. *Mirror Image.* A mirror image backup does exactly what it describes and backs up a mirror image of the disk drive—including the disk flaws. These are usually the fastest backups to make, but are not recommended. If a spot on a disk should go bad between the time the backup is made and the time the data is restored, the information that is restored to the bad spot on the disk is lost. Another problem with mirror image backups is that they cannot often be restored to different disks.

2. *File-by-file.* A file-by-file backup is also a descriptive name—the backup is made on a file-by-file basis. This can either be a complete backup of the entire disk or by directory. Sometimes the backup software allows certain files to be designated for backup. Although this type of backup takes longer than a mirror image backup, it is more flexible and can be restored on another type or size of hard disk.

3. *Incremental.* An incremental backup is one in which only the files that have been changed since the last backup was made are backed up. This can be a quick way to backup, but relies on previous backup tapes to restore the data in a complete manner. How many tapes need to be restored depends on the number of incremental tapes made since the last complete file-by-file backup.

The best type of backup to make is usually a combination of a complete file-by-file and incremental. Remember that the whole point of backups is not to make the backup easy, but to make the restore as easy as possible. However, there is a trade off in the frequency of restores that need to be made and the amount of tape to be used in backups. The method most professionals favor is something like that shown in figure 4.5.

Note that a different tape is used for each Friday's backup so that there are always complete file-by-file backups going back four weeks. Also note that one backup from each month is saved for a year.

You should tailor the backup method that best suits your comfort level and site. You may want to keep the weekly tapes going back for six or eight weeks.

Figure 4.5

The Fine Art of Backups.

Save for one year ───────

	MON.	TUES.	WED.	THURS.	FRI.
	COMPLETE	INCREMENTAL	INCREMENTAL	INCREMENTAL	COMPLETE
	TAPE 1	TAPE 2	TAPE 3	TAPE 4	TAPE 5
	COMP.	INC.	INC.	INC.	COMP.
	T-1	T-2	T-3	T-4	TAPE 6
	COMP.	INC.	INC.	INC.	COMP.
	T-1	T-2	T-3	T-4	TAPE 7
MONTH: APRIL	COMP.	INC.	INC.	INC.	COMP.
	T-1	T-2	T-3	T-4	TAPE 8

	M	T	W	TH	F
	COMP.	INC.	INC.	INC.	COMP.
	T-1	T-2	T-3	T-4	T-5
	COMP.	INC.	INC.	INC.	COMP.
	T-1	T-2	T-3	T-4	T-6
	COMP.	INC.	INC.	INC.	COMP.
	T-1	T-2	T-3	T-4	T-7
MONTH: MAY	COMP.	INC.	INC.	INC.	COMP.
	T-1	T-2	T-3	T-4	T-9

Save for one year ───────

NOTE

Remember that just like the albums or tapes of music that get worn out from frequent playing, your tape backups are no exception. Be safe and get new daily backup tapes after about a year. If you feel wasteful, unwind the old ones and use them for office party decorations.

If you would have a higher comfort level making complete file-by-file backups every night, then by all means, do so. You should implement the backup plan that will help you sleep better at night.

Offsite Storage

It is a really good idea to keep some of your complete file-by-file tapes in a place other than your office. This is called *off-site storage*, and it is a very important part of being able to make a good recovery in case your office burns down, your office experiences some type of theft or vandalism, or a natural disaster. For more information on off-site storage, see Chapter 11, "Disaster Planning and Tape Backups."

UPS

UPS does not mean the United Parcel Service when it comes to networks. It means Uninterruptible Power Supply. PC-based computers are pretty hearty and healthy pieces of equipment, but they are more sensitive to variations in power than other appliances like your toaster.

A sudden loss of power is capable of causing great damage to the data on your fileserver, not to mention the workstations. The reason is that they could be right in the middle of writing information and whamo!—the power goes out. Unless the complete file had a chance to get written to disk, chances are very high that the file is *corrupted*.

In addition to complete power outages, other things can go wrong with electricity. There might be "brownouts," where the power level doesn't fail completely, but falls below normal levels, or "spikes," where you get too much power (as in a lightning hit).

A really good UPS will protect against things like brownouts and spikes in the electricity. The only problem is that a UPS of that type can be very costly. Before you make that kind of purchase, you may want to have the electricity going to the fileserver tested. But not by the company that sells the really nice UPS systems, although they will be likely to offer such a service. The electricity going to your fileserver may be just fine, falling into normal fluctuation levels.

At the bare minimum, a UPS should provide about five or ten minutes of power to the fileserver in the case of a power outage. That allows you to perform a proper shutdown on the fileserver, making sure that all the data is written to the disk in a nice, controlled, manner. Any other "bells and whistles" that you want on a UPS unit are up to you.

WARNING
Never plug the fileserver into the same electrical circuit that the copying machine uses. In some offices, even using the same circuit as a coffee maker is enough to cause problems. At the very least, you should make sure the fileserver is on a dedicated circuit so that no other electrical equipment or appliances have any effect on, or a chance to interfere with, normal operations.

You should definitely consider buying a UPS with an interface card that goes right inside the fileserver. It will interact with NetWare and you can set it up so that NetWare will perform a graceful shutdown all by itself when it receives the right information from the UPS interface card. The number of minutes before a shutdown is performed after the power is disturbed is determined by the network administrator.

Printers

The printers you need to select for a network will depend totally on the size of your office, the type of application software being used, and the physical location of the workstations.

Laser

In the past few years, the prices of all types of laser printers have dropped considerably, and there is no reason not to add one to the network. Laser printers have the highest printing quality of most any type of printer and produce some really nice looking documents.

The thing to keep in mind when considering a laser printer for the network is that several workstations will be sharing it, and you should consider purchasing one that is bigger, better, and faster than you would normally purchase for just one person. Remember that the paper trays will empty faster, and with several people likely to send work to the printer at the same time, speed, and memory can be important factors.

It is not unreasonable to buy a laser printer that has two 500 sheet bins and can print 17 pages per minute or more. Such a printer will probably be heavier duty than a single-user laser printer and can stand up to the abuse of printing for most of a business day. No personal laser printer is designed for eight hours of continuous printing.

When selecting a laser printer, it is a very good idea to visit your computer dealer so that you can see the quality of the output from several models at the same time and make comparisons. Also remember that laser printers need regular care and feeding. Neglecting proper cleaning and service can cause poor quality output.

Dot Matrix

Dot matrix printers come in all shapes and sizes and can be very useful and good office workhorses, particularly the type that print a whole line or page at a time. Once again, comparisons are important, as well as regular care and feeding.

The big advantage of dot matrix printers is that they cost a lot less than lasers to operate. Figure under a tenth of a cent per dot matrix page versus three or four cents for a laser printout. For big reports that don't need laser quality, dot matrix printers are a great alternative.

Dot matrix printers will also print from a wide variety of form types, including carbons, wide paper, green bar, individual labels, and so on. You have a lot of options that aren't available for lasers. It's usually difficult to print a single label on a laser printer, for example.

Just as with laser printers, heavy duty dot matrix printers are available and are usually worth the added cost. Often, high-speed dot matrix printers are called "line printers." Dot matrix printers can be purchased with just about any performance characteristics you require (and are willing to pay for).

Modems and Faxes

If your office needs communication with the outside world, a communications server or fax server will be an important part of the network equipment.

Don't be fooled by the terms "gateway" or "communications server" or "fax server." These are just nerdspeak for a workstation that is attached to the network just like any other workstation. The difference is that it is dedicated to providing a certain type of service. For instance, a communications server that can handle four "sessions" is basically four PC-based machines in one box. It would be like stacking four machines on top of each other.

As a matter of fact, if your communication needs are modest, it is usually cheaper just to buy one or two workstations, but only one keyboard and one monitor to share between the two. Load them with a communications software program always set to receive incoming calls, put a NIC in each machine and attach them to the network like any other workstation.

To let users dial in to one of these PCs, use remote access software such as PC Anywhere or Carbon Copy. Or you can buy a network modem package to enable LAN users to dial out through a modem on the LAN.

For network fax needs, check the software carefully. Some things to look for are ease of use in sending faxes and routing incoming faxes and so on. The big gotcha with network fax isn't sending, it's receiving. The fax server can't read the fax cover page to see who the fax is addressed to. (Some fax servers are trying for character recognition, but the technology has a long way to go.) Make sure that it's easy for a fax administrator to route incoming faxes without it becoming a full-time job.

Once again, getting "real world" experience from other users is a valuable purchasing tool. See Chapter 14 for more information.

Chapter 4, Short and Sweet

This chapter covered some tips and hints to keep in mind when selecting hardware for the network.

1. If you can make most computer purchases that will suit your needs for the next three to five years, you are pretty good and might want to consider a new career in computers.

2. A fileserver should be the most powerful computer on the network because it will be the real "workhorse" machine.

3. Purchasing two computers in the fileserver "class" won't hurt so that you can always have a backup machine at hand. Using one as a workstation until it is needed for service puts the extra machine to good use.

4. If you cannot purchase two fileserver "class" machines or if you want to add to fileserver redundancy, consider disk duplexing (two drives, two controllers) or disk mirroring (two drives, one controller).

5. Network Interface Cards (NICs) need to be more powerful for the fileserver than the workstations. You can put more than one NIC in a fileserver to help split the network load or to support two or more different networking topologies at the same time.

6. The settings on the NICs need to be good neighbors with the settings on the other interface cards in the computer and not conflict with anything else.

7. Wiring should be installed by a professional because wiring is very picky about where it goes and how connections can be made. Wire can be difficult to troubleshoot.

8. Tape backups are one of the most important jobs the network administrator has. Do 'em.

9. There are many different ways to perform tape backups, but you should pick the method that lets you sleep comfortably at night, knowing you can restore easily and completely, as well as quickly.

10. A UPS (Uninterruptible Power Supply) is another sleeping aid. It can save the integrity of the information on your fileserver in the case of power outage or fluctuation.

11. Select the printers for the network wisely because they will be used heavily.

12. Communications servers, fax servers, and gateways are basically special purpose workstations.

NOS Software

(Or, Now You're Ready To Look at NetWare)

Now that you know some things to check for in the hardware that goes on a LAN, it's time to look at the software. This chapter discusses such exciting topics as:

→ The Network Operating System—what it is and what it does

→ The workstation networking software

→ Some things to consider when you select applications software

→ A few guidelines for when you plan the file server disk and memory requirements

These topics might not sound lively now, but no doubt you will soon order your very own N.E.R.D. button (Network Emergency Repair Dude—or Dudette). That's when you know you're hooked on networking.

Building a Computer Part or Program

Before you explore networks further, you should get acquainted with another nerdy term—*architecture*. In computer terms, the meaning is very similar to the normal use of the word. In the real world, *architecture* is used to describe the design and construction of a building.

In the hardware world, *architecture* describes the design and construction of a computer chip. The architecture refers to the way the chip handles addressing memory, how much information it can work with at one time, and so on.

In the software world, *architecture* refers to the way the program is designed from all sorts of aspects, like how well it utilizes different aspects of the hardware, how well it performs the job it was designed to perform, and certain aspects of its functionality.

You need to know this word, because you're going to use it right away!

Network Operating Systems

Obviously, if you are reading this book, you have selected, or are thinking of selecting, Novell's NetWare version 3.11 or 3.12 for your network operating system, but it is worthwhile to look at some of the other NOSs available and understand them a little bit.

Other NetWare Options

Chapter 2, "How Does a Net Work?" mentioned the different versions of NetWare, but it is good to be aware of their place in life before you make your final selection—if you haven't already.

Although Novell is still selling NetWare 2.*x*, don't buy it unless you only have an 80286-based computer to work with for the fileserver. The way the 80286 chip handles memory has certain architectural limitations that a NOS runs into pretty fast. Although the NetWare 2.*x* operating system works fairly well with those limitations, why bother unless you really have to? Because most manufacturers have ceased manufacture of 80286-based machines, the days of Novell even offering NetWare 2.*x* are limited.

NetWare 3.x is an excellent choice for when it is the only fileserver in the office, or the only fileserver that most users need to talk to. In some offices, users need to be connected to two or more fileservers at the same time, and for those occasions, better options than NetWare 3.x exist.

NetWare 4.x is the NOS of choice for large numbers of users connected to two or more different servers at the same time, or for an administrator administering to an environment spread over multiple physical locations.

Other NOS Options

There are other NOS options. After all, Novell only has a corner of about 65 percent of the network market, according to several market survey companies.

One of the newer entries into the NOS arena is Microsoft's NT/AS (Advanced Server). Even though this operating system is brand new, several serious network gurus are reporting excellent results. This is a GUI-based NOS and works well with Microsoft's Windows-centric view of the world.

Banyan VINES is another contender in the network market. Until the introduction of NetWare 4.x and NT/AS, it was the largest contender in the market for administrating several servers at the same time, and is still considered one of the tops for tying together many varied types and sizes of computer equipment (mainframes, minis, and PCs) into a reasonable network.

Microsoft's LAN Manager and IBM's LAN Server have been vying for a piece of the network market, but it has usually been a fairly small piece. Microsoft seems to be putting most of its NOS efforts into NT/AS, and IBM is authorized to sell NetWare.

What's a Protocol?

Before you dive into protocols, you should know that you can run your NetWare network all day everyday, and you don't have to know or care what a protocol is. The following information is included so that if you do run into these things in the Novell documentation or other places (like network magazines) you can have a "heads up" on the reference. If you want to skip it now, go ahead, and it will not affect your ability to perform your NetWare administration duties.

A *protocol* is the down-and-dirty bits and bytes part of how communication occurs between two computers. Before you read about how NetWare fileservers communicate with workstations and workstations talk back to fileservers, it helps to know about networking protocols.

Incidentally, NetWare's standard protocol is called IPX, for Internetwork Packet Exchange. NetWare supports many other protocols, but IPX is the one examined in this book.

OSI Model

In 1978 the International Standards Organization (ISO) undertook the development of a standard for computer communications protocols. What they came up with is the Open Systems Interconnection (OSI) Reference Model. The OSI Model defines seven layers or functions that any product from any vendor needs to fit into to have at least half a chance of communicating with other products from other vendors. The seven layers of the OSI Model are shown in figure 5.1 and explained in the table and list that follows.

Figure 5.1

The OSI Reference Model.

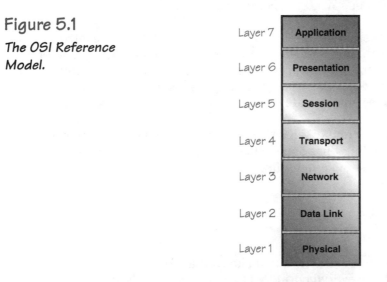

Layer 7	Application
Layer 6	Presentation
Layer 5	Session
Layer 4	Transport
Layer 3	Network
Layer 2	Data Link
Layer 1	Physical

→ **Physical Layer.** In this layer, the transmission parameters are defined for talking to the wire—the electrical and mechanical stuff.

→ **Data Link Layer.** The Data Link layer's purpose in life is to make sure that the information is packaged in the proper packets and arrives at its destination without errors. This layer depends on the Physical layer and has many protocols.

→ **Network Layer.** When networks get large and complex, this layer ensures that a message is routed through the many possible routes to its destination.

→ **Transport Layer.** Complete messages can be thousands or millions of bytes long. Networks, however, deal in small messages. 512 to 4,096 bytes at a time are typical. The Transport layer takes messages from the Session layer and breaks them up if necessary before passing them to the Network layer. The broken up message parts are frequently called *packets* or *frames*.

→ **Session Layer.** This layer manages communications between applications. You might call it the dialogue control traffic cop, because it makes sure that one end is listening if the other is transmitting.

→ **Presentation Layer.** This layer is the translator between different types of communications that go on between two computers. It ensures that the communicating devices speak the same language, important when different brands of computers are connected.

→ **Application Layer.** The Application layer doesn't include the applications you might immediately think of, like word processors. Instead, it ensures that applications have a standard way to talk to the network. The Application layer ensures that applications don't need to know how a network works before being able to send data on the network.

Don't worry about memorizing this stuff. Some basic information you should come away with follows:

→ A set of layered protocols that works in this way is commonly called a *protocol stack*.

→ Layered models allow you to assemble various protocols in various ways. Imagine a stack of Lego blocks. It is especially common to switch protocols around at the Physical and Data Link layers.

→ In a protocol stack, each layer is concerned only with the layers immediately above and below it. Protocols at the Session layer don't care, for example, about what is happening at the Physical layer.

The only real reason for beginners to worry about this stuff is that it helps to understand how NetWare communication components fit together.

NetWare and OSI

Figure 5.2 shows the way NetWare relates to the OSI model. In this figure, you see several NetWare protocols that are commonly mentioned in discussions about NetWare.

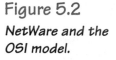

Figure 5.2

NetWare and the OSI model.

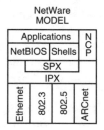

NCP stands for NetWare Core Protocols. The *NCP* defines a set of rules that enable outside resources to submit service requests to the NetWare kernel. The kernel itself is the very heart of NetWare, and you must perform communication with it in an orderly fashion. You can see that NCP covers two layers of the OSI model: application and presentation. It also covers a bit of the session layer. NCP and IPX are the only protocols NetWare needs to implement a basic network.

IPX (Internet Packet Exchange) is NetWare's main protocol for the way messages are managed on the network. IPX is optimized for high performance, and it takes some shortcuts. One shortcut is that IPX assumes that every message it sends is received. This saves overhead otherwise required to track each message and verify reception. Because LANs are very reliable, it is usually a safe assumption that messages are delivered successfully.

If absolute reliability is required, another protocol is added. *SPX (Sequenced Packet Exchange)* adds many checks and balances, which causes some performance loss.

Together, IPX and SPX are the NetWare protocols at the Transport and Session layers.

The modularity of the protocol stack approach is demonstrated at the Data Link and Physical layers. NetWare can work with many different protocols. In Chapter 3, you learned about Ethernet, Token Ring, and ARCnet. In figure 5.2,

802.3 refers to the most prominent standard for Ethernet, and 802.5 refers to a similar standard for Token Ring. You encounter 802.3 and 802.5 frequently when you work with NetWare, and it's useful to remember which network protocols they relate to.

Figure 5.2 shows that NetWare can easily interchange Physical and Data Link protocols. In fact, many other protocols can be supported at these layers. The figure shows only the most common. This flexibility is the explanation for the power of a layered network model.

No matter what kind of network operating system you buy, none of them has a one-to-one relationship with the OSI model. But, to an extent, each of them follow the OSI model, because the purpose of the OSI model is to provide a guideline for basic communication services. In other words, it is a guideline to follow so that with the help of other pieces of software, the different network operating systems can talk to each other.

NOTE

When OSI was developed, there was no such thing as a Local Area Network. The concept for OSI was to provide guidelines for worldwide mainframe-based communication networks.

NetWare—The Big Picture

This is a little overview on NetWare that might help you with the planning, planning, and planning phases of network installation (discussed in Chapter 3). Figure 5.3 is a model of NetWare's basic structure.

NLMs

NetWare was designed to be a very flexible and modular operating system. You've heard of modular furniture, where it is easy to add and subtract pieces to make a piece of furniture functional? NetWare is the same, only it's done with software rather than cubes or cushions. By being able to add NLMs (NetWare Loadable Modules) to NetWare, each different installation can expand the base program and customize it to its needs, without having to make room (on disk or in memory) for things they might not ever use.

Figure 5.3
The NetWare
structure.

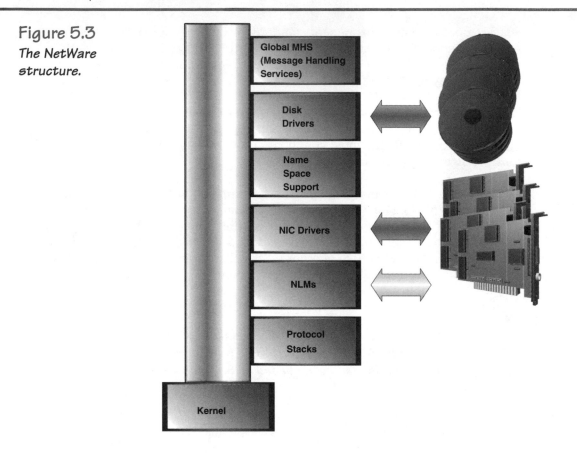

NOTE

The basic NetWare components are referred to as the kernel.
This is the heart of the operating system.

NetWare Loadable Modules (NLMs) are software programs that run on the
server where they hook into the base NOS and add functionality. NLMs are
not stand-alone programs. In other words, you can't run an NLM without the
basic NetWare program already running.

One of the really clever things about NLMs is that most features can be
added, modified, or deleted without stopping NetWare. In the past, it was
usually necessary to stop a NOS, reconfigure it, rebuild the program files,

reinstall it, and restart the server, just to add a feature. The process of rebuilding the operating system with new features was called NOS *regeneration* (the buzzword is "regen"). Changes that take minutes with NetWare 3.11/3.12 can take hours with operating systems that require regens.

Actually, a NetWare server isn't much good until at least a few NLMs are loaded. NetWare can't talk to the disk drives until a disk driver NLM is loaded. NetWare can't work with an NIC until a network driver is loaded.

To add NLMs to NetWare is very easy. First, you start the NetWare server by executing the command SERVER at the DOS command line. That's right, before you start a NetWare server, you boot the server with DOS. The SERVER program starts NetWare. You know the server is running when you get the : console prompt. (The server is also called the console.)

After the base NetWare starts up, you tell NetWare to load any NLMs that you want. You already know that some NLMs are required to support disk drives and network cards. Other things that NLMs are used for include adding the capability to talk to Macintosh computers, additional printing capability, and database capabilities.

Partitions

The space on all hard drives is organized in partitions. If a drive has one partition, it can support one operating system. Or, a drive can be set up with two or more partitions to support more than one operating system.

Each disk on a NetWare server can have one NetWare partition. Normally the entire disk is partitioned for NetWare. Otherwise it's not of much use to the server.

The first disk in the system, however, usually has two partitions: a small one for DOS and a large one (the rest of the disk, in fact) for NetWare. 5M is about right for the DOS partition. The NetWare partition can be as large as the largest disk drives manufactured.

Volumes of Data

Another NetWare term you need to know is *volume*. The dictionary definition of volume says that it denotes a collection of written or printed sheets bound together. That's a good way to think of volume in NetWare terms also—sort of a super directory. A *directory* is an area on the hard disk used to hold and organize program and data files. However, unlike a regular directory, a volume also denotes physical space on a disk. Because you can set Rights by volume, it's a good top-level way to manage access to the different parts of the network.

Some people confuse NetWare volumes with physical disk space or with partitions. Although it is quite common for people to make one physical disk drive equal to one volume, they don't need to. As a matter of fact, a volume can be spread across two or more different physical hard drives. Doing so, however, is only recommended if you also mirror your hard drives. One physical disk drive cannot have more than eight volumes on it. The last rule about volumes is that while you can name the rest of them anything you want, you must name the first one SYS.

NOTE

SYS is the most important volume on any NetWare server, and every server has a SYS volume. SYS stores the NetWare operating system files. It is also the home for print queues.

It's worth summarizing this discussion. Each NetWare partition is set up with one or more volumes. You cannot use partitions to store files unless you create these volumes.

Dynamic Configuration

NetWare 3.11/3.12 is the operating system for people on the go. You can change many of the configuration parameters while the operating system is up and running. Changing hardware still usually requires that you turn the server off. However, after you plug in the new hardware, you can bring the system up and let the users work on the system while you configure any necessary software.

Some of the things you can do while your system is up and running include:

➔ Configure additional disk drives or NICs (providing you turn off the fileserver when you physically add them)

➔ Change operating system parameters (buffers, caching, and so on)

➔ Load and unload NLMs

WARNING

Before you change volume sizes or anything that affects the disk drive, make sure you have at least three good (current) backups of the data on the drive that you want to mess with. If you change parameters that affect the disk; it can cause the data on it to be destroyed or lost forever. You need to restore your data from the backup tapes onto the reconfigured drive.

The way NetWare and the NLMs work together is that whatever the NLMs are doing is not fully determined until they are loaded into memory, which is why you can load many NLMs with command-line parameters. For instance, you can load NIC driver NLMs with parameters that provide IRQ and DMA addresses.

It is helpful that you can also unload NLMs when you want to free up more fileserver memory. You might want to do this if you have an NLM running to support Macintosh name space, but all the people who need to use it have gone home for the day, and you want to make use of the remote management capabilities. Unload the Macintosh name space support and load up the remote management NLMs.

Cache In

When NetWare is started up on the fileserver, it sets aside a certain amount of memory as a Cache Buffer Pool. You pronounce cache just like the green stuff: cash.

Cache memory is used for several different things in NetWare, most notably the following:

➜   **FAT and directory tables.** When NetWare starts up, it loads as much information as it can about the files stored on each volume. That way, it doesn't have to spend time sending the disk drive out to read this information from disk when files are requested.

➜   **Parts of files.** If you use certain files, or parts of files, frequently, NetWare makes adjustments as everyone works and tries to store as much of the files as it can in memory, which saves it from going out and physically reading it from the disk drive.

NetWare likes to keep certain things in cache memory for faster response time for the users of the system. The less time it has to go out and read from the disk drive, the faster response time the users have. So it is important to plan your memory carefully, and some guidelines are given later in this chapter.

User Privilege Structure

The Overseer and Keeper of the Keys of a Novell network is the NetWare administrator, which NetWare calls "Supervisor." (I prefer "Lady and Mistress of All She Surveys"—but that's a little long.) The Supervisor is the only user who can go anywhere and do anything on the network. Of course, multiple users can be assigned Supervisor rights, if that's the way you want to set up your system, but it's not advised.

Rights is the lingo NetWare uses to indicate various privileges a user can be assigned for any given part of a NetWare network. Although a complete discussion is in Chapter 6, "Security," an overview of the types of rights follows:

➡   **Look but Don't Touch.** In this category, you have Read (open the file and look at the contents) and Scan (see the file or directory in a directory listing).

➡   **Touch and Play.** In this category, you have Create (create new file or directory), Delete (get rid of file or directory), Write (edit an existing file or directory), and Modify (rename files or directories).

➡   **I'm in Control.** In this category, you have Modify (alter file attributes) and Supervisory (complete control of file or directory where this right has been granted).

There are some fine points to rights in NetWare, such as the fact that users cannot access a file they have created unless they also have Read or Write privileges. But this should help you get started.

Guidelines for Planning Disk and Memory Requirements

Before you read about actual disk and memory requirements for networking, it can't hurt to perform a quick overview of how those things are measured and the difference between them.

Measuring Up

The computer programs you work with and the accompanying data and information files need a place to reside, just like people need a home. That place is on the disk—either hard or floppy. The amount of space the programs and data take up is measured in bytes.

NOTE

The architecture of the Intel-based series of chips that are used to run NetWare is built around the fact that eight bits equal one byte. A bit is one binary digit and represents either on or off. An easy way to think of a byte is that one byte roughly equals one character. Don't forget that things like spaces, tabs, periods, and other punctuation marks are also represented with a byte.

Because things on a computer are either on or off, computer types have found it convenient to measure things on computers in multiples of two. That's why the binary numbering system is used. Because the measurements are starting with a base 2 instead of a base 10 numbering system, the numbers are a little off.

For instance, the prefix kilo- means a measurement of one thousand (for example, kilowatt, kilohertz, and so on), so when you put kilo in front of bytes, that means you have one thousand bytes—almost. Actually, you have 2 to the tenth power, or 1,024 bytes. A kilobyte is usually abbreviated by "K" or "KB."

Megabyte is the next commonly used measurement, which can be abbreviated as MB, MByte, or just M and is usually pronounced meg. "Mega" is a prefix that means one million, but because of the base 2 system, it is really equal to 1,024 x 1,024 or 1,048,576 bytes.

The next form of measurement is the gigabyte, and then the terabyte. For those who don't want the math, think of it as a *gigantica* of information.

NOTE
If you're used to 100-200M hard drives on personal computers, gigabytes might sound like an absurd number of bytes. But servers with several gigabytes are quite common. And NetWare is capable of managing four terabytes of information on a server. There's not a server alive that can currently support four terabytes of hard drives, so there's a little room for growth here.

RAM

Computer memory uses the same measurements that hard and floppy disks do, but it is a different physical type of storage for computer programs and data.

Computer memory is only temporary storage for your programs and data—sort of like a vacation home is to people. For the programs and data on your disks to actually do anything, you must load them into memory, or RAM, as those in the know call it. (Now you know, too.) RAM stands for random-access memory. As soon as your computer is turned off—or loses power—anything in RAM is gone. A computer can access whatever is stored in memory much faster than it can access something stored on disk. The reason is that a disk is a piece of mechanical equipment, and the disk driver heads (much like a needle on a record player) must find the information before the computer can read it.

Now some programs, including Windows and OS/2, can use disk space as though it were RAM for certain tasks. When something that the operating system is keeping track of in memory is not used very often, it is written to disk temporarily. That way the operating system can still access the information, but it doesn't need to get at it as fast as the other information in memory. Using disk space as a substitute for RAM is called *paging* or *swapping*. (These temporary files are automatically erased by the operating system when the computer shuts down properly.) Because using RAM is a whole lot faster than accessing things from the disk, paging can slow things down. That's why most operating systems run faster and happier with more RAM. If your workstations are running either Windows or OS/2 and using the fileserver for disk space, you need to count on more space than you normally have.

However, there is a diminishing return on RAM. What that means is that past a certain point, doubling the amount of RAM does not double the performance of the operating system—only by three or five percent, for example. In some cases, performance actually slows, which is why you should estimate the amount of RAM you need in the fileserver and workstations before you buy the additional RAM. Prices of all sorts of computer equipment are cheaper than they used to be—but they still aren't free.

Disk Space

Your server isn't likely to end up with an unusable surplus of space even if you overbuy at the beginning. Nevertheless, it's time to sit down and plan.

Building Blocks

A disk drive works much like a record player; the head on the drive is similar to the needle on a record player. Information is organized on the disk in concentric rings, called *tracks*. The disk drive arm moves in and out to locate the track on which the required data is stored.

NetWare further subdivides the tracks into blocks. When a disk drive is told to read or write information, it does so in *blocks*. Just how much information is in a block varies by operating system. With NetWare, you can control the size of a block during installation.

The thing to remember with blocks is that all files are written in multiples of the block size. For instance, if the block size is 1K (1,024 bytes), a one-character file still takes up 1,024 bytes on the disk. If you have a 1,025 byte size file, it takes up 2,048 bytes on the disk, or two blocks. Therefore, it is helpful if you can determine the average size of the files that your office produces.

It might appear, then, that small blocks are best. Then less disk space is wasted for files that don't fit precisely in blocks. However, NetWare performs a trick to improve performance. Each storage block has a corresponding entry in the directory area on the disk. NetWare tries to load as much of the directory information into memory as possible to make accessing files on the hard disk faster. (That way, it doesn't have to wait for the disk drive head to move to the directory entry as well as to move to the appropriate spot on the hard drive to read the information). This affects the amount of memory your fileserver needs.

To run efficiently, NetWare requires large amounts of RAM. NetWare servers with 128-256M of RAM are surprisingly common. Smaller blocks mean more blocks, more to put in memory, and still more RAM. So, to conserve memory, it's common to use a middling to large block size.

A good compromise is to use 4K blocks (4,095 bytes), which is the default block size on NetWare. If most of your work is one or two page letters, 4K is a very inefficient block size for your fileserver, and you should consider using 1K or 2K block sizes. If most of your work deals with large databases, the default of 4K size blocks is probably a good choice.

If your applications work with larger file sizes, and you select a small block size, the performance can degrade. It simply takes more time to read a large file in smaller chunks than it does in bigger chunks. Databases are probably the applications that generate the largest files on your LAN. A database file can be millions or even billions of bytes in size. When only large files are stored in a partition, large storage blocks reduce RAM requirements, and transfer the information more efficiently to the network.

NOTE

Both DOS and NetWare make use of FATs. This has nothing to do with too much cholesterol—a FAT is a File Allocation Table. A FAT has information about the files on the disk, and it's a quick index to where information on the file and the physical location on the hard disk are stored.

Hot Fix!

Another thing to make room for on the fileserver disk is the Hot Fix area. Hot Fix is a very cool feature in NetWare. Any magnetic medium tends to wear out, and hard disks are no exception. A hard disk is rarely perfect straight from the factory, and it is likely to have some "bad" spots on it where information cannot be written to or read from correctly. As time passes, the bad spots on the hard disk tend to increase in number. This can be nasty and cause you to lose data you thought was fine.

Novell knows that the information on your fileserver is important to you, and they allow for an area on the hard disk to be set aside to make allowances for the hard disk imperfections as they are detected. If the disk drive on the fileserver encounters a spot that it finds it cannot write to properly, it marks that spot as bad (and promises never to write there again) and writes that block of information to the Hot Fix area. This all happens "on the fly," and you never know about it. Ever after, the information is read from and written to the Hot Fix area.

The Hot Fix area is one that you should check up on regularly. Hard disks tend to develop problems slowly at first, but can go down hill fast. If the Hot Fix area starts to fill rapidly, it's time to shop for a new hard disk.

> *Don't be too alarmed about the hard disk going bad, though. The first Novell network I installed in 1987 is still going strong—complete with original hard disks! (Not every disk drive is that good.)*

NOTE
When you create a NetWare partition, two percent of the disk is set aside for Hot Fix. If you work with a large disk, this is far more space than you need to allocate. Be conservative, but don't let the Hot Fix hog valuable disk space. Large in this context is over 100M. One percent or less is more appropriate for the Hot Fix area on a disk of this size.

Print Queues

Print queues also require room on the fileserver's SYS volume. When a job is sent to print on a network, it does not go directly from Point A (the workstation) to Point B (the printer). Because the printer is part of the networking services, the print job (or file) has to pass through the network to get information about the printer.

The print job is spooled to the print queue. Basically, spooling means that the print job is printed on the hard disk before it goes to the printer. There needs to be plenty of room on the SYS volume to enable the print jobs to spool. After the job spools to the print queue on SYS, a print server sends the data to the required printer. After the job prints, it is automatically deleted from the hard disk.

If insufficient room is allocated on the hard disk for the spooling, serious problems can develop on the fileserver, not to mention that print jobs tend to disappear (poof!). Once again, this is an area that you need to determine according to your particular needs.

Interoperability—Name Space

Here's a word almost guaranteed to glaze the eyes of all but the most hearty—*interoperability*. This networking term means that different operating systems can interact with each other in such a way that the interaction is transparent to the user. NetWare has NLMs that enable it to interoperate with other types of operating systems such as Macintoshes and Unix.

If you plan to integrate your NetWare network into these other types of environments, the disk space needs to be planned accordingly. For instance, a file name for a Macintosh takes up quite a bit more room than for a DOS workstation. However, if you plan to integrate other types of systems with NetWare, you should consult a specialist and read the documentation. Interoperability is outside the scope of this book.

NOTE

The NLM that is loaded to handle other types of naming conventions (besides those used in DOS) to support other file types on the NetWare fileserver is called Name Space. These modules have different names, but all have an .NAM file extension.

Your Fileserver Disk Space Requirements

Although disk space requirements are unique to each site and their own specific applications, it still helps to have a worksheet to help guide your own planning.

Your Fileserver Memory Requirements

Novell documentation helps you calculate the amount of memory you need by the amount of disk space on all your mounted volumes. NetWare's file system cannot use a dismounted volume. When the volume is mounted, the volume's file directories are loaded into RAM so that performance is optimized.

The size of the volumes being mounted, along with the block size on the volumes are factors to consider when you calculate memory requirements for your server.

Another factor is the NLMs. You can find the amount of memory required by an NLM in the documentation for the particular NLM.

NetWare Operating System (3.11/3.12) 13M

(If you think you might upgrade to NetWare 4.01 anytime soon, remember that it takes 65M of disk space.)

NLMs for your site   _____

Hot Fix Area   _____

Print Spooling   _____

(Estimate the size of some of your largest printing jobs and allow for several print jobs to hit the spooler at the same time.)

Disk space taken up by all applications that will reside on server. (Old and New)   _____

Disk space taken up by all the data the applications produce.   _____

"Home" disk area set aside for each user of the system. (Allow for additional employees, if applicable.)   _____

Add up disk space listed in previous 3 blanks and double that number.   _____

Now double the number in the previous blank for total disk space required for applications, users, and data.   _____

Add 15 percent cushion   _____

Total fileserver disk space: _____

The basic formula to determine the memory required to support each volume on your server follows:

$(.023 \times \text{volume capacity in megabytes}) / \text{block size in K}$

If there is a name space on a volume in addition to DOS you use .032 as the multiplier rather than .023.

Total the memory requirements for each volume and add 4M to support NetWare. Then add the memory required for any additional NLMs you install. Round the grand total to the next higher 4M boundary that makes sense given your hardware. The final number is the memory you should install on your server.

Here is an example that, for a server with a 1G hard drive, would help you calculate the space you might require:

1. Determine the memory required for a 1G (gigabyte) drive:

    $(.023 * 1024) / 4 = 5.88$ (round up to 6M)

2. Add 4M for the operating system and 1M for NLMs:

    $6 + 4 + 1 = 11$

You can install three sets of 4M to get 12M of memory. It makes much more sense, however, to install a set of 16M chips. It shouldn't cost much, if at all, more, and 16M gives you room to grow. It probably also improves your server's performance.

Here is another example with a server that has a 1G disk drive with Mac name space. The volume is configured with the default 4K block size. NLMs that run require 1M of RAM

$((.032 * 1000) / 4) + 4 + 1 = 13$ M of RAM.

Again 16M is the sensible memory choice.

If you have more than one volume, calculate the sum of all the volume requirements. Then add 4M for the NOS and the memory required for NLMs.

Remember that all the preceding calculations get you a minimum RAM requirement only. From there you need to check Resource Utilization (discussed in Chapter 13) to make sure you don't go under the Novell recommended 50 percent RAM for cache buffers. The SysOps on NetWire, who deal with their own servers and other peoples' constantly, recommend that you have enough memory for 65 percent RAM for Cache Buffers.

Workstation Software

The workstation software is minimal compared to the NOS. The software takes up approximately 80K of memory and minimal space on the hard or floppy disk.

Loading Workstation Software

You might have heard something about extended or expanded memory and loading the NetWare drivers high. Although extended and expanded memory are discussed in the next section, you don't need to have any more than 640K of memory to use NetWare and most of your regularly used programs. If you don't use some of these memory helpers, the 80K that the NetWare drivers take up is just less room for the data that your programs normally use.

Extended Memory

Extended memory is real memory above 1M. It is addressed linearly (sequentially), in a straight line without gaps. In other words, you can address extended memory directly with the CPU; you don't have to look elsewhere, like expanded memory.

On PCs, extended memory exists only in Intel-based 80286 and higher machines. Those are the only Intel CPUs that have sufficient address space for real memory addresses above 1M.

NetWare servers can work directly with this extended memory.

On DOS workstations, however, there's a problem. DOS was written in the bad old days of the 8088 and 8086 Intel Microprocessors. Those primitive beasts couldn't work with more than 1M of RAM, so that limitation was built into DOS as well.

To make extended memory available to DOS applications, you must run a DOS system driver such as the MS-DOS EMM386.EXE.

Microsoft Windows is the best-known program that makes use of DOS extended memory. Windows can easily manage many megabytes of memory, and 8 to 16M of memory is common on PCs running Windows.

Expanded Memory

It's expanded memory. (Not extended. It's easy to miss the change of a few letters.) Expanded memory was invented in the days of fairly primitive PCs that could work only with 1M of memory. That just wasn't enough for the large spreadsheet models being developed on Lotus 1-2-3, and Lotus worked together with Microsoft and Intel to develop the LIM Expanded Memory Specification (EMS).

The 8086 and 8088 processors and DOS versions that were current couldn't work with memory above a meg, so the LIM process worked by swapping chunks of memory from an option board into the memory that DOS could read. Although cumbersome, this swapping process enabled applications to work with much more data if properly managed. Expanded memory isn't very necessary these days, but it's the only way to push old 8086 and 8088 memory up above a meg.

Any Intel-based 80x series chip can support expanded memory. If you have a PC with an 8086, 8088, or 80286 processor, you need to use an add-in expanded memory board. Frankly, though, these PCs should be pretty much regarded as obsolete.

Beginning with the 80386 processor, it became possible to have expanded memory without expanded memory boards. By running an expanded memory program, any extended memory on the PC can be made to emulate expanded memory. The same chips you use to provide extended memory can be allocated in whole or in part for providing expanded memory service.

To do this, you need to have the EMS driver. An EMS driver comes with MS DOS 5.0 and above and DR DOS 6.0 and above.

Workstation Network Software

Your workstation needs to run network software to activate its NIC and enable applications and DOS to exchange data with the network. Novell calls its standard for workstation software ODI, Open Data-Link Interface.

ODI is the method by which NetWare allows multiple protocols to be mounted onto a single network adapter. Protocol in this context refers to being able to talk to a Unix machine, for instance, with the same NIC that you use to talk to NetWare. Although this book deals only with workstations talking to NetWare, lots of folks need to be able to talk to many different types of networks, and NetWare ODI drivers enable that to happen.

The NetWare software that you load on a workstation is composed of the following components:

→   Link Support Layer

→   NIC driver

→   IPX Protocol driver

→   NetWare Shell (3.11) or the NetWare DOS Requester (3.12)

Figure 5.4 shows how these pieces hook together to connect your applications to DOS and the network.

Figure 5.4

How the workstation network software components communicate.

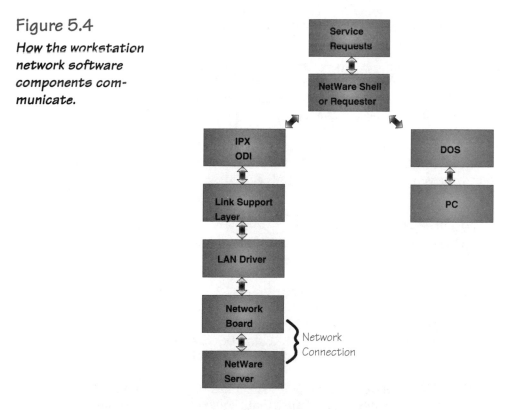

The Shell and Requester function as traffic cops. If you request a directory of your C: drive, the shell/requester makes sure that the service request goes to DOS. If you want to run an application stored on the server, the shell/requester directs the service request to the network drivers.

Several layers of software are encountered before a message can get to the network:

1. First is the IPX protocol layer. Remember that IPX is NetWare's standard protocol. IPX makes sure that the message is properly managed on the network. The program that runs the IPX protocol is called IPXODI.

2. A link support layer serves as an interface between IPX. This layer is provided by a program called LSL.COM.

3. Finally a LAN driver program actually understands how to talk to the particular model of NIC that is installed in the workstation. Each model of NIC requires a different LAN driver program. The names of these drivers generally reflect the model numbers of the cards. The driver for Novell's NE2000 NIC is called NE2000.COM.

The reason for all these layers relates back to the earlier discussion about the OSI network model. Modular construction makes it easy to plug in and play with different components. If you change the NIC in your workstation, only the LAN driver program changes. You don't need to change LSL.COM or IPXODI.EXE.

Similarly, if Novell makes a change to IPXODI.EXE, you usually don't have to contact your vendor to obtain a new LAN card driver program.

DOS Shell or DOS Requester

Older versions of NetWare, including NetWare 3.11, used software called the DOS Shell, which came packaged in a program file named NETX.EXE.

New versions of NetWare, including NetWare 3.12, use a different program that Novell calls a DOS Requester. The DOS Requester uses virtual loadable modules (VLMs) to make system configuration more flexible, similar to NLMs on the server. Instead of NETX.EXE, the DOS Requester uses a file named NETX.VLM, which is installed by a VLM loader program.

Regardless of whether you use the older shell files or the Requester, the purpose is much the same. Both ensure that requests for services on your PC are handled by DOS and that requests for services from NetWare are sent through the network to the server. The differences are technical and qualify as nerdy details if ever anything did.

That doesn't mean that you shouldn't plan to change your older workstation shell files to the new Requester design. It's always a good idea to have all your workstations using the latest network drivers known to be stable—which in this case means the DOS Requester included with NetWare 3.12. Eventually you will put an application on your LAN that requires the latest drivers. If you've already upgraded, the application is a cinch to install. If not, you have to upgrade all of your workstations in a hurry.

Be Aware of Applications

Many applications today are made strictly to run on a network or are network-aware. *Network-aware* means that you can install them on either a stand-alone computer or on a network and that they can use some of the network resources, such as shared printing. Network-aware applications are generally easier to install and configure on a network than applications that are not network-aware.

Chapter 5, Short and Sweet

This chapter covered the software side of a network and a few related considerations. The following list breaks them down.

1. Where NetWare version 3.11 and 3.12 fit into the family of NetWare products and the situations in which each one might be applicable.

2. Other networking operating systems that you might want to consider from Banyan, Microsoft, and IBM.

3. An executive overview of the different types of rights that users can have on NetWare (see the following list):

   → Access Control

   → Create

   → Erase

   → File Scan

   → Modify

   → Read

   → Supervisory

   → Write

Don't worry about memorizing these, there is no test.

4.   How you can use volumes to help segment the fileserver into logical working areas—and help control access at the same time.

5.   How NLMs (NetWare Loadable Modules) help build the basic core services of NetWare and adapt the NOS to your environment.

6.   Although having enough workstation memory is optimal for loading the NetWare drivers into high memory, many folks have no trouble working their applications with a minimum of 640K.

7.   Hard or floppy disks are where your programs and data reside when they are not in use. Any program or data currently being used by the processor is worked on in computer memory, or RAM.

8.   The way that disks and memory are measured are with kilobytes (K), megabytes (M), gigabytes (G), and terabytes (T).

9.   The NetWare Operating System can use different sizes of blocks to store the files on the fileserver, but selecting the right size depends on your data.

10. Print Spooling is when the data you want printed is sent to a print queue (which is like a subdirectory on the hard disk) and then sent to the network printer. Print jobs cannot go directly to the printer without going through the server to get the information from NetWare about the printer.

11. Some of the things you need to account for when you calculate fileserver disk space are block size, printer spooling, NLMs, user work space, applications, and data.

12. The amount of memory the fileserver needs depends on the size of the disk drive, block size, the amount of memory your NLMs take, and whether you use Name Space.

Security

(Or, Taking Care of Business)

Keeping your network secure from unintentional, as well as intentional, threats is an issue that every administrator needs to address. This chapter will cover the following areas:

→ Where to look for threats to your network security, and what to do about them

→ Viruses and how you can deal with them

→ The different aspects of NetWare security and how to utilize it to protect the network, including using passwords

→ NetWare rights and how to utilize them

Chapter 6

Key Terms to Look for:

→ Access rights:
  supervisory
  read
  write
  create
  erase
  modify
  file scan
→ worms
→ trojan horse
→ data integrity program
→ virus scanning program
→ Supervisor
→ Guest
→ SYSCON (system console)
→ trustee assignment (TA)
→ Inherited Rights Mask
→ cascading

When you look at security issues, it's important to remember that you need to protect your system, but not at the cost of making it user-hostile and difficult for users to access or get their work done. Security and ease of access are mutually exclusive—the more of one, the less of the other—and the network administrator's job is to strike an appropriate balance.

Threats to Your Security

You may think you don't need much in the way of security. After all, you know everybody in the office, and they're a great bunch! But are you all that sure that no one is going to quit and take important data with him or her, your customer list, for example? Or that no one is going to log in with a supervisor ID and infect your whole network with a virus? Or that no one's snoopy enough to read other people's electronic mail? You need security on your LAN. Accept this fact and read the rest of this chapter as though it could save your life, your *professional* life.

The only way to *really* protect your company's data is to lock the fileserver in a closed room and not allow any access to it. Obviously, that would defeat the whole purpose of a network, so let's see if a compromise can be reached on allowing access and maintaining system integrity.

Actually, one of the absolute best ways to maintain security on a NetWare fileserver *is* to put the fileserver in a locked room. While still allowing users to log on, of course. Novell has actually requested that people try to "hack" their way into a NetWare system (they call such a team of potential crackers a *Tiger Team*) so they can check for security "holes." The only way it has been accomplished within a reasonable period of time so far, has been when the intruder has had physical access to the fileserver.

Ooops!

The biggest threat to network data is the uneducated or sloppy user. These types of users erase files, accidently overwrite files, and spill coffee and colas in their keyboards. These types of errors are totally inadvertent and non-malicious, but can cause quite a bit of damage.

Computer support folks call these "pilot errors." Nice support folks, that is. The not-so-nice call these types of users "computer-impaired" and worse.

The best protection against pilot errors is to segregate the areas on the fileserver where users have write and erase privileges as much as possible. This is one reason why most "network-aware" programs accommodate putting the program files and data files in two different places on the fileserver. Write access to the program and initialization files can be limited to the Supervisor, so that the careless user cannot harm them.

Backups also play a vital role in protecting against the careless user. You will know you are a full-fledged network administrator the day a user comes to you with a wild-eyed, panic-stricken look on their face. "I've just erased all my files!" he'll gasp helplessly, close to tears. Naturally, this is your moment of glory when you can turn to him and tell him calmly that you can restore his data from the backup tapes within a half-hour. In his relief, the user may offer his first-born as a token of his appreciation.

It is usually better to hold out for cash—or at least an expensive lunch. But don't hold out too long. Note that the user, after looking at the restored data made from the backup the night before, will be unappreciative because you didn't make the backup five minutes before they trashed their directory— you are, obviously, an unresponsive network administrator no matter what you do. (Okay, most users aren't this bad, but sometimes we administrators *do* feel like Rodney "I don't get no respect" Dangerfield...)

Disgruntled Employees

Another threat to computer systems comes from disgruntled employees. They tend to do nasty things like erase files on purpose, falsify data, change passwords without telling anyone, and generally try to make life miserable for their employers as long as they have access to the employer's comput- ers. Some of them consider it to be "fun" to make trouble for others.

Some companies escort newly fired employees to their desks to pick up any personal belongings and then escort them out the door. Whether or not that is your company policy, one of the best things to do to protect against a disgruntled employee is to be fanatical about backups. With proper backups, your system can always be restored to a previously unaltered state.

Make sure to change a newly fired employee's access to the network immedi- ately. Speak to personnel and make sure that if an employee is being fired you know about it before it happens or while it is happening. You may be able to change the network password while personnel gives the employee the bad news.

Once again, limiting write and erase privileges can also prevent damage from attacks. In addition, making use of the other NetWare security features can help limit damage (see the section under *NetWare Security*).

Viruses

Since viruses are a topic that few people are familiar with, people are naturally leery of any real or imagined threats. Two basic questions need to be answered here: the first is what the heck is a virus, and the second is where do they come from?

What Is a Virus?

Computer viruses are named after their biological counterparts. A *virus* is a software program that tries to infect other software programs or data. In computer terms, infecting means that a virus will replicate itself into another program, making another infectious copy of itself and tagging along on a previously clean program. Some viruses damage programs, data, and even hardware, others do not. In the same vein are worms and trojan horses. *Worms* don't require a host program (executable file) in order to reproduce themselves like viruses do. Instead, they use system resources, such as memory and network connections, to both "live" in and to do their utmost to make your life miserable. *Trojan horses* are so named because they distract the user with some type of nifty display while they do their damage.

Where Do They Come From?

Viruses are written by juvenile-minded programmers, companies that sell virus protection programs (very rare), and supposedly inspired programmers who don't stop to consider the damage their little creation may do to other computer users if it gets away from them. The most feared (and also the most publicized and yet least common) virus writers are basically on the same level as saboteurs and vandals—they get their jollies from doing huge amounts of damage to the property of others. The most likely places to pick up a virus are (in order of probability):

1. **Shrink wrap software**. Large numbers of infections come from the disk duplicator hired by major software vendors, who then inadvertently infects 20,000 or more disks at a time. These disks end up on the shelves in your local computer store.

    In addition, many vendors have a generous return policy on software. These companies have a shrink-wrap machine in their back room and simply take the returned disks and repackage them. Reputable vendors will mark the repackaged programs so that the buyer will know it is a returned package. Many, though, do not. In other words, a shrink-wrapped package does not mean that the software came directly from the manufacturer. Even if it does, it is not a guarantee that it is virus-free.

2. **Computer repair folks**. These people visit a lot of different offices and put their diagnostic disk in a lot of machines. Computer repair folks have been known to have inadvertently passed around viruses. It is a good idea to make sure your computer repair diagnosticians use a virus scanning program on their own disks.

3. **College campuses**. If someone in your office is attending college and wants to use the same disk at both the office and in the PC lab on campus, it would probably be a good idea to have a data integrity program or virus scanning program on that person's office computer. Colleges often try to protect against viruses, but it wouldn't hurt to provide your office with a little extra protection.

4. **BBS (Bulletin Board System)**. One of the *least* likely places to get a virus is from a BBS. Unfortunately, rumors and misinformation still abound that this is one of the most likely places, which is in fact totally false. The reason is that the folks who run both small and large BBSs know that their systems are vulnerable to viruses and as a consequence they are very aggressive in protecting against infection. The procedure on nearly every BBS in the known universe is to allow users to upload files all day long. The BBS operator does not, however, allow these files to be available for download by other users until these files have been scanned for viruses. Most BBS operators use at least two or three virus checking programs.

5. **Shareware programs**. Often people will confuse shareware with BBS programs and therefore, just as they are misinformed about the viruses with regards to BBSs, they're also misinformed about the non-threat shareware offers to the user. Shareware is distributed in two ways: first, through BBSs for evaluation copies of the program. The second way is through your mailbox or overnight courier, direct from the manufacturer when a happy shareware user registers the software. Since the software comes directly from the vendor, it is in that vendor's best interests to make sure that no infection exists on disks sent out. The Association of Shareware Professionals says that there are no known infections caused by any of their author-members' programs to date.

Viruses and NetWare

Remember that the only program that is ever executed on the NetWare fileserver is the NOS itself. Therefore, the only way to infect the fileserver is for a virus to be written to specifically infect the NOS. To date, no such virus has ever been written.

Basically, the fileserver is a holding place for programs and data. What *can* happen is that an infected program can be loaded onto the fileserver and then accessed by the workstations, infecting the workstations. These nodes then, in turn, infect more files residing on the fileserver and so on.

Your first line of defense is to utilize the NetWare access rights to your advantage in further protecting data that is stored on your network. If users do not have Write rights, for instance, then they cannot write to a file on the fileserver and corrupt it. Minimizing Write and Create rights access to the data on your network can really help in protecting against viruses that might try to infect the programs and data residing on a NetWare fileserver.

Virus Protection Programs

One of the better forms of protection against viruses is a data integrity program rather than a virus scanning program. These programs constantly check file sizes to detect whether or not the executable programs have been modified. They also check your computer system's memory while you are working to look for any bad guys there.

Checking the file size to look for modification in the code is not always reliable, so these types of programs also take a "signature" check of the programs on the disk, making a unique signature for each program on your disk. Such a signature will change if the program ever gets infected by any virus or is otherwise tampered with, and the user is notified immediately when such a change occurs.

Other anti-viral programs are known as "scanners" that look for certain character sequences, or "code strings." These strings are actually snippets of known computer viruses: programs containing these strings at the right place are most likely infected with a virus. If those "signatures" are found, then a known virus has been found, and it's time to call in the anti-viral SWAT team (more on that in the next section).

Why are data integrity programs better than virus checking programs? The reason is that almost by definition, virus checking programs are coded to look for certain virus "strings." Since new viruses can pop up at any time, virus programs can quickly lose their effectiveness. In order to keep your anti-virus scanner current, you have to be prepared to get an update every few months; if the vendor hasn't released an upgrade in the last six months, then any new virus of the last six months will never be found by that scanner. Data integrity programs don't need the same kind of regular updates that a virus-checking program does at all.

NOTE

Data integrity programs are the only way to protect against the latest "polymorphic" viruses. These viruses change themselves every time they infect a file, so they don't have a consistent signature for a scanning program to look for. The only way to know you have one of these buggers is to catch it in the act of modifying a file. That's what a data integrity program is best at.

If you absolutely have your heart set on getting a virus scanning program, here are some guidelines that you will need to follow in order to make the program effective:

1. **Updates**. This aspect is often overlooked, but is what makes virus scanning software expensive: you will need to get periodic updates from the vendor. Quarterly updates are the minimum that you should expect from the vendor, and monthly updates are better. Many vendors post their updates on a company BBS so that it is easy to keep your software current.

2. **Multiple programs**. The serious system administrator will need at least two different scanning programs from two different companies. The reason is twofold: what one program misses, the other is likely to catch; and, it is possible to get a "false positive" from one scanner and another will be needed to double check.

3. **Don't wait for trouble**. Although many viruses attack as soon as they enter your system, others viruses are time bombs: they wait until your system is thoroughly infected before they blow up. These programs get on your machine and don't make themselves known until every .EXE and .COM file is infected. And they'll infect every

floppy disk you give to a friend so that they can spread to other machines as well. Then a special event, often a predetermined date, will trigger the virus, and it will make its presence known. One day your computer behaves normally; the next it's got bouncing balls on the screen, and your data files are being trashed.

The time between the initial infection and the explosion of a time bomb is the period when you have a chance to remove the virus with a scanning and repair program. Scan early, scan often, and button up your overcoat when the wind blows free.

If the Computer Gets Sick

If you believe that your computer programs have been infected with a virus, here are some guidelines to follow:

1. **Don't Panic**. And *don't reformat the drive or erase all the files*! This is a common mistake. Until a virus triggers, it has caused no purposeful malicious damage to the data on your disks—although since beta-testers for new viruses are scarce, some new viruses may cause inadvertent damage.

2. **Disconnect the machine from the network**. This will minimize the chances of infecting other workstations if there is really a virus on the workstation.

3. **Boot the machine from a virus-free floppy**. You should always have a "safe" floppy boot disk in your troubleshooting kit, thoroughly scanned and carefully guarded. If it will fit, a copy of your virus scanner should be on the floppy so that it can't be detected or infected by a virus that gets on your C drive. Make sure the floppy is write-protected and use it to boot the infected PC.

4. **Look for the bug**. Use the virus scanning software to check for infection on the computer. If you do not have a virus scanning program, proceed to the next step, but be sure to get a virus scanner the next time you go cruising the safer-than-*your*-network-BBSs.

5. **Double-check**. Double-check the program that gave you cause for suspicion. You'll occasionally get a system user who's *convinced* a virus—and not any possible pilot error—is the root of all PC mishaps.

6. **Back up**. Back up the contents of the hard disk from the infected machine to floppy disks. Don't forget to mark the disks clearly to indicate that they might be infected.

7. **It's all right to ask for help**. You may feel better if you call in the help of a professional to disinfect the computer. However, many professional-grade anti-viral software packages are available at a reasonable price, and you should be able to clean up any infection yourself. If you make a mistake and trash the computer, be glad you followed the directions of step six, and have an up-to-date backup.

You don't ordinarily need to reformat your hard drive, and you should never need to if your virus is a time bomb that hasn't yet caused any damage. Virus programs can only infect other programs. If a virus has your system, start by reinstalling the operating system and the affected applications. Don't forget to replace any device drivers you may be using. Examine your CONFIG.SYS file for DEVICE= statements, and make sure that each of the .SYS and .EXE files called in the statements are replaced. Then rescan with your virus program to see if you've gotten everything.

If you've been making your backups, just restore an earlier backup that you made before the system was infected. Do you need another reason to make backups?

Some viruses infect the boot tracks of the infected disk. These are the tracks that contain the system files for your operating system. When you use FORMAT /S or the SYS command, you are installing the boot files. So you might find it necessary to reinstall the operating system to replace infected boot files with clean ones.

Remember that the best protection against viruses is simply practicing safe computing and using some common sense. A good data integrity program running on your LAN's workstations is the best defense. There are many good data integrity programs available, including some shareware, as well as commercial vendors.

Oh, yes, good security helps too.

NetWare Security

NetWare has some excellent security measures built-in, but it is up to the network administrator to utilize all of them to properly protect the network. The tools that NetWare provides are summarized here and discussed fully in the remainder of the chapter:

→   Passwords

→   User rights

→   Intruder Detection Lockout

→   Login time restrictions

→   SECURITY program and SECURE CONSOLE utility

When NetWare is installed, two users are automatically created. The first one is SUPERVISOR, and the other one is GUEST. The SUPERVISOR password should always be changed immediately, but don't forget about the GUEST userid. Anyone familiar with NetWare knows this userid exists, which is why the first thing to do is to delete it. By doing so, you have just eliminated one possible security loophole in the system. If your system does have a need for the occasional guest user, simply create that user when needed and make sure the password expires after the ID is no longer needed.

Passwords

The following is a re-creation of a memorandum I once sent to the users on one of my systems under the SUPERVISOR userid:

In an effort to protect the security of the network, I would like to make the following suggestions:

1. *Please note that passwords on this network must be a minimum of 6 characters in length. They can be longer if you want, but cannot be shorter than 6 characters. You can use any combination of alphabetic or numeric characters.*

2. *When selecting a password, please observe the following guidelines:*

    i.   *Do not use your name, your wife's name, your children's names, or pet names as passwords.*

ii. Do not use the name of your hobby as a password (that is, "tennis," "golfer") if it's a common one. If your hobby is appropriately archaic, a certain obscure element or aspect of the hobby would be fine.

iii. Do not use birthdays (yours or members of your family).

iv. If your typing speed is not particularly fast, consider using a password that can be typed with one hand, so that you can type it in faster. This will help eliminate people from deciphering your password if they are standing near you when it is typed in.

3. Make sure your password is easy enough to remember so that you will not need to post yellow stickies anywhere on or in your desk as reminders.

4. If you do need a memory jogger, please write the password in such a way that it is not recognizable as such, that is, a phone number, embed it in a sentence, and so on.

5. To set your password, type **SETPASS** at the DOS command line when you are connected to the fileserver.

Thank you for your cooperation.

As can be surmised by the contents of this message, I had seen a number of things in going to people's offices in the course of providing support and answering their questions. Everything from yellow stickies in prominent places in their offices to watching executives type in their passwords at the speed that grass grows.

As a result of this message, everyone on the system cleaned up their act. How did I receive such massive cooperation?

➔ The element that is not obvious is that sending messages to the users on the system under the Supervisor identity is used sparingly. Doing so adds to the effectiveness of any such communication since it is a rare occurrence, and as such, people tend to sit up and take more notice. (This has nothing to do with network security, but has everything to do with part of being a successful administrator.)

→   Notice that the overall tone of the memorandum is very polite.

→   Especially notice that at no time was anyone directly accused of any sloppy actions. Had the memo read "I have noticed that some of you type so slow I thought you had gone into a coma," or "I can't believe it, but many of you actually had yellow stickies prominently displayed," it would hardly have been received with the same spirit of cooperation.

→   Note that the recipients were asked to "observe... guidelines." No one was told that "These are the rules." A certain spirit of cooperation was asked for—not demanded. It makes a difference.

Why all the stress on eliminating familiar dates and names from passwords? If someone is acquainted with the person, it makes guessing that person's password fairly easy. Why the use of six characters instead of four or eight? Because the more characters used, the less chance of someone getting the combination correctly. Six is a good compromise and more user friendly than requiring eight or more characters, but naturally you're free to go with what you think will work best on your LAN.

Other Password Hints with NetWare

Make use of the NetWare password settings. To change these settings, start the SYSCON utility (type SYSCON at the DOS command prompt). Then select User Information from the SYSCON menu. Highlight a user name from the list you see and press Enter. Now you will see a User Information box with all the options you need for setting up users. You'll see this box in figure 6.1.

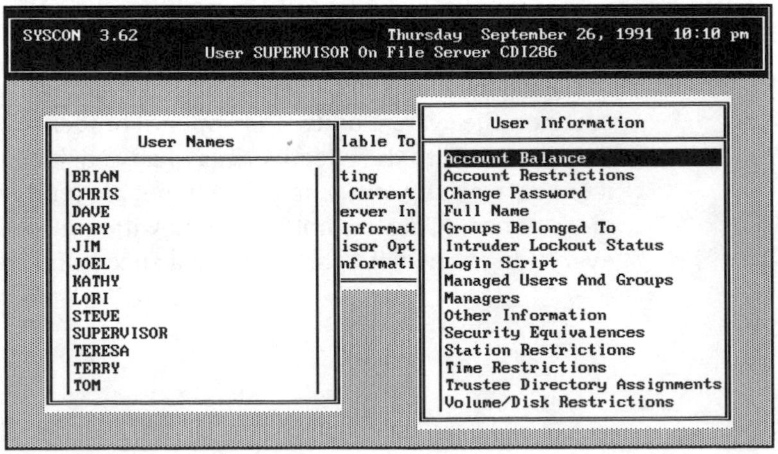

Figure 6.1

The SYSCON User Information screen.

```
 SYSCON  3.62                          Thursday  September 26, 1991   10:10 pm
                        User SUPERVISOR On File Server CDI286


                                              |                 User Information
           ┌─────────────────────────────┐  |lable To ┌───────────────────────────────┐
           │        User Names        ·   │  |         │Account Balance                │
           │                              │  |ting     │Account Restrictions           │
           │ BRIAN                        │  |  Current│Change Password                │
           │ CHRIS                        │  |erver In │Full Name                      │
           │ DAVE                         │  |Informat │Groups Belonged To             │
           │ GARY                         │  |isor Opt │Intruder Lockout Status        │
           │ JIM                          │  |nformati │Login Script                   │
           │ JOEL                         │  |         │Managed Users And Groups       │
           │ KATHY                        │  |         │Managers                       │
           │ LORI                         │  |         │Other Information              │
           │ STEVE                        │  |         │Security Equivalences          │
           │ SUPERVISOR                   │  |         │Station Restrictions           │
           │ TERESA                       │  |         │Time Restrictions              │
           │ TERRY                        │  |         │Trustee Directory Assignments  │
           │ TOM                          │  |         │Volume/Disk Restrictions       │
           └─────────────────────────────┘  |         └───────────────────────────────┘
```

The option you want is labeled Account Restrictions. Choose it, and you will see the screen in figure 6.2. This screen enables you to change several values related to passwords:

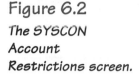

Figure 6.2

The SYSCON Account Restrictions screen.

```
SYSCON  3.62                    Thursday September 26, 1991  10:11 pm
                      User SUPERUISOR On File Server CDI286

                  Account Restrictions For User STEVE

        Account Disabled:                   No
        Account Has Expiration Date:        No
  BRIA    Date Account Expires:
  CHRI  Limit Concurrent Connections:       Yes
  DAVE    Maximum Connections:              1
  GARY  Allow User To Change Password:      Yes
  JIM   Require Password:                   Yes          s
  JOEL    Minimum Password Length:          5
  KATH  Force Periodic Password Changes:    Yes          ps
  LORI    Days Between Forced Changes:      40
  STEV    Date Password Expires:            November 5, 1991
  SUPE    Limit Grace Logins:               Yes
  TERE       Grace Logins Allowed:          6
  TERR       Remaining Grace Logins:        6
  TOM   Require Unique Passwords:           No           gnments
        Limit Server Disk Space:            Yes          ns
        Maximum Server Disk Space (KB):     10240
```

➜ **Allow User To Change Password**. Absolutely, how else do you expect them to remember passwords without writing them down if you assign them? The only instance you would not want them to be able to change a password is if, for whatever reason, you have set up a userid that two or more people share.

➜ **Require Password**. Certainly this should be set to Yes, unless you really want anyone to have unlimited access to the network.

➜ **Minimum Password Length**. Passwords can be up to 128 characters long. That could be a mite user-hostile, but the length you set is dependent upon the nature of the information on the network and sensitivity of the environment.

➜ **Force Periodic Password Changes**. The default is 40 days, but 60 or 90 might be more reasonable and user-friendly. Once again, the time is up to you and your network's situation.

➜ **Limit Grace Logins**. How many times do you want to allow the user to log in after the old password has expired? It is considerate to allow two or three logins in case the user is in a time crunch at the time they log in and their password has expired. It also gives the user a little flexibility and time to think up a new password that fits any guidelines you have set.

➡   **Require Unique Passwords**. The default setting does not require that users use a different password each time they are required to change them. NetWare remembers eight previous passwords used. But what's the point in requiring passwords if the user is allowed to use the same one over and over? Setting this field to Yes is recommended.

NOTE

SYSCON stands for System Console. That term is sort of a holdover from the old mainframe days when the only way the administrator could access the system with special privileges was from the console (or terminal) hooked up to the computer in the computer room. Any user can invoke the SYSCON command, but only the Supervisor has all privileges needed to make the changes mentioned here.

System Security

Passwords aren't the only security blanket that NetWare provides. Some other security options that can be invoked are default time restrictions, intruder detection lockout, physical locks, and NetWare utilities.

Default Time Restrictions

The Supervisor Options option from the SYSCON main menu leads you to a menu that, among other things, enables you to set some default options for your users. One of these options sets default time restrictions that apply to all users of the network or to an individual user. The screen that is used to set default time restrictions is shown in figure 6.3.

If an asterisk (*) is present in a half-hour block, users can be logged in at that time. Just put a space in a block to prevent logins at that time.

The default setting is no time restrictions, but it never hurts to set certain restrictions that won't inhibit valid usage by the users, but will deter intruders. For instance, you may want to disallow access from midnight to five a.m., or something along those lines. People do physically break into offices to steal data (and computers, in which case the time restriction isn't much help. It does, however, discourage the casual intruder).

Figure 6.3
*The SYSCON Default
Time Restrictions
screen.*

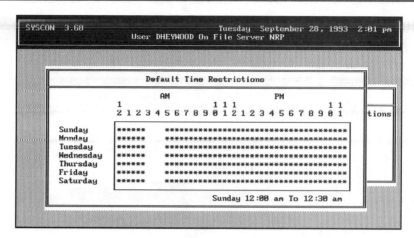

Keep a couple of things in mind when setting any restrictions here. First, the Supervisor userid will probably be performing unattended backups at some time during the night, so don't forget to un-restrict the proper userid in that particular individual user profile. The second is to make sure that everyone is aware of any limitations set here. Users tend to get a little testy if they have made plans to stay late and get locked out during a critical point in their program, or if they come in early and can't get into the system at all.

Intruder Detection Lockout

Another option under Supervisor Options in the SYSCON utility is used to activate the Intruder Detection/Lockout feature. This is a particularly nice option to set if your system has a modem, which in turn enables anyone in the outside world with a modem to stumble across your network.

Intruder detection is there to record any login attempts with an incorrect password—and lock the account if the attempts exceed a certain number. In the screen shown in figure 6.4, the Incorrect Login Attempts option is set to seven attempts, and the Bad Login Count Retention Time default is 30 minutes. That means that if someone tried to log in with the incorrect password seven times in 30 minutes, the account is locked for 15 minutes (Length of Account Lockout). Those are all quite generous numbers. If you are serious about security, you might want to tighten these numbers up to something like three incorrect login attempts in 30 minutes, which locks the account for four hours. At that rate, it would take a very persistent person until the polar cap melts before he or she broke into your system (if your users follow good password guidelines also).

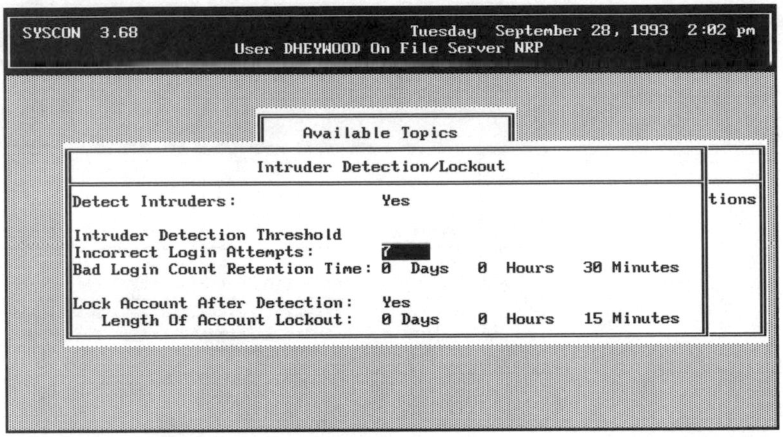

Figure 6.4
*The SYSCON
Intruder Detection/
Lockout screen.*

```
 SYSCON  3.68                          Tuesday  September 28, 1993  2:02 pm
                        User DHEYWOOD On File Server NRP


                              ┌─────────────────────┐
                              │   Available Topics   │
                              └─────────────────────┘
              ┌───────────────────────────────────────────┐  ┌──────
              │         Intruder Detection/Lockout         │  │
              ├───────────────────────────────────────────┤  │
              │Detect Intruders:          Yes              │  │tions
              │                                            │  │
              │Intruder Detection Threshold                │
              │Incorrect Login Attempts:  7                │
              │Bad Login Count Retention Time: 0  Days  0  Hours   30 Minutes │
              │                                            │
              │Lock Account After Detection:   Yes         │
              │   Length Of Account Lockout:  0 Days  0  Hours   15 Minutes │
              └───────────────────────────────────────────┘
```

The Supervisor can unlock any account that has been locked with the Intruder Detection/Lockout feature. If someone makes a legitimate mistake and gets locked out, you can unlock that userid immediately.

Physical Locks

If you can arrange it, it never hurts to place the fileserver in a room that can be physically locked. If you do so, make sure that the room has adequate ventilation, air conditioning, and heating. This applies to all your PCs. A computer placed up against a wall might hamper the ventilation to the computer's fan. As hearty as PC-based computer equipment is, it cannot function properly (and sometimes not at all) in extreme temperature conditions. To find out what the best operating temperature is, check the documentation that comes with your equipment.

NetWare Utilities

Novell's NetWare provides a few standard utilities that help out in the security arena:

➔   SECURITY is a utility that is run from the DOS command line. It isn't perfect, but it wouldn't hurt to run it periodically. The information provided includes information about passwords (none, insecure), privileges (Supervisor equivalence, Root directory, excessive), and login scripts. Use common sense when looking at the results of running this program. Direct the results of the program to a file so you will be able to read it at your leisure. At the command line, type **SECURITY > SECURE.TXT**, and then print the file SECURE.TXT.

→ SECURE CONSOLE is a console command. Use this to prevent people from accessing the OS debugger (which enables knowledgeable techies to do anything they want to your system). It also prevents people other than the console operator from changing date and time so that they can bypass Intruder Detection/Lockout or Default Time Restrictions. SECURE CONSOLE also prevents NLMs from being loaded from other directories than the SYS:SYSTEM so that no one can load a program that is designed to break into your system.

NOTE

The console referred to here is the monitor directly attached to the fileserver. A person with access to the console can access many features in NetWare that are best left to trained and trusted personnel—in other words, the system administrator.

Other NetWare utilities have some security aspects, but these are the main ones that deal with system security.

Setting the Right Rights

Rights define what a user can do on your LAN. Can they change files? Delete them? Copy them? Setting up rights properly is an extremely important task for a supervisor.

NetWare is very flexible in the different ways that rights can be set. There are three levels in which rights can be set, and eight (that's right, 8) different access rights that can be given at the directory or file level.

The Bill of Rights

This isn't Social Studies 101, but rather NetWare's list of rights, and some ideas on how each would be used.

Supervisory

There is a user named Supervisor (Lord and Master of All Surveyed), but there is also a privilege named Supervisory. If someone has Supervisory rights to a directory, that person has all rights to files in that directory and in all the subdirectories beneath it. The person with this right needs no other permissions to grant others access, take away access, modify, delete, write, create, erase, or anything else. In other words, give this right sparingly because real havoc could be wrought from an inexperienced or untrustworthy person.

To revoke the Supervisory right, it can only be taken away from the directory where it was granted, not a subdirectory or file.

Read

This is a directory-level right and grants the right to open files and read them or execute programs in a given directory.

Write

If a user has Write rights in a directory, existing files can be opened and modified. The user can't make new files, though, without the Create right.

Create

The right to create files in a directory means that users can make new files, but without the Read right, they cannot actually read the file there. Adding the Write right would mean they could modify the file. This also allows a file to be salvaged after it has been deleted.

Interestingly, it is possible for a user to create a file that the user then can't read or modify. This can happen if the user has Create rights but not Read rights in a directory. This is a good way to set up an archive directory to hold, say, correspondence records. Users can save record files in the archive directory, but they can't be altered thereafter.

Erase

The Erase right enables someone to erase subdirectories, files, or directories. It's powerful, so grant it sparingly.

Modify

Modify means the owner of this right can grant the right to change directory and file attributes. It also means that the person can rename directories, files, and subdirectories. It does *not* mean that a person has a right to change a file's contents.

File Scan

This enables users to see files in a directory when they issue a command that lists, such as DIR, NDIR, and so on. It also allows the right to see the directory structure, so that if there are subdirectories in the directory, those will be seen.

Without File Scan rights, the contents of a directory are hidden from a user. That's a good way to keep users from snooping around on the server. They can still read and write files even if they can't see the directory entry, but it is harder for the reader to access data they shouldn't if they can't hunt for it.

Trustee Assignments

The terminology that NetWare uses when you do grant rights to your users for directories or files is *Trustee Assignments*, usually shortened to TA. Just like a banker who is the trustee over a special fund (and as such holds a position of trust), NetWare's Trustee Assignments grant special privileges and rights to your users on the system. So, if you grant someone the right to Read, Write, and Create in a directory (for example), those rights are referred to as that person's Trustee Assignments.

As suggested in the NetWare documentation, this is something that you want to sit down and work out on paper before you actually set about to implement it on your fileserver. Since each user is limited to a total of 32 Trustee Assignments, this is not something that you want to do "on the fly." On a poorly planned system, you could run out of Trustee Assignments quickly.

Playing Around

It also helps to "play" with these rights on a fake user that you create and add to your system. Working with something firsthand is the best way to learn it, and the documentation—and even this book—might not be totally clear until you play around with it.

TIP

Before I set about to "play" with something on my fileserver, I always create a user with Supervisor equivalences. In the course of testing things out, it's easy to forget who you are logged in as (Supervisor or Daffy Duck?) and accidently take away your own Supervisor rights or access.

By creating another user with Supervisor equivalences, it's easy to back out of any sticky situation you may get yourself into by logging on with this userid and making the necessary adjustments. I tend to name the other user with the equivalences something obvious like GOD or DEITY so it will catch my eye and I can remember to erase it when I'm finished playing. Using this trick is especially helpful when toying with the Time Restrictions mentioned earlier.

Don't forget to use the handy dandy command line utility WHOAMI. It tells you who you are logged in as and what fileserver you are attached to. It's very helpful when logging in as different users to test things out.

The Three Assignment Levels

You can set Trustee Assignments at three levels, really. The first place is at the volume or directory level with something called the *Inherited Rights Mask* in the utility FILER. We'll get to that in a minute.

The other two levels where rights are set are for *Groups* and individual *Users*. Groups are a collection of individual users who all happen to need the same access to the same directories or files. By making up groups, like accounting, or marketing, you can lump a whole bunch of people together, give the group the rights, and add individuals to the group. This saves considerable time in going in and setting the exact same rights to a whole bunch of individuals. It also saves considerable wear and tear on you, the NetWare administrator, in trying to figure out who has access to what.

Setting Up

In order to demonstrate just how the rights work and how you would go about setting things up, let's take the case of our hypothetical law firm, Lucky Litigators (remember Chapter 3?).

We know that each administrative assistant needs a directory to call home. In each home directory, these assistants can tuck away correspondence, memos, and anything they don't want other people on the network peeking at. As a matter of fact, NetWare kind of figures that you might want to do that, and as you create each new user on your system, it will pop up a dialog box asking if you want to create a directory with the user's name. Novell calls these *Home* directories in their documentation.

So, we have Home directories for the administrative assistants. We'll go ahead and make Home directories for everyone on the system. Even the attorneys.

Another area we'll need is one where all the bookkeeping programs and records are kept. After all, we don't want Lucky Litigators to keep poor records and become victims of IRS litigation. Only a few select people will have access to this area. It will be called \ACCT.

Next, we know there will be a "working area" set aside. This will contain all the forms and briefs and agreements having to do with each client that Lucky Litigators was lucky enough to get and represents all their "work in progress." We'll call this \WORK.

Finally, we know that there will be a "final document" area set aside where nearly no one can write, but everyone can read from, so that copies of final documents can be used as templates to draft new ones. This is called \FINAL.

Without needing any further directory structure detail at this point, we can see that we have a structure like something shown in figure 6.5.

Groupies

Next, we group people according to the access they will need on the system.

We know that the administrative assistants will need Read, Write, Create, and File Scan rights in the \WORK directory. They will also need Create, Read, and File Scan rights in the \FINAL directory. Remember, we don't want anyone to be able to actually write modifications to this area once a file is there, so administrative assistants don't need Write permissions there.

Figure 6.5

The Big Picture

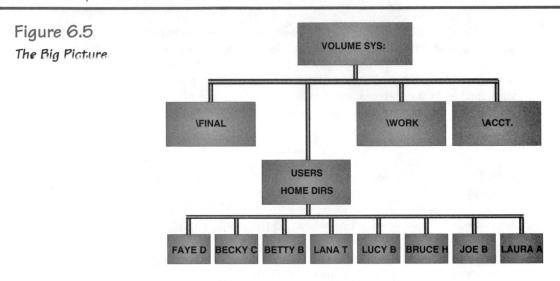

The bookkeeper and office manager are the only ones who will need any type of access in the \ACCT directory; they will need permissions that the accounting program calls for which are Read, Write, Create, and Erase. They will also need to see the files there, so they get File Scan, also. They need to be able to look at documents occasionally, too, so we'd better add Read and File Scan rights to the \WORK and \FINAL directories for them.

The attorneys at the Lucky Litigators law firm are enthusiastic computer users, but careless, so we had better only give them Read and File Scan capabilities in the \WORK and \FINAL directories. We don't want them to be able to write modifications to documents in either directory.

Everyone gets all permissions in their Home directories, of course.

Let's set up some groups here, then, and see what permissions those groups will need. By looking at our worksheet (fig. 6.6), we can see that every person in Lucky Litigators needs at least Read and File Scan rights in the \WORK and \FINAL directories. Since everyone will need those permissions, we will take advantage of using the group EVERYONE that is automatically created when NetWare is installed. All we need to do is to set the group EVERYONE with Trustee Assignments of Read and File Scan in both the \WORK and \FINAL directories.

Figure 6.6

The Grouples at the Lucky Litigator Firm.

GROUPS	DIRECTORIES	PERMISSIONS
AA (Administrative Assistants)	\WORK \FINAL	R W C F R C F
ADMIN (Bookkeeper and office manager)	\ACCT \WORK \FINAL	R W C E F R F R F
ATTORNEYS	\WORK \FINAL	R F R F
R = Read W = Write C = Create E = Erase F = File Scan		

Right now, we really don't have a need to make a separate group for attorneys. If we need to make a separate group at a later date, we can do so.

What is left, then, is a need for two groups. One called AA for administrative assistants, and one called ADMIN for the bookkeeper and office manager. AA will be assigned Trustee Assignments of Write and Create in the \WORK directory and Create in the \FINAL directory.

The ADMIN group will be assigned Read, Write, Create, Erase, and File Scan rights in the \ACCT directory.

NOTE

A person's Trustee Assignments for a given directory or file are the SUM of that person's group and individual user assignments. In this case, since the people in the groups AA and ADMIN also belong to the group EVERYONE, we don't need to duplicate the rights they already have as members of another group.

So, the groups that we need for now are shown in figure 6.7.

Figure 6.7

The final roundup of Groups .

GROUPS	DIRECTORIES	PERMISSIONS
EVERYONE (Already on sytem)	\WORK \FINAL	R F R F
AA	\WORK \FINAL	W C C
ADMIN	\ACCT	R W C E F
R = Read W = Write C = Create E = Erase F = File Scan		

User Rights

Although NetWare, ever the flexible NOS, enables you to set rights for individual users, you want to do that sparingly. Naturally, individuals will have rights to their individual directories, but where possible, stop there. Try to create groups that make logical sense on your fileserver, and if two or more people need the same permissions, then you have the need for a group.

By utilizing groups for setting permissions, the security on your system will be a lot easier to track—especially if you give it some thought.

NOTE

The Group and User rights "cascade." This means that if you give a group or user a right in one directory, those rights will cascade down to any subdirectories.

This is also known as rights inheritance. A subdirectory inherits the rights that are effective in the parent directory.

See the next section, Inherited Rights Masks, on how to keep rights from cascading, and why you might want to do so.

Inherited Rights Masks

There may be occasions when you do not want the rights assigned in a parent directory to cascade, or filter down, into subdirectories. Think about some of the subdirectories that applications programs create that you don't necessarily want people to be able to write to. You still realize, however, that they need to read the files from the subdirectories in order to run the program.

A case in point might be the accounting program that is used at the Lucky Litigator law firm. It creates a subdirectory called TABLES that contains tax tables for calculations. If one of these should get written to by accident, Lucky Litigators could pay the wrong taxes and might end up being Unlucky Litigatees.

You could create another Trustee Assignment for the ADMIN group for the \ACCT\TABLES directory and only assign them Read and File Scan rights there. But then you would be using up one of your 32 Trustee Assignments. You don't need to do that; instead, you can control access to that subdirectory with NetWare's Inherited Rights Mask.

The Inherited Rights Mask is a way of putting masking tape over some of the rights that were previously granted (in the directory above) and saying, "I don't care what rights you had in the directory above me, you aren't getting them here unless I say so or unless they're specifically granted here."

When a directory is created, all rights are available in the Inherited Rights Mask. In other words, no rights are masked out. In order to mask the rights you do not want filtered through, you need to go into the utility FILER and take away the rights the group or user had in the directory above. In this case, you would do the following.

1. At the command line, type **FILER**, press Enter, select `Current Directory`, and type **SYS:ACCT\TABLES**. See figure 6.8. Press Enter to bring up the Available Topics menu shown in figure 6.9.

2. Next, select Current Directory Information to display the Directory Information screen shown in figure 6.10.

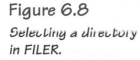

Figure 6.8

Selecting a directory in FILER.

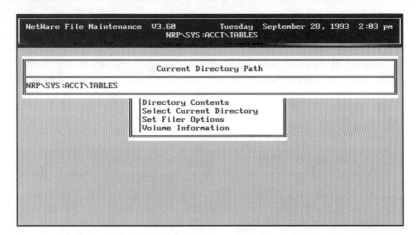

Figure 6.9

The Available Topics menu in FILER.

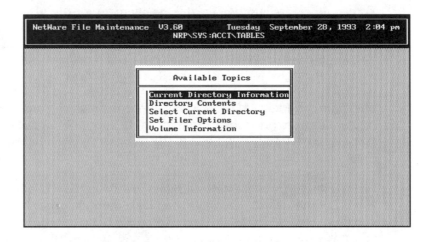

Figure 6.10

The Directory Information screen in FILER.

3. Scroll down to the Inherited Rights Mask field and press Enter. A box will show all of the rights that are in the current Inherited Rights Mask for the directory. To remove a right from the list, highlight the right and press Delete.

   In this case, you would select the Write, Create, and Erase flags. A shortcut is to highlight each right in turn and press F5 to select it. The items selected are shown as blinking. Then press Delete to remove all of the selected rights at once.

4. Exit the FILER utility (press ESC).

In this example, you left the Read and File Scan rights, but took away the other rights that the group ADMIN would normally have "inherited" in this directory. The group ADMIN's rights for \ACCT and \ACCT\TABLES are shown in figure 6.11.

Figure 6.11

ADMIN's Inheritance.

```
DIRECTORY \ACCTS

INHERITED
RIGHTS MASK:
[SRWCEFMA]

GROUP ADMIN:
[   RWCEF   ]

EFFECTIVE RIGHTS
[   RWCEF   ]
                              DIRECTORY\ACCTS\TABLES
                              INH.RTS.MASK:[ R  F      ]
                              GROUP ADMIN:[ NONE      ]

                              EFFECTIVE
                              RIGHTS:          [ R  F      ]
```

This example illustrates that the rights available in any one directory are a combination of the Inherited Rights Mask, Group Trustee Assignments, and Individual User Assignments.

TIP

The SUM of the Trustee Assignments assigned by Group and User override a specific Inherited Rights Mask in a directory. In the preceding example, if the Inherited Rights Mask had been Read and File Scan at the \ACCT directory, the specific rights granted in group ADMIN would have overridden the Inherited Rights Mask for that directory.

Be sure to check your NetWare documentation about Rights. There are several examples given to work through, but with the information given here, and a bit of testing on your own, you'll get the hang of it in no time.

Chapter 6, Short and Sweet

NetWare offers some great security protection features, but they don't all come set at the toughest levels, so you need to understand and make use of them. This chapter covered all aspects of security, including the following:

1. The only really secure system is the one that is kept in a locked closet with no user access. A NetWare system administrator has to find a happy medium between security and allowing the users to get their work done.

2. The biggest dangers to any network are careless and uneducated users. You can help keep accidents down by limiting access everywhere on your fileserver (and by educating your users).

3. Deliberate malice is the next major threat to any computer system, but with company-wide cooperation, those incidents can be kept to a minimum or completely stopped. By deleting userids and changing sensitive passwords immediately, damage can be controlled or stopped.

4. The hazard of viruses has been over-publicized in the past few years by a handful of firms who specialize in making money from virus scanning software. Yes, viruses are out there and can be spread, but a good data integrity program is a much better investment than a virus scanning program. Considerably less expensive also, since a data integrity program doesn't need constant updates in order to do its job.

5. Disk duplicating machines, as well as companies that re-shrinkwrap returned software, are good sources of viruses.

6. BBSs (Bulletin Board Systems) and Shareware are the safest places and ways around to get clean software.

7. Following good password guidelines and avoiding such things as family names, birth dates, hobbies, and so on will make your system more difficult to break into.

8.   The Default Time Restrictions settings in SYSCON can be utilized to keep unauthorized people from trying to even begin to log in after hours.

9.   Intruder Detection Lockout can be a big help in securing your system against people who might randomly try to log in.

10. Lock your fileserver in a well-ventilated room.

11. NetWare has a utility that will help you close loopholes in the way your system is set up, called SECURITY.

12. Understand and utilize the rights that NetWare enables you to assign to directories and files to protect your information and control access to your fileserver.

13. Group and individual User rights cascade down to subdirectories. Use Inherited Rights Mask to change access to subdirectories.

14. Access to any given directory, subdirectory, or file is controlled by the SUM of the Group and User rights assigned in that directory. If no assignments are made in a particular directory, the rights from the parent directory are filtered through the Inherited Rights Mask.

15. Utilize additional settings in SYSCON to control access by the number of stations logged into and the address of stations.

16. Workgroup Managers and Security Equivalencies can help control access to certain areas of the fileserver.

Chapter 7

Key Terms to Look for:

→   directory trees
→   volumes
→   FILER
→   directory blocks
→   root

Disk and Directory Management

(Or, Volumes and Volumes of Data and Data)

Okay, now let's go over the ways you can put your data onto your fileserver, how you can manage the data, and how that affects the way your users see that data. Before you can use the fileserver effectively for storing and retrieving files you need to set up some kind of logical structure by which to group the particular files and directories. This is known as setting up the *directory tree*, because you start at the root and branch out to new directories from there.

Throughout this chapter we will discuss the following things:

→   What is a volume

→   Ways to design the directory tree

→   Using FILER to manage files and directories within the tree

→   Purging and salvaging deleted files

How Big Is My Volume?

The first thing you have to do before being able to store anything on the fileserver is to define your volumes. Volume size, and physical properties of the volume (volume name, disk block size, Hot Fix table size, and so on), are defined when running the INSTALL process on the fileserver. Defining a volume for NetWare is similar in concept to creating a DOS partition using FDISK for your workstation. It sets up a logical relationship between the physical disk information and the usable capacity assigned to it.

Also contained in the volume information are the maximum number of assignable directory blocks, those areas of the disk that can contain directory list information including file names and subdirectory names; and the name spaces the volume supports, which by default is DOS but which can also be OS/2, Macintosh, and NFS among others. All of these things can affect the way in which you set up your volumes. For example, you may want separate volumes for DOS and Macintosh system and user files, or you may want your users on one volume and all applications on another. As stated before, this is very similar to putting partitions onto your DOS workstation's hard disk, and you can think in the same terms that for each volume defined you will most likely need or want to assign a separate drive letter when making your drive mappings. One last thing, as was stated elsewhere in this book: volumes are not limited in size to the physical disk capacity because you can span a volume across multiple physical disk drives. The only limitations on volume-specific information are the following NetWare maximums:

➜   32 Terabyte physical addressable disk capacity

➜   32 Terabyte logical volume capacity, either on a single physical disk or spanned total capacity across multiple physical disks

➜   A spanned volume cannot cross more than eight physical disks

➜   A physical disk can not have more than eight volume segments on it

➜   4 Gigabyte single file size

The only volume requirement on a NetWare server is that the primary, or first, volume on the fileserver must be named SYS, and that it contain all the NetWare-specific utilities and system files.

If a Tree Falls...

Now that we have our volume, or volumes, defined, we need to start putting things onto it. We do this by creating directories, into which we can copy and create files. Making a directory on a NetWare volume can be as easy as making one on a DOS disk on your workstation's local drives. You would use the MD <directory_name> command from the DOS prompt. As stated before, the initial volume that gets created is the SYS volume, so we will be using that in the examples in this section (since we know these will always exist).

When you look at the NetWare directory you start with the volume name, SYS: in this case, which is the ROOT of the directory tree. It is called the *root* because this is where everything else starts from. When the SYS volume is created, several directories are created automatically. These are the ETC, LOGIN, MAIL, PUBLIC, and SYSTEM directories in the root. Within some of these directories are more subdirectories. This produces a directory TREE off the root of the volume that looks like this:

SYS: (ROOT)

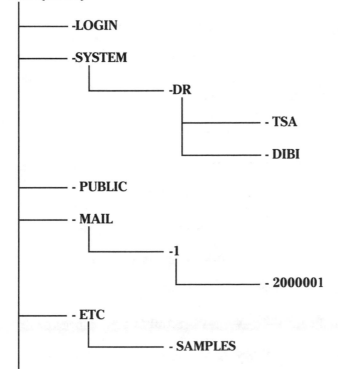

This basic directory can be expanded by adding more directories and subdirectories. You will need to carefully plan where you want your own directories to be stored. For example, where are the users' home, or personal, directories going to be. Where are you going to put applications on the network, what about shared data file access, and so on.

To this end, you may end up taking the previous directory tree and modifying it so that it ends up looking like this:

SYS: (ROOT)

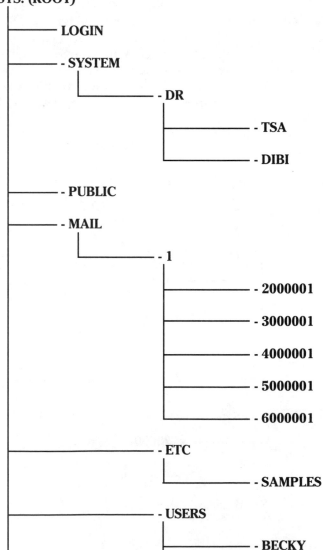

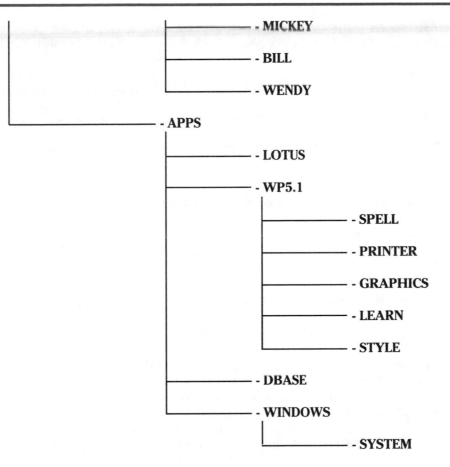

- MICKEY
- BILL
- WENDY
- APPS
  - LOTUS
  - WP5.1
    - SPELL
    - PRINTER
    - GRAPHICS
    - LEARN
    - STYLE
  - DBASE
  - WINDOWS
    - SYSTEM

NOTE

The MAIL subdirectories get created automatically when you create additional users on the network. You can also configure SYSCON to create a default USER HOME DIRECTORY when creating new users. These are the only directories that NetWare will create for you automatically after using the INSTALL utility.

One thing to keep in mind is that many applications will create the directories they need as part of their installation. Usually all you need to worry about creating is the main directory that you want to load them into, like the APPS directory as shown in the preceding example.

As you can see from these examples, you use the ability to make directories to logically group similar information. All the users wind up in subdirectories below USERS, all the applications below a subdirectory called APPS, as shown in the example. And you can see how the directory tree grows as you add things to it. By default, NetWare 3.1*x* will allow you to go as far into the tree as 25 levels deep. You can change this number using the appropriate SET command, as detailed in the NetWare system administration manual.

Forest for the Trees

Once the basic directory tree is in place, it's time to start filling up the directories. Keep in mind that directories can be thought of as nothing more than a filing cabinet into which you place file folders. Each specific subdirectory can be thought of as a drawer in the cabinet holding specific file folders that are somehow related to that drawer or other information contained in the drawer. Application and data files can be thought of as the file folders that you would store in the cabinet.

Users may put files into a particular directory because that's where their applications expect to find them, or they had the option of stating a destination address. Applications may create temporary files, copies of files, and any number of variations on the above. Although there is no real limit on the number of files that can be stored in a single directory, it is best, for DOS workstations, to try and keep the number of files in a single directory below 1,000 file/directory entries. This is more due to the way MS-DOS seeks files in a directory and the performance hits imposed when you have a larger number of files in the directory.

Also, there is no real limit imposed on the total number of files and subdirectories you can define on the network, although by default you can only use 13 percent of the total number of disk blocks for directory blocks.

NOTE
What this means in real terms can be shown using the following conceptual statement:

If a volume were to be defined to have a total of 78,023 blocks (using 4K block size by default) to make a 304M total volume capacity, then you can have a maximum number of

10,143 of those blocks, using the default 13 percent, for directory blocks.

Each directory block is capable of storing a total of 128 DOS directory and file names each.

What this means is that, theoretically, you can have a maximum number of 1,298,304 total subdirectory and file names on that 304M volume. Just a few trees in that forest. What it also means is that the maximum total number of directory entries is a function of the volume capacity used on the drives; the larger the total volume capacity, the more directory entries you can have. You can also change the maximum percentage of disk blocks that can be used as directory blocks using the SET commands, as detailed in the NetWare system administration manual.

How you set up your particular directory tree will be dependent on the ways your users access and make use of the network resources. Please refer to Chapter 3 while working out the size of your volume.

What's a FILER?

So, now that you have your directory tree defined and set up on your fileserver, how do you suppose you'll manage it? Let's look at one of the utilities that Novell provides specifically for managing your files and directories on the NetWare volumes: FILER.

FILER is one of Novell's Menu programs, that is, it is a menu driven utility and not a command line function. You would use it to perform many of the day to day tasks that one would encounter when running any computer. These tasks include:

- → Creating directories on the disk

- → Copying files and directory structures

- → Deleting files and directories from the fileserver

- → Viewing directory contents (list files and directories)

→   Viewing directory information

→   Viewing volume information

→   Setting directory and file attributes

During this part of the chapter, we will be showing screen images of the
FILER utility as examples.

Things to Do

First, let's look at the FILER main menu and discuss what each item does.
Some of the items only have one or two options attached to them, so we'll
look at those things first, even if they're out of order according to the menus.

First, the main menu (see fig. 7.1):

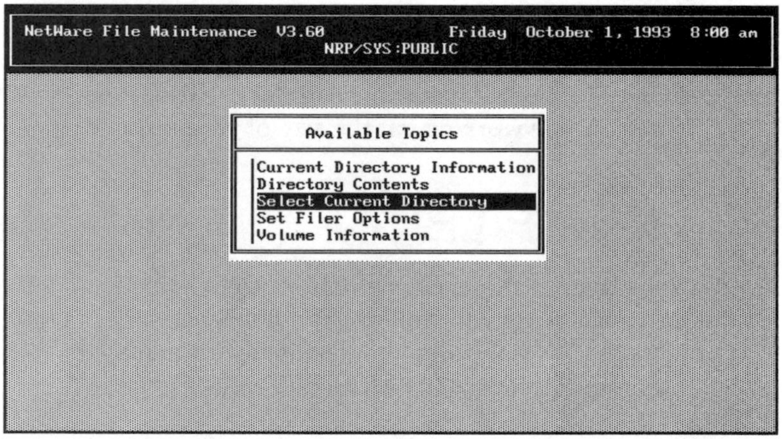

Figure 7.1

The Filer main menu.

```
NetWare File Maintenance   V3.60              Friday  October 1, 1993  8:00 am
                              NRP/SYS:PUBLIC

                          ┌──────────────────────────┐
                          │     Available Topics     │
                          ├──────────────────────────┤
                          │Current Directory Information│
                          │Directory Contents        │
                          │Select Current Directory  │
                          │Set Filer Options         │
                          │Volume Information        │
                          └──────────────────────────┘
```

Current Directory Information

This shows and allows you to set such things as Directory Owner, Creation
Date and Time, Directory Attributes, Inherited Rights Mask, and Trustees
(see fig. 7.2).

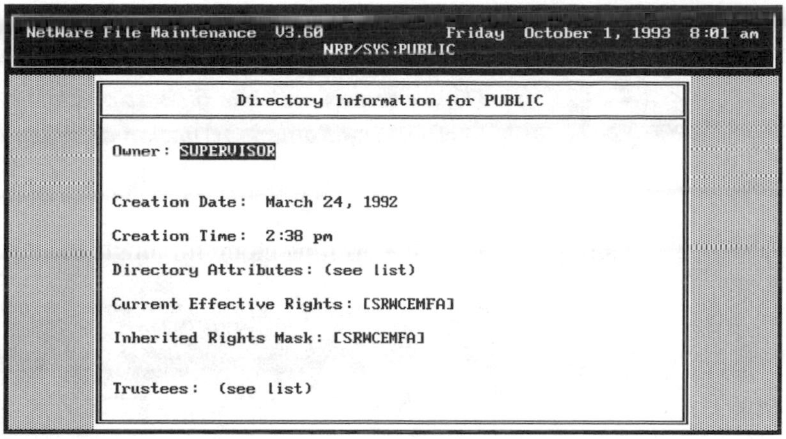

Figure 7.2

*The Current
Directory Information
screen.*

```
NetWare File Maintenance  V3.60        Friday  October 1, 1993  8:01 am
                         NRP/SYS:PUBLIC

          ┌─────────────────────────────────────────────────┐
          │          Directory Information for PUBLIC         │
          │                                                   │
          │  Owner: SUPERVISOR                                │
          │                                                   │
          │  Creation Date:  March 24, 1992                   │
          │                                                   │
          │  Creation Time:  2:38 pm                          │
          │                                                   │
          │  Directory Attributes: (see list)                 │
          │                                                   │
          │  Current Effective Rights: [SRWCEMFA]             │
          │                                                   │
          │  Inherited Rights Mask: [SRWCEMFA]                │
          │                                                   │
          │                                                   │
          │  Trustees:  (see list)                            │
          │                                                   │
          └─────────────────────────────────────────────────┘
```

Directory Contents

This is a directory listing of all the files and directories in the current directory (see fig. 7.3). When you bring up the file list you will have different
options based on whether you have tagged a group of files or are highlighting a single file. Besides the menu options that are listed in the following
example, you can easily manipulate the directory tree at this point. By
pressing the INS key while in the Directory Contents screen, you can create a
new subdirectory below your current directory. Pressing the DEL key while
highlighting a file name, or tagged group of file names, allows you to delete
those files. Pressing the DEL key while highlighting a directory name, or
tagged group of directory names, allows you to delete all the files and
subdirectories below and including that directory.

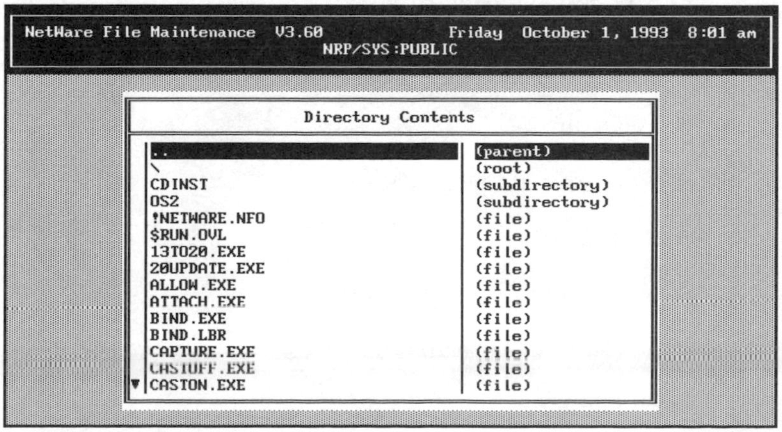

Figure 7.3

*The Directory
Contents screen.*

```
NetWare File Maintenance  V3.60        Friday  October 1, 1993  8:01 am
                         NRP/SYS:PUBLIC

          ┌─────────────────────────────────────────────────┐
          │              Directory Contents                   │
          │                                                   │
          │ ..                        (parent)               │
          │ \                         (root)                 │
          │ CDINST                    (subdirectory)         │
          │ OS2                       (subdirectory)         │
          │ †NETWARE.NFO              (file)                 │
          │ $RUN.OVL                  (file)                 │
          │ 13TO20.EXE                (file)                 │
          │ 20UPDATE.EXE              (file)                 │
          │ ALLOW.EXE                 (file)                 │
          │ ATTACH.EXE                (file)                 │
          │ BIND.EXE                  (file)                 │
          │ BIND.LBR                  (file)                 │
          │ CAPTURE.EXE               (file)                 │
          │ CASTOFF.EXE               (file)                 │
          │▼CASTON.EXE                (file)                 │
          └─────────────────────────────────────────────────┘
```

NOTE

When using Novell's Menu Driven utilities, you can press the F5 key to tag multiple files at one time. This allows you to perform the same instruction on many files or directories at once.

Figure 7.4 shows the options menu for single file access:

Figure 7.4

The File Options box.

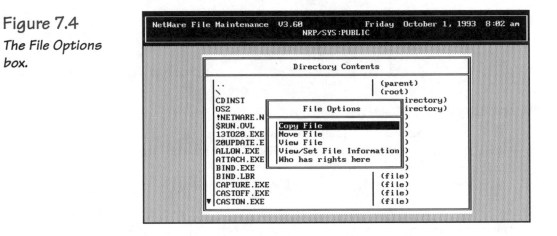

The functions provided by Copy File, Move File, and View File are fairly self-explanatory and equivalent to DOS functions of the same or similar names.

View/Set File Information for a single file specification at a time includes a list of the following information:

→   Attributes

→   Owner

→   Inherited Rights Mask

→   Trustees

→   Current Effective Rights

→   Owning Name Space

→   File Size

→   EA Size

→   Short Name

→   Creation Date

→   Last Accessed Date

→   Last Archived Date

→   Last Modified Date

When working with multiple tagged files, you have a slightly different group of options available. Check the menu of currently available options shown in figure 7.5:

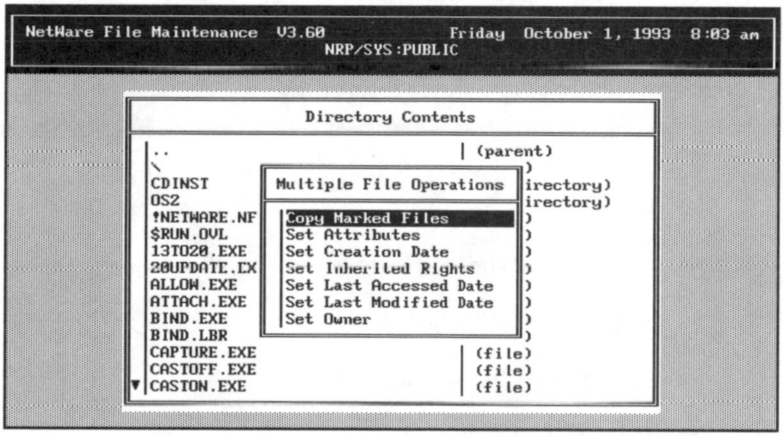

Figure 7.5

The Multiple File Operations box.

Also under this option from the main menu is the ability to look at, create, and delete directories. Again, you have the ability to work with a single directory entry or work from a tagged number of subdirectories (see fig. 7.6).

Figure 7.6

The Subdirectory Options box.

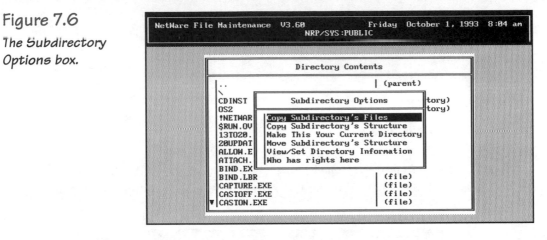

View/Set File Information for a single directory specification at a time includes a list of the following information:

→   Owner

→   Creation Date

→   Creation Time

→   Directory Attributes

→   Current Effective Rights

→   Inherited Rights Mask

→   Trustees

Just like when working with multiple tagged files, with multiple tagged directories you have a slightly different group of options available. Check this menu of currently available options (see fig. 7.7):

Figure 7.7

Options Under Multiple Subdirectory Operations.

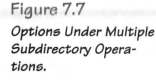

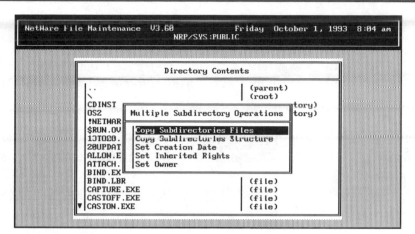

Figure 7.7

Options Under Multiple Subdirectory Operations.

Select Current Directory

This option sets the working directory that you are positioned in.

Set File Options

This menu selection lets you set the options that you want to use while in this FILER session. FILER does not store the configuration options you choose, so you have to reset the options each time you run FILER. This is where you set what options FILER will use to search for and display files and directories, including whether to show Hidden or System flagged files and directories. Following are the Filer Settings menu options (see fig. 7.8):

Figure 7.8

The Filer Settings box.

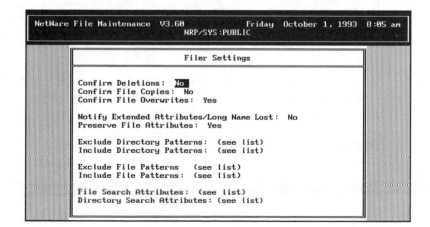

Volume Information

This option shows you the specific information about the defined volumes on the fileserver. As shown in figure 7.9, it includes information about volume size, number of available directory entries, and number used as well as the name spaces used on the volume.

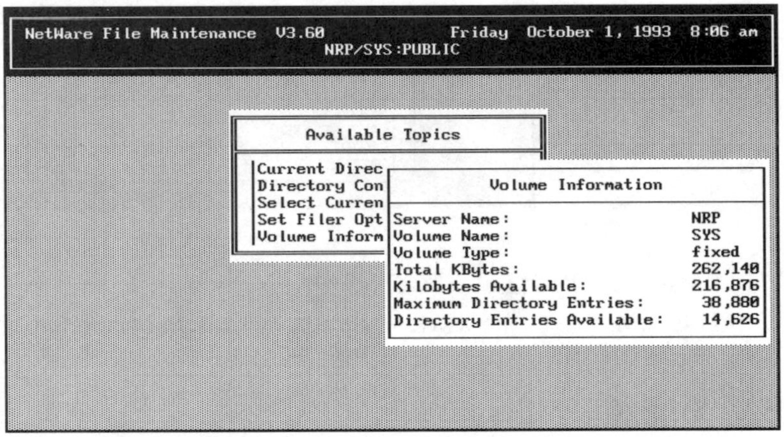

Figure 7.9

The Volume Information box.

```
NetWare File Maintenance   V3.60           Friday  October 1, 1993  8:06 am
                              NRP/SYS:PUBLIC

                      ┌──────Available Topics──────┐
                      │ Current Direc              │
                      │ Directory Con    ┌──────Volume Information──────┐
                      │ Select Curren    │                             │
                      │ Set Filer Opt    │ Server Name:         NRP     │
                      │ Volume Inform    │ Volume Name:         SYS     │
                      └──────────────────│ Volume Type:         fixed   │
                                         │ Total KBytes:        262,140 │
                                         │ Kilobytes Available: 216,876 │
                                         │ Maximum Directory Entries:  38,880 │
                                         │ Directory Entries Available: 14,626 │
                                         └─────────────────────────────┘
```

Recovering from Something You Didn't Mean to Do

NetWare 3.1x has a very powerful ability to recover deleted files from the fileserver's hard disk. NetWare can use up to 85 percent of the available unused disk space to store files that have been deleted from the disk. This allows you to recover those files should it be discovered that you didn't mean to type DEL *.* from the root of your home directory.

When you delete files from the network hard disk, they actually get flagged to be purged when more disk space is needed and are moved to a hidden directory that is in the root of each volume on the fileserver called DELETED.SAV. Even though this directory is flagged as Hidden, you can change to the directory by typing the following:

```
CD \DELETED.SAV
```

Do this from the DOS prompt on your workstation, assuming you have sufficient rights to be able to get into the root directory on that particular volume.

While files are in this directory, they are referred to as salvageable files. They use this term because the utility you use to recover the files is called SALVAGE. Although this utility has several options, the two you should be most concerned with are Select Current Directory, which allows you to choose which directory you want to salvage files in, and View/Recover Deleted Files. When you select the View/Recover Deleted Files option, you will be asked the file specification you wish to try to recover; the default is *, which is NetWare's way of saying All Files.

After you select the file spec you want to use, and press Enter, you will be faced with a list of all the salvageable files. You can either recover the files you want one by one by paging through the list and pressing Enter on each file, or you can use the F5 key to tag a group of files to salvage; when you press Enter, you will be asked if you want to recover the whole group of files. You also have the option of performing a PURGE of files from the list of salvageable files by either highlighting a particular file or using F5 to tag a group of files and then pressing the DEL key.

I'm Sorry Cap'n, I Cannot Do That

Although SALVAGE is a very powerful utility, there are some conditions that will prevent it from operating. Most of these are conditions that the system administrator needs to enable, but some can happen out of carelessness.

Instant Death

The first, and most critical, is that the Fileserver Console command that follows,

```
SET IMMEDIATE PURGE OF DELETED FILES=ON
```

was either issued at the fileserver console or through RCONSOLE, or that it was added to the fileserver's AUTOEXEC.NCF file and executed during system startup. This command causes *every* file that is deleted to be purged from the fileserver immediately, and there is no possible recovery, unless a tape or disk backup of the file is available.

A Little Instant Death

The next possible condition that would prevent you from recovering files is that someone either executed the command that follows,

```
FLAGDIR <directory_name> P(urge)
```

or used the FILER program to set a directories attributes for Purge.

This instructs the fileserver that whenever a file in this directory is deleted it should be purged from the system immediately. You would normally use this command on the Print Queue directories in the SYS:SYSTEM directory, or for directories that applications use to create and delete a large number of temporary files. This command is very useful in maintaining a manageable number of directory blocks by preventing the system from using directory entry slots to hold large numbers of deleted/waiting for purge temp files.

A Very Little Instant Death

The last of the user settable, permanent options is to use the following command

```
FLAG <file_name.ext> P(urge)
```

or the FILER program to set a file's attributes to Purge.

This does the same as the previously mentioned option, but for one specific file only.

Forced Retirement

As stated in the preceding section, you can force files to be purged using the Salvage utility to delete files from the Salvagable Files List. You can also remove files manually by issuing either the command PURGE which purges all deleted files from the directory you happen to run the program in, or PURGE/ALL.

PURGE /ALL not only removes all the files from your current directory, but also all the files in all the subdirectories below your current directory.

Why Doesn't This Thing Work?

There is one condition that can occur that can bring major grief and aggravation to a network administrator: when someone deletes all the files and directories for something important, and when they run the SALVAGE utility to recover the files they get a message telling them that they don't have sufficient rights to recover the files. This is especially disconcerting when the person running the Salvage utility is a Supervisor or Supervisor Equivalent.

What has really happened in this case is that the special hidden directory, DELETED.SAV, has somehow been deleted from the root directory on that particular volume. This isn't necessarily as bad as it may sound, since you can rebuild the directory, but you will not be able to recover the files that were lost.

To rebuild the DELETED.SAV directory, you issue the following commands from the volume that is experiencing the problem:

```
CD \
MD DELETED.SAV
FLAGDIR DELETED.SAV H
```

This will make the directory in the root of the volume, and then flag the directory as Hidden.

Chapter 7, Short and Sweet

To review, in this chapter we've learned about the following things:

1. What a volume is.

2. What things a volume contains and how it affects your fileserver.

3. Maximum capacities for the NetWare Disk Support services, including the maximum supported disk capacity and largest supported file size.

4. Directory structure concepts, including the concept of a directory tree.

5. How to create directories from the command line.

6.   What the NetWare SYS Volume directory tree looks like on a newly installed fileserver, and what it may look like after you've made changes to it.

7.   How to determine the theoretical maximum number of directory entries you can have on your volume.

8.   What FILER is and what it is used for.

9.   How to recover deleted files using the SALVAGE utility.

10.   What would prevent you from being able to recover files.

PART THREE

Where Every NetWare Guru Starts

Doris pointed out to Norene that, over a period of time, Joe had taken to wearing armbands and demanding that he be called not Joe, but Mr. Exalted, Guru of the LAN.

Printing

(Or, Getting Ink on Paper)

Chapter 8

Key Terms to Look for:

→ dedicated print server
→ PSERVER
→ print queue
→ PCONSOLE
→ parallel printers
→ serial printers
→ remote printers
→ baud rate
→ parity
→ stop bits
→ data bits
→ handshake

So, the time has come, the network administrator said, to speak of many things; of sealing wax and print services, of shared laser printers and kings. This chapter discusses the different methods of printing on your network, the basics of how they work, and why you might prefer one method over another. Topics include:

→ Types of print services

→ Setting up Novell's print services

→ Alternative print services

→ Print job definitions

Printing just happens to be the one topic that confounds network administrators more often than any other topic in networking.

Who, What, When, Where, Why, and How

Well, like that age-old adage about trying to decipher a problem, the concept is the same. Someone wants to print (Who) some document they have been working on (What) as soon as they press Print (When) to some printer on the network (Where) so that they can justify their salary (Why) using NetWare's print services.

Before exploring the How of printing on a network, it is probably best to explain a little bit about the What of printing on a network. Because several methods exist for getting printed data from the workstation to that printer that happens to be sitting at Sally's desk, you want to make sure you use the most sensible method. The very basic concept of printing on the network is this:

"I have this document that I need to print and somewhere out there on the network is the printer I want to print to."

That's it. Simple concept.

So, you need to examine Where the printers can be on the network and Who can use them. Along the way, the differences in performance of some of the options are covered.

By its very nature, NetWare provides the capability to share some set of resources among all the workstations on the network. Usually those resources reside on the NetWare fileserver, but with some options in the available print services, you can share printers anywhere on the network.

Where Can I Print This Thing?

NetWare's print services enable you to attach printers:

→ **Directly to the fileserver.** Printers attached to the LPT or COM ports on the fileserver itself.

→ **To a dedicated print server.** A *dedicated print server* is a workstation set up specifically to run Novell's PSERVER.EXE print server software, and whose sole purpose in life is to print. No one uses a print server to perform daily work.

→ **To workstations.** Under this arrangement, the person who sits at the workstation and the other people in the office can print to the printer attached to the workstation because Novell's RPRINTER.EXE software is running on the workstation in addition to the network shells.

NetWare doesn't discriminate—it enables printers to be shared from DOS/ Windows workstations, OS/2 workstations, Macintosh workstations, and host systems. It also enables any workstation to use a shared printer anywhere on the network. This enables you, as the network administrator, the greatest flexibility when you determine the physical placement of the printers, as well as when you determine which printers should be set up as shared.

You can print on the fileserver by using Novell's PSERVER NLM (NetWare Loadable Module). You can set up additional print servers by using PSERVER.EXE, which is run on a dedicated workstation.

PSERVER NLM requires a NetWare 3.x fileserver to operate in and about 500K of fileserver RAM. When you calculate the amount of RAM your fileserver needs, add this 500K amount to the calculation as an added NLM requirement.

PSERVER NLM does not take a user connection slot on the NetWare 3.x server, which means that when you look in MONITOR at the Connection Information list of users, PSERVER NLM uses a connection number higher than the User Count of your NetWare. For example, in a 10 User NetWare server, PSERVER NLM appears in the Active Connection list as a number higher than 10 listed as the name of the Print Server you defined. This enables you to run a print server without having to give up a workstation connection.

A computer running PSERVER can support 16 printers and 32 queues, of which 5 can be locally attached printers (printers connected directly to the print server ports, LPT 1 through 3 and COM 1 and 2) and 11 RPRINTER remote printers. Each printer can support multiple print queues. With this limitation, if you need to support more than 16 printers you need to run more than one PSERVER.

To install the PSERVER NLM, you must make sure that it is in a directory you can load from your fileserver hard disk.

Setting Up Network Printing

You follow four major steps to set up NetWare printing:

→   Define print queues. You do this first so that the queue definitions are available for the later steps.

→   Create the print servers.

→   Define the printers.

→   Set up the printers.

These steps are explained in the following sections.

Defining the Print Queue

The *print queue* is the directory space on the server's hard disk that stores the data being sent to the printer until the application has finished sending the complete print job, or until the defined destination printer becomes available.

After you install PSERVER, you must define print queues and print queue users. These tasks are performed by using the PCONSOLE menu utility. You should define one print queue for each printer, but each printer can service multiple queues, and you can assign a queue to multiple printers at different priority levels (the position on the ladder at which things should be done).

1. Log in to the network as SUPERVISOR or equivalent and run the PCONSOLE program from the DOS command prompt.

2. At the PCONSOLE Main Menu, choose the Print Queue Information option. If any queues are already on your server, they appear in the list.

3. Press the Insert key to add queue names, or highlight a queue name and press the Delete key to remove them.

4. After you press the Insert key, a box prompts you for the New Print Queue name. Type the name of the new queue—QUEUE 0, for example—and press Enter. Choose a queue name that makes sense to

you and your users; for example, LJ4_3RD_W for the LaserJet 4 on the 3rd floor West side. Or, you might want to name the queues CURLY, MOE, and LARRY because you taped name tags onto the printers, and you know exactly where they are.

5. After you enter the new queue's name, it appears in the list of queues in the Print Queues box.

Repeat this process until you define all your print queues.

PCONSOLE automatically assigns SUPERVISOR as the queue operator and the group EVERYONE as queue users. Queue users can send jobs to the queue. Only queue operators can kill jobs or issue other queue control commands.

If you want to modify operator information for a queue, highlight the queue name in the Print Queues list.

Select the Queue Operators or the Queue Users options. Then use the Insert and Delete keys to define the queue operators and users. Both groups and individual users may be specified in the operators and users lists. The operators and users you define must be valid users or groups as defined in SYSCON.

You probably want to assign another Queue Operator so that more than one person can perform management tasks, such as deleting unwanted print jobs from the queue list or reordering print jobs, in the event that someone needs to print something out of order.

Often you just put the group EVERYONE in the queue users list because you seldom need to restrict printer use. You can remove the group EVERYONE from the Queue User List if you do want to restrict printing to a few users. One example of a printer that might need to be restricted is a high-quality color printer, which can cost a dollar or more per page to operate. Certainly you don't want an unwanted printout going to this printer.

You define the queues first so that when you go into the Print Server definition and are ready to define printers, the Queues are available to assign to
the printers.

Defining the Print Server

The next step is to define the print server itself.

1. Choose the Print Server Information option from the PCONSOLE
    Available Options menu.

2. To define a new print server, press Insert and enter a new name.
    Each print server requires a unique name to identify it to the
    fileserver. After you enter the print server name, you are returned
    to the Print Servers box.

3. To delete a print server, highlight its name in the Print Servers box
    and press Delete.

After a print server name is entered, you need to configure the printers and
other resources, which is discussed in the next section.

Attaching Printers to Queues

Well, thus far you have created print queues and print servers, but they have
no idea how to talk to each other; that is, how *do* you accomplish the actual
transfer of data from the queue to the printer?

To start, you must define the printers that the print server services.

1. From the Print Servers list, highlight the print server you want to
    work with and press Enter.

2. Select the Print Server Configuration option from the Print Server
    Information menu. The Print Server Configuration menu appears.
    From this menu, select the Printer Configuration option. This pro-
    vides a list of Defined Printers.

3. In a new print server, all printers are labeled as Not Installed. High-
    light the printer number, from 0 to 15, that you want to add or
    modify, then press Enter. You are presented with the configuration
    choices menu.

Enter a name to identify the printer and move to the Type field. In the Type field, press Enter for a menu of printer types. Four general types of printers can be defined:

→ **Parallel (LPT) or Serial (COM) Printers.** Parallel and serial printers are attached directly to the print server's ports.

→ **Remote Parallel (LPT) or Serial (COM) Printers.** These remote printers are attached to workstations that run the RPRINTER TSR to service printers remotely on the network.

→ **Remote Other/Unknown Printers.** Remote printers are used with RPRINTER when the port type isn't known in advance. You might want to be able to assign any printer on short notice and have both LPT and COM printers available on different ports, for example.

→ **Printers Defined Elsewhere.** This designation is used when print servers send jobs to printers on other fileservers.

After you select the printer type, enter the appropriate data for the port definition. The ports you have available are the LPT (parallel) or COM (serial) ports on the fileserver, dedicated print server, or workstation to which you are going to attach the printer. Some things to consider when you define printers and their ports follow:

1. If you choose a Parallel port, remote or local to the server, the only configuration options you need to deal with are the Interrupts and Buffer Size. You have the option with a local printer of entering No in the Use Interrupts field. Then you don't even need to worry about interrupts.

2. If you define a Remote LPT, you must choose to use the proper Interrupt (IRQ) for that port. Ordinarily, LPT1 uses IRQ7, as does LPT3. LPT2 uses IRQ 5.

3. If you define the printer as local to the fileserver or dedicated print server, then you should define the port as using No Interrupt. If problems arise, you can change No Interrupt to the proper interrupt.

4. If the port you choose is a COM Serial port, you must choose the proper operation mode for the port. This includes the following configuration options:

Baud Rate. The speed at which data flows through the port.

Parity. The method with which data integrity is checked between the computer port and the printer.

Stop bits. The number of bits added to the data to indicate spaces between valid data.

Data Bits. The amount of data sent to the printer in each timing cycle.

Handshake. The way the port controls the data flow between the computer and the printer.

These parameters are determined by the printer you use. If the printer is defined as a Remote printer on one of the workstations, be aware that you must use a true Serial Printer cable and not a generic serial data cable. After you define the necessary printers, press Escape. The printer's new name appears in the Configured Printers list.

After you define the print server, you can assign print server operators and users by selecting the appropriate options from the Print Server Information menu. You also can restrict access to print servers by assigning passwords. Again, PCONSOLE assigns SUPERVISOR as the printer server operator and the group EVERYONE as users.

NOTE

You also can set up Printer Notification in the event that a printer needs service (out of paper or jammed). In most installations, however, the network supervisor is notified by users quickly enough. To enable notification, select the Notify List for Printer option and select the appropriate printer number. Press Insert to open the Notify Candidates box and select the users or groups you want to notify if the printer needs attention. You need to define the time interval, in seconds, at which the notification should be performed (wait for first notification and time between notifications).

Press Esc to Exit, and select Yes to save the configuration. As when you add users to the Queue Operators list, this eases the management of the printers and queues.

Assigning Print Queues to Printers

The next step is to assign print queues to the printers.

1. From the Print Server Configuration menu, select the Queues Serviced by Printer option.

2. Select a printer and press Insert to select the appropriate queue name from the Available Queues list.

If you are assigning one queue to each printer, use a priority of 1 for all queue assignments. If a single printer will service multiple queues, set the appropriate priority levels. After you assign the queues to the printers, press Esc.

Getting This Thing Started

To enable the changes made in PCONSOLE, you must reload the PSERVER program. If you are currently running PSERVER, be sure to shut down the print server by using PCONSOLE (access the Print Server Status/Control menu and select Print Server Information).

If your print server is an NLM running on a NetWare v3.x server, enter the console command UNLOAD PSERVER to shut down the print server. Then enter the LOAD command to reload PSERVER. For example, the following command loads a print server named PSERV1:

```
LOAD PSERVER PSERV1
```

A print server status screen appears, listing the printers you defined for this print server, along with a status message for each printer. If the printers appear as they should, they are ready to print on the network.

Now that you've read about how to set up printing on your fileserver, you should look at the alternatives.

→   Printers on other fileservers

→   Printers on dedicated PSERVER print servers

→   Printers on users' workstations

→   Alternatives to Novell's Print Server

PSERVER on Multiple Fileservers

A single PSERVER can manage queues on several fileservers. To define a print server for an additional fileserver, you need to run PCONSOLE and attach to the desired fileserver.

1.   Select Print Queue Information and define the queues.

2.   Then, select the Print Server Information option and define a print server with the same name as you defined on the first fileserver.

NOTE
You can assign passwords and change or add operators and users. If you are using print server passwords, they must be the same for the print server on all fileservers. If you define PSERV1 on fileserver ONE and PSERV1 on fileserver TWO, for example, the passwords for PSERV1 on both servers must match.

3.   Next, select Printer Configuration and then choose the printer you want to define. Use the same printer number as defined on the first print server's printer definition list. The printer name also should be the same.

4.   Select Defined Elsewhere as the printer type.

5.   Assign the queues to the printers by selecting the Queues Serviced by Printer option.

6.   Select the appropriate printer and queue.

Again, you need to shut down the print server to make the changes effective.

NOTE

Even though you defined a PSERVER that supports queues on two different NetWare fileservers, you run the PSERVER program only once. You do not have to, for example, LOAD PSERVER on the second fileserver. In fact, you can't.

PSERVER.EXE on a Dedicated Workstation

To run PSERVER.EXE, a workstation must have access to the following files:

IBM$RUN.OVL

PSERVER.EXE

SYS$ERR.DAT

SYS$HELP.DAT

SYS$MSG.DAT

All these files are found in the SYS:PUBLIC directory. Here are two good ways to make these files available to your print server workstation:

➜   Copy all the files to the workstation's root directory.

➜   Copy all the files to the SYS:LOGIN directory. All files in this directory can be read by all users, regardless of whether they are logged in. Flag all files in this directory as Shareable Read Only (SRO) so that users can't inadvertently—or advertently—remove them.

Use a text editor to create a file on your boot disk, named NET.CFG. This file must have at least the following commands:

```
SPX CONNECTIONS = 75
SPX ABORT TIMEOUT = 2000
SPX LISTEN TIMEOUT = 300
SPX VERIFY TIMEOUT = 200
```

These commands increase the minimum number of connections to the print server and extend the timeouts that packet collisions/reconfigurations under heavy load can cause. These are times on the cable when the packets can become lost or removed so that data signals can be restarted.

Also, use a text editor to create an AUTOEXEC.BAT file on this workstation; it looks similar to the following example. Chapter 5 explains how these commands are used to connect a workstation to the network.

```
@ECHO OFF
LSL
NE2000
IPXODI
NETX
PSERVER PSERV1
```

Now, attach the workstation to the network and reboot it. PSERVER.EXE should start, read the definitions you establish in PCONSOLE, and display an active status screen. If all the printers you define for this PSERVER appear, your print server is ready to go.

Using a Printer on a Workstation

You know that one possible type of printer is remote. A remote printer is attached to a user workstation, but configured as shareable by other users on the network.

After you define a printer as REMOTE COMx or REMOTE LPTx in PCONSOLE's Printer Definition menu, you must assign the appropriate interrupt and port specific information. Interrupts are not optional for remote printers.

The next step is to set up and run RPRINTER at the appropriate workstations. To run RPRINTER, the following files must be available:

IBM$RUN.OVL

RPRINTER.EXE

RPRINTER.HLP

RPRINT$$.EXE

SYS$ERR.DAT

SYS$HELP.DAT

SYS$MSG.DAT

Copy these files to the workstation's hard drive or to the SYS:LOGIN directory. If you put them in SYS:LOGIN, flag them as Shareable Read Only (SRO). Putting the files in either of these locations enables the RPRINTER to start on the workstation without having to log a user into the network. RPRINTER does not require a user to be logged in to operate. IPX/SPX, however, must be loaded.

Use a Text Editor, like MS-DOS's EDIT or DR-DOS's EDITOR, to change the AUTOEXEC.BAT file on the RPRINTER workstation's boot disk. If RPRINTER and the other files are in SYS:LOGIN, AUTOEXEC.BAT is similar to the following:

```
@ECHO OFF
LSL
NE2000
IPXODI
NETX
F:
:START
RPRINTER PSERV1 0R
IF ERRORLEVEL 1 GOTO START
LOGIN
```

Several things in this file might need to change, depending on your setup.

1. Replace F: with the appropriate letter for the drive to which you copied the RPRINTER files. Normally, SYS:LOGIN is set to the F: drive after NETX is executed.

2. Replace PSERV1 with the name of the print server you have defined. Replace the number after PSERVE1 with the number of the printer as you defined it in PCONSOLE. After RPRINTER has established a connection with the PSERVER, take a look at the PSERVER's monitor

display. The status for the printer should have changed from Not Connected to Waiting for job You also might see the message Out of paper.

NOTE

The line containing IF ERRORLEVEL deserves some explanation. If the PC running RPRINTER is rebooted, the PSERVER doesn't immediately release the printer connection, and the RPRINTER command can't attach to the printer. If this is the case, RPRINTER returns an error code of 1 to DOS, which you can detect by an IF ERRORLEVEL statement. If the error code is 1, the GOTO command loops to the :START label and tries the RPRINTER command again. Eventually, PSERVER frees up the connection and RPRINTER succeeds in starting up. RPRINTER then returns an error code of 0 and the GOTO is ignored so that execution of the batch file can continue.

These are the basic instructions for loading, defining, and starting a PSERVER system for local and remote printing. Everything discussed is available in detail in the NetWare Print Server and Installation manual provided with NetWare.

Now What?

Now that you have your print server, print queues, and printers defined, configured, and installed, what can you do to actually get data to the printers? Well, you have several options:

→   CAPTURE

→   NPRINT

→   Applications printing directly to the queue

CAPTURE is Novell's parallel port redirector. It uses memory space in the NetWare shell to tell the shell where to transport printer data that was originally destined to a local LPT port so that it prints off the proper queue. CAPTURE is not a TSR program, but rather, just a utility to set flags and pointers in the shell that is resident in memory on the workstation it's run from. Following is a common CAPTURE command line:

```
CAPTURE NB NT NFF TI=45 Q=<queue_name> L=1
```

This command instructs Capture to produce NoBanner, do No Tab expansion (maintain a ByteStream flow of data in its original binary format), do No Form Feed (preventing an additional blank sheet of paper to be ejected from the printer at the end of the print job), provide a timeout of 45 seconds (this is the amount of time the queue waits for MORE data from a print job before it assumes the job is done and closes the queue, thus starting a NEW job if more data is sent to the queue), send to the Queue that is named, and reroute data that was originally intended for LPT1: on the workstation.

CAPTURE also has the capability to reroute printer output to a disk file on the network using the CR= switch; for example, CAPTURE NB NT L=1 CR=F:\TEST.FIL sends the print job to the file TEST.FIL in the root of drive F. The only exception to using CAPTURE is if an application prints directly to the printer port hardware instead of using the computer's BIOS functions to print.

NPRINT is Novell's equivalent to MS-DOS's PRINT utility. It's a command-line utility that enables you to print a disk file directly to the print queue. All the CAPTURE command-line switches apply to NPRINT with the exceptions of L= and TI=. Use this to print pregenerated ASCII files, like DOC and README files that come with applications or updates, or to print files you create by using the CAPTURE CR= command or files that are created by applications that print directly to a disk file. You use it as follows:

```
NPRINT <filename.ext> NB NT Q=<queue_name>
```

You can use wild cards as part of the file name or extension; for example:

```
NPRINT *.DOC
```

The preceding example sends all the files with the DOC extension to the printer.

Many applications are capable of printing directly to the NetWare Queues. These applications do not require the use of the CAPTURE command, nor the utility of NPRINT because they use NetWare's function calls to send print data directly to the defined queue. This is significantly faster than using CAPTURE to redirect printer output, and more functional than using NPRINT. Applications that support printing directly to the queue include WordPerfect, Quattro Pro, and Microsoft Windows (hence all programs that print through the Windows Print Manager). Each application implements the function a little differently than the others, so you find that some applications use an intuitive function to define print queue output, while others require some work to get network printing properly configured.

Common Problems

The following are common problems encountered with printing on a network.

RPRINTER prints very slowly. This problem usually indicates one of the following:

The remote printer is defined in PCONSOLE as not using IRQs.

The port that the printer is attached to does not fully support hardware IRQs.

NOTE
RPRINTER requires hardware support of the IRQ's lines to signal the print server when it is ready for more data. If the port doesn't have true hardware support of the IRQ's line, RPRINTER has to wait for the CPU to become completely idle before it can request more data.

Graphics are corrupted. This problem usually indicates that the NT command-line option was not included in the CAPTURE command. The NT option tells the print server not to expand tab characters. An example of a valid CAPTURE command for printing graphics across the network follows:

```
CAPTURE NB NT NFF TI=45 Q=<queue_name>
```

The preceding command tells the system to capture data 1.) without a banner (NB); 2.) with No Tab Expansion, which maintains a binary data stream; 3.) with No For Feed to prevent an additional blank page to be ejected at the end of the print job; 4.) with a Timeout of 45 seconds, which is the length of time the queue will continue to accept data from a particular print job before assuming the job has ended and it closes the queue. Whew.

When a serial printer is used on an RPRINTER port, characters are lost, or data is corrupted. This problem usually indicates that the serial cable isn't providing the proper line support for the printer to send a serial signal to the port. In most cases, this problem has been solved by changing from a generic serial cable to a true HP, IBM, or Apple serial printer cable.

Other Tips:

Remember that RPRINTER requires the following:

IRQ lines are enabled

LPT1 is IRQ 7

LPT2 is IRQ 5

COM1 is IRQ 4

COM2 is IRQ 3

Avoid conflicts with your network adapter cards and other devices.

RPRINTER cannot support LPT3 if LPT1 is also used as a remote printer.

RPRINTER can support multiple printers on a single workstation if RPRINTER is loaded multiple times (the appropriate print server name and printer number must be used each time RPRINTER is loaded).

RPRINTER uses about 9K of RAM each time it is loaded on a workstation.

RPRINTER does not work well with Windows and does not work well when it is loaded into high memory with programs such as QEMM (Quarterdeck) or 386 Max (Qualitis Software).

Alternatives to Novell's Print Services

There are limitations to what you can do with Novell's Print Services. PServer allows only 16 printers per dedicated print server, and its maximum throughput is about 120kb/s. PServer EXE requires a dedicated PC on the network. These limitations have led to a remarkable business in alternatives to PServer and Rprinter.

Among the alternatives are Queue Service applications, which operate through the network from a dedicated print server or a workstation running a TSR print-sharing application. Examples of this type of print-sharing product are PS-Print from Brightwork Development and IQueue! Server from Infinite Technology.

Other alternatives include hardware-based print servers. These include devices like Hewlett-Packard's JetDirect line of network interface cards for the LaserJet family of printers. These are dedicated devices that install directly into the printer, providing a direct network connection for that printer. These devices usually have the capability to operate in Queue Server mode—which usually is faster, but requires a user login on each file-server it is servicing queues for—and Remote Printer mode, which is a dedicated version of RPRINTER using the Defined Elsewhere option in PCONSOLE's Printer Definition menu.

Another hardware-based option includes products like the Castelle LANPress and ASP JetLAN products. These are external dedicated print servers, providing up to eight printer ports through a single network connection. As with the JetDirect cards, these devices have the capability to operate as a Queue Server or a Remote Printer.

A major benefit to these types of devices is ease of installation. With most of the dedicated hardware options, you usually just have to plug in the print server, run the utility disk to create a print queue, make the logical assignment to the print server's port, and turn on the hardware—usually a 5 to 10 minute task. Another benefit is the improved overall performance in printing. Because you have a direct network attachment to the printer, data can stream into the printer at rates much faster than PServer or Rprinter normally can provide. In high volume or large graphic situations, this can mean a reduction in terms of minutes lost waiting for a print job.

Chapter 8, Short and Sweet

OK, now everyone on your network can print.

1. There are at least five ways to set up printing on your network:

    → PSERVER NLM on the fileserver

    → PSERVER EXE on dedicated print servers

    → RPRINTER EXE on workstations around the network

    → Third-party software print-sharing applications on workstations

    → Third-party hardware print-sharing devices installed directly in the printers, or dedicated to multiple printers

2. A Print Queue is configured using PCONSOLE.

3. Print Servers are set up using PCONSOLE.

4. To print, you need to assign a Printer to a Queue and attach that Queue to a Print Server.

5. You can configure a workstation as a dedicated PServer print server.

6. You can also set up a workstation as a remote printer using Rprinter.

7. You can troubleshoot common printer problems on the network.

8. Two basic NetWare Commands send printer output to a Queue:

    CAPTURE

    NPRINT

9. Some NetWare-aware applications have the capability to print directly to the NetWare queue. If an application has this capability, it should be configured to use it.

Chapter 9

Key Terms to Look for:

→ authentication
→ system script
→ user script
→ default script

Login Scripts

(Or, You Have To Start Somewhere...)

Before you talk on the phone, you have to dial a number; before you visit another household, you knock on the door; before you speak to most people, you get their attention. Okay, these are loose analogies, but the point is that logins have to do with the protocols of interaction, like the items just mentioned. And this chapter is all about logins, covering the following:

→ What login scripts are and how they run

→ What login scripts actually do

→ How to write them yourself

→ How to learn from sample login scripts

Logging in is the process of starting a conversation with a server. First, a network connection must be established between the workstation and the server. Then the user must be given permission to use the server's resources.

When the supervisor creates a new user on the LAN, the user is assigned a user name (an identification or id) and, usually, a password. When the user executes the LOGIN command, a series of events takes place:

1. The user enters his or her login id and password.

2. The server checks to ensure that the id belongs to an authorized user and that the password checks out.

    If everything is OK, the server grants the user access and continues the rest of the login process. In NetWare terminology, the user has now been *authenticated* to the server.

    If either the user id or the password are invalid, the server says "Get outta here" and denies the user access. (The actual message is "Access to server denied.")

3. If a user has been authenticated, NetWare then runs a series of login scripts. These scripts contain a variety of setup commands that define the user's network environment. After the last login script runs, the user is fully logged in.

Think of it like this: loading the LAN drivers and shells enables your workstation to talk to the fileserver, whereas running LOGIN tells the fileserver who is using that connection and lets you go inside. Okay, let's try that another way...

Loading the LAN drivers builds a house on a street in the city. Loading the NetWare shell gets it an address (321 Elm Street). When you log in to the network, it's like someone moving in and letting the post office know they now live there so that they can get mail—there's a name associated with the physical address (The Smiths).

After you are fully logged in, you need to have something happen so that you can actually use the resources of the fileserver. That's where login scripts come in.

Login Scripts? I Don't Need No Stinkin' Login Scripts!

To begin with, it probably would be best to explain what login scripts are and why you would want to use them. In NetWare 3.1*x*, there are three types of login scripts:

→   SYSTEM SCRIPT

→   USER SCRIPT

→   DEFAULT SCRIPT

Each of these performs some level of environment configuration for users, providing them logical drives on the network or running specific utilities to enable network functionality (such as capturing). They can be thought of as the network version of the CONFIG.SYS file on your workstation's boot disk, in that they automatically perform some set of instructions to get your workstation ready to run the applications you wish to run.

What They Are

Each login script operates for specific conditions, but all are based on individual users logging into the network. In other words, you can't create a login script for a group of users, although a group of users can execute specific commands in a script based on their group membership.

→ **SYSTEM LOGIN SCRIPT.** This script runs for each user logging into the network. It generally contains all the generic commands that every user logging into this fileserver would need to make use of this server's resources. The SYSTEM LOGIN SCRIPT is maintained in the SYS:PUBLIC directory in the file NET$LOG.DAT. It is a standard text file and can be edited using any text editor, including MS-DOS's EDIT and DR-DOS's EDITOR.

→ **USER LOGIN SCRIPT.** This script is specific to a particular user. It sets specific environment information for that user that is unique to that user; an example is the DOS environment variable for WordPerfect that contains the three-letter username. The USER LOGIN SCRIPT is maintained in each user's personal MAIL directory in the file LOGIN. It also is a standard text file.

→ **DEFAULT LOGIN SCRIPT.** This is run only if there is no USER LOGIN SCRIPT defined for a particular user and if there is neither an EXIT nor a NO_DEFAULT command in the SYSTEM LOGIN SCRIPT. The Default Login Script is programmed into the LOGIN.EXE program and sets up what Novell has determined is a minimum number of environment settings to function on the network.

See How They Run

Now that we know what they are, let's look at when they run and in what order. This is the part about NetWare that befuddles a lot of people. We'll start with the "easy" one.

1. The DEFAULT LOGIN SCRIPT runs only in the event that there is no USER LOGIN SCRIPT and if there is neither a NO_DEFAULT nor an EXIT command in the SYSTEM LOGIN SCRIPT. If any of these three conditions exists, the DEFAULT LOGIN SCRIPT will not execute.

2. The USER LOGIN SCRIPT executes if it exists as long as there is not an EXIT command in the SYSTEM LOGIN SCRIPT.

3. The SYSTEM LOGIN SCRIPT always executes if it exists.

NOTE
With the latest versions of the LOGIN.EXE utility, it is possible to define a LOGIN SCRIPT that should be executed for that particular login event. This option will bypass all the preceding LOGIN SCRIPT options. You invoke this option by issuing the command:

```
LOGIN /S <script_name> <server_name>\<user_name>
```

Also, if someone uses the ATTACH.EXE utility to connect to the fileserver, it will not execute any of the LOGIN SCRIPT options.

In most cases you would use a combination of the SYSTEM LOGIN SCRIPT and USER LOGIN SCRIPTS to set each user's particular environment when he or she logs in to the network.

Why Login Scripts?

Now that we've discussed what they are and how they run, you may be wondering why you need login scripts. As mentioned earlier, they are used to set the user's operating environment while they are on the network. Some of the things you can set in a login script include the following:

→ Logical drive mappings. These are the commands that assign a drive letter to different areas of the fileserver's hard disks, thus allowing you access to the files stored on that fileserver.

→ Search mappings. These are the commands that assign drive letters to different areas of the fileserver's hard disks as PATHed drives. This enables you to run applications that are stored on the fileserver without having to be in the particular directory on that fileserver.

→ Capture printers. This enables you to print to a networked printer as soon as you login without having to run a capture by hand.

→ Set DOS environment variables. You can then use them as conditionals later for applications, or for applications that look specifically in the DOS environment for configuration parameters, such as WordPerfect.

→ Select your starting drive letter designation.

→ Branch off to additional commands based on any number of conditionals.

→ Attach to other fileservers on your network.

→ Launch a start-up batch file to get you into your basic application or Menu system.

What Can They Do?

Okay, now it's time to get into the specific script commands, what they do, and how you would use them. There are 25 script commands; many of them are similar, if not the same, to their DOS equivalents in the CONFIG.SYS or AUTOEXEC.BAT on your workstation's boot disk. The commands are as follows:

(Executes an external command)

ATTACH

BEGIN ... END

BREAK

COMSPEC

DISPLAY

DOS BREAK

DOS SET

DOS VERIFY

DRIVE

EXIT

FDISPLAY

FIRE PHASERS

GOTO

IF ... THEN ... ELSE

INCLUDE

MACHINE

MAP

NO_DEFAULT

PAUSE

PCCOMPATIBLE

REMARK

SET_TIME

SHIFT

WRITE

What Does It All Mean?

Okay, so now that we've listed them for you, we'll explain what each one does and give examples of how you would use them. One thing to keep in mind is that it's best to issue all login script commands, identifiers, and variables in uppercase only.

# #

This command executes a command external to the login script. This means it will run any .COM or .EXE file that either is in the workstation's search path or that has been explicitly stated on the command line. Use this to run programs like CAPTURE or an anti-virus program (like Central Point Software's Anti-Virus, CPAV) during the login process.

WARNING

Do not, under any circumstance, run or load a TSR (Terminate/Stay Resident) program (Borland's SideKick or Novell's RPRINTER, for example) from inside a login script. Note the following from The Novell Installation Manual, Appendix A (Login Scripts):

"The login script is held in memory when the # command is run. The login script is not released from memory until you return to the script and complete it or exit the script."

What this means to you is that if you load a TSR from inside the Login Script, LOGIN.EXE as well as the script itself remains in your workstation's RAM memory until you unload the TSR. This can waste over 100K of workstation memory each time you log in to the fileserver.

You would use the # command in the following manner:

```
#CAPTURE NB NT TI=45 Q=PRINTQ_0
```

NOTE

You can use this command to run DOS batch files from inside the login script by using the following command:

```
#<d>:\<path>\COMMAND /C <BATCH_NAME>.BAT
```

Where <d>: is the drive letter and <path> is the directory that you have COMMAND.COM stored—usually your boot disk in the root directory.

ATTACH

This command enables you to connect to multiple fileservers at one time without having to enter your user name or password (this assumes that you have the same user name and password on each fileserver). It also enables you to connect to other fileservers without losing your connection to your primary server.

Use this command in the following manner:

```
ATTACH <server_name>
```

Where <server_name> is the name of the other fileserver you want to connect to. If you have a different user name or password on the other fileserver you want to connect to, then you would use this command in the following manner:

```
ATTACH <server_name>\<user_name>
```

You can't pass passwords to fileservers through the login script, contrary to Novell's documentation.

BEGIN / END

This command set enables you to embed subroutines in the login script. This usually is used in conjunction with IF .. THEN commands.

Use this command set in the following manner:

```
BEGIN
        DO SOMETHING
END
```

BREAK

This command enables you to turn ON or OFF the capability to stop login script execution using the Ctrl-C or Ctrl-BREAK keystrokes. This has no effect on your computer's DOS CONTROL BREAK checking.

When you turn BREAK ON in the login script the keyboard's buffer is not saved.

Use this command in one of the following ways:

BREAK ON	Enables you to abort the login script.
BREAK OFF	Prevents you from aborting the login script.

COMSPEC

This is equivalent to the DOS command "SET COMSPEC=". This sets the computer's environment so that it knows where to find the DOS COMMAND.COM command processor if it needs to reload DOS after any particular application.

Use this command in the following manner:

```
COMSPEC <d>:\<path>\<filename.ext>
```

In which <d>: is the drive letter, <path> is the directory in which you can find the command processor, and <filename.ext> is the file name of the command processor itself (usually this will be the root directory of the workstation's boot disk, and the file COMMAND.COM).

NOTE

Although Novell's manuals state that you should set a COMSPEC to be equal to a directory on your fileserver's hard disk, this is not recommended unless you are using remote boot (diskless) workstations. If your workstation boots from a floppy or hard disk, it is best not to set a COMSPEC to your network drives.

DISPLAY

This command enables you to show, or type, a text file to the workstation's monitor screen each time a user logs in to the fileserver. This can be used to send company or workgroup information to all the users on your network, and ensures they have the opportunity to see it when they log in.

This command does no filtering of the data in the file it is displaying, and so will pass "garbage" characters, such as word processor format codes, to the monitor screen. This command does not generate an error message if the file stated is not found.

Use this command in the following manner:

```
DISPLAY <d>:\<path>\<filename.ext>
```

Where `<d>:` is the drive letter, `<path>` is the directory in which you can find the text file, and `<filename.ext>` is the file name of the text file itself.

DOS BREAK

This command is equivalent to the DOS BREAK command that can be issued from a DOS batch file or the DOS prompt. It enables or disables the capability to use the Ctrl-C or Ctrl-BREAK keys to stop DOS application execution.

Use this command in one of the following ways:

`DOS BREAK ON`	Enables you to abort DOS application processing.
`DOS BREAK OFF`	Prevents you from aborting DOS application processing.

DOS SET

This command is equivalent to the DOS command SET NAME = VARIABLE. Use this command to assign some value to an identifier in your PC's DOS environment. You can use this command to set variables for later use within the login script, or batch files to start applications from the DOS prompt.

Use this command in the following manner:

```
DOS SET <name> = "<value>"
```

Note that you must use the quotation marks before and after the value you want to use. Some examples of what you would do with this command are as follows:

```
DOS SET USER_NAME="%LOGIN_NAME"
DOS SET NODE="%P_STATION"
DOS SET LOCAL_PRINTER="NO"
DOS SET X="1"
DOS SET %<X> + 1
```

NOTE

You can prefix the SET command with the TEMP option when using the DOS SET command to inform the login script that the variable will only be used within the script and not to save it in the DOS environment space. (For example: TEMP SET NODE="%P_STATION").

WARNING

Because the DOS SET command uses the DOS environment space, you must ensure that you have a large enough environment defined to the PC. This space is defined in the CONFIG.SYS file using the command

```
SHELL=<d>:\COMMAND.COM /E:ssss /P
```

In which <d>: is the boot disk drive letter that your workstation uses, /E:ssss tells DOS how large to make the environment in BYTES, and /P tells DOS to make the changes permanent.

If the DOS environment size is not large enough, you will get errors on your workstation similar to the following:

```
Can't expand DOS environment space
```

and changes you want to make will not be saved.

DOS VERIFY

This command is equivalent to using DOS's VERIFY command or the /V switch on the DOS COPY command. Use this to set the workstation to enable or disable the DOS file verification when copying files to a local hard or floppy disk on the workstation. It does not affect files copied with the NetWare NCOPY command, which defaults to having verification enabled.

Use this command in the following manner:

```
DOS VERIFY ON
```

Enables file copy verification.

```
DOS VERIFY OFF
```

Prevents file copy verification.

DRIVE

This command is used to set the default drive you will use on the network. Before you can issue this command, you must properly map the drive letter you want to use.

Use this command in the following manner:

```
DRIVE <d>:
```

Enables you to map a specific drive letter.

```
DRIVE *<n>:
```

Enables you to map the logical network drive number.

EXIT

This command is used to terminate execution of the login script. It allows for several options when you terminate the script depending on the specific syntax used with the command. This command completely exits from the login script, without the capability to process other login scripts down the chain. In other words, if you have an EXIT command in the SYSTEM LOGIN SCRIPT, the USER LOGIN SCRIPT is bypassed completely.

Use this command in one of the following manners:

`EXIT`	Drops to the DOS prompt.
`EXIT "<filename.ext>"`	Stuffs the keyboard buffer with the file name specified and then executes that file.
`EXIT "<DOS command>"`	Stuffs the keyboard buffer with the DOS command specified and then executes that command.

Note that you must use the quotation marks before and after the file name or command that you want to use. Some examples of what you would do with this command are as follows:

```
EXIT "START.BAT"

EXIT "DIR"

EXIT "MENU MAIN"
```

FDISPLAY

This command enables you to show, or type, a text file to the workstation's monitor screen each time a user logs in to the fileserver. This can be used to send company or workgroup information to all the users on your network, and ensures they have the opportunity to see it when they log in.

This command filters and formats the data in the file it is displaying, and so will not pass "garbage" characters, such as word processor format codes, to the monitor screen. This command does not generate an error message if the file stated is not found.

Use this command in the following manner:

```
FDISPLAY <d>:\<path>\<filename.ext>
```

Where `<d>:` is the drive letter, `<path>` is the directory in which you can find the text file, and `<filename.ext>` is the file name of the text file itself.

FIRE PHASERS

This command enables you to generate sound from the computer's speaker.

Use this command in the following manner:

```
FIRE PHASERS <x> TIMES
```

GOTO

This command is equivalent to the DOS batch file GOTO command. It enables you to jump to some other part of the login script, and usually is used in conjunction with IF ... THEN commands.

Use this command in the following manner:

```
IF <something> THEN GOTO <label>
```

You identify labels in login scripts by using a colon (:) after the label name, as in the following example:

```
LABEL:
```

IF ... THEN ... ELSE

This command set enables you to test the validity of a condition and do something if the condition is true, or do something else if the condition is false. You can use logical arguments (AND, OR, NOR) to chain multiple conditions, and you can use one of several system identifiers as conditions to test. (Identifiers will be discussed later in this chapter.) You also can use DOS environment variables as conditionals, and you can test for the reverse of the condition using the NOT option.

Examples of how to use this command set are found later in this chapter during the discussion on identifier variables.

INCLUDE

This command enables you to add subscripts to the login script you are executing. These would be standard text files stored on the fileserver's disk in a directory the users can access, that include valid login script commands. One of the main reasons you would use INCLUDE is to maintain modular login scripts and increase the total number of commands you can have executed in the script. You also can use INCLUDE based on IF ... THEN conditional testing.

Use this command in the following manner:

```
INCLUDE <volume>:<path>\<script_name.ext>
```

Where <volume> is the NetWare volume name, <path> is the directory name, and <script_name.ext> is the file name you have set up as the file to be included.

MACHINE

This command is used to set a NAME to your computer.

Use this command in the following manner:

```
MACHINE="name"
```

MAP

This command, and its variations, enables you to make several changes to the environment, including the following:

→ Make logical assignments between drive letters and directories on the fileserver's hard disks

→ Assign drives and add them to the search path

→ Delete specific drive-letter mappings and search drive mappings

→ Show drive mappings during the execution of the login script, or hide them

→ Insert Search Mappings into specific positions in the PATH

→ Assign drives as False Roots so that users can't easily move up the directory tree

There are several MAP options when using the MAP command:

→ **DISPLAY [ON/OFF]** Enables or disables the displaying of drive mappings from the login script itself

→ **ROOT** Assigns a drive letter as a False Root drive

→ **ERRORS [ON/OFF]** Enables or disables the displaying of login script error information

→ **INS** Inserts a search drive into a specific location within the DOS path

→ **DEL** Removes a logical drive letter or a search drive from the current drive list

You also can use any of the login script identifier variables within your MAP commands.

Use this command in any number of possible configurations, including the following:

```
MAP F:=SYS:\PUBLIC

MAP *1:=SYS:\PUBLIC

MAP ROOT INS S1:=SYS:PUBLIC

MAP INS S2:=SYS:\PUBLIC\%MACHINE\%OS\%OS_VERSION
```

For more information on using the MAP command in login scripts, refer to the *NetWare Installation Manual*, Appendix A (Login Scripts).

NO DEFAULT

This command instructs the SYSTEM LOGIN SCRIPT to bypass the DEFAULT LOGIN SCRIPT even if there are no valid USER LOGIN SCRIPTS or an EXIT command in the SYSTEM script.

Use this command in the following manner:

```
NO_DEFAULT
```

PAUSE

This command enables you to place the script processor on hold while waiting for the user to enter a keystroke. You can substitute the command WAIT in the login script.

Use this command in the following manner:

```
PAUSE
```

PCCOMPATIBLE

This command ensures compatibility with various DOS versions and PC BIOS variations. You can substitute the command COMPATIBLE in the login script.

Use this command in the following manner:

```
PCCOMPATIBLE
```

REMARK

This command' makes comments in the login script. You can substitute the REM, *, or ; commands in the login script.

Use this command in one of the following manners:

```
REMARK Make changes to something here

; Make changes to something here

* Make changes to something here
```

SET TIME

This command enables or disables the resetting of the workstation clock by the LOGIN.EXE during the login process.

Use this command in one of the following manners:

SET_TIME ON	Enables the workstation time to be reset.
SET_TIME OFF	Disables the workstation time to be reset.

SHIFT

This command is equivalent to the DOS command SHIFT used in batch files. It enables you to move through a string of command-line arguments up to 10 deep. You usually use this in conjunction with an IF ... THEN GOTO loop.

Use this command in the following manner:

```
SHIFT n
```

In which n is equivalent to the number of positions you want to move over by, usually 1.

WRITE

This command is equivalent to the DOS command TYPE used in a batch file, and displays a single line of text on the monitor during the login process. You can use standard text messages, embed super-characters (including the capability to force a line feed or beep), and impose one of several operators to produce compound strings. You also can use any of the login script identifier's variables.

Use this command in the following manner:

```
WRITE "text string"
```

Variations on a Theme

Table 9.1 shows the login script identifier variables. These are used in conjunction with many of the login script commands to test the condition of the workstation's environment, or some external value, including such things as date and time. You can use these to provide the capability to automate tasks for specific users, based on specific dates, day of week, or time, as well as any information on the workstation's address itself. Many of the variables require the use of the % (percent sign) identification marker to let the login script parser know how to interpret the commands; you would use the %ERROR_LEVEL or %<env_var> identifiers within the login script, for example.

Table 9.1
Login Script Identifier Variables

Identifier Variable	Display
CONDITIONAL ACCESS_SERVER	Returns a true state if issued on an Access Server
ERROR_LEVEL	0 if TRUE or no errors, 1 if FALSE or errors

Identifier Variable	Display
MEMBER OF "group_name"	Returns a TRUE if the user is a member of the stated group, otherwise FALSE

DATE

DAY	Day number (01 through 31)
DAY_OF_WEEK	Day name (MONDAY, TUESDAY, etc.)
MONTH	Month number (01 through 12)
MONTH_NAME	Month name (JANUARY, FEBRUARY, etc.)
NDAY_OF_WEEK	Day position number in week (Sunday=1, Friday=7)
SHORT_YEAR	Year in short format (93, 94, etc.)
YEAR	Year in long format (1993, 1994, etc.)
DOS ENVIRONMENT	Enables you to use a DOS environment variable as a login script variable

NETWORK

NETWORK_ADDRESS	LAN segment address (8 digits, hex address)
FILE_SERVER	Fileserver name

TIME

AM_PM	Day or night, AM or PM
GREETING_TIME	Morning, afternoon, or evening
HOUR	Hour in 12-hour notation (1 through 12)
HOUR24	Hour in Military notation (00 through 23, Midnight = 00)
MINUTE	Minute (00 through 59)

continues

Table 9.1
Continued

Identifier Variable	Display
SECOND	Second (00 through 59)

USER

FULL_NAME	User's full name, as defined in SYSCON, User Information
LOGIN_NAME	User's unique login name
USER_ID	NetWare's internal identifier for each user

WORKSTATION

MACHINE	The machine the shell was written for; default is IBM_PC
OS	The workstation's operating system; default is MSDOS
OS_VERSION	The workstation's OS version in Vx.yy format
P_STATION	Workstation's physical node address, 12-digit hex format
SMACHINE	Short machine name; default is IBM
STATION	Workstation's logical connection number to the fileserver

Other Options

Besides the script commands and variables, there are many logical operators, several of which have different ways of expressing the same option.

EQUAL can be defined as IS, = , ==, EQUALS

NOT EQUAL can be defined as IS NOT, != , <> , DOES NOT EQUAL, NOT EQUAL TO

IS GREATER THAN can be defined as >

IS LESS THAN can be defined as <

IS GREATER THAN OR EQUAL TO can be defined as >=

IS LESS THAN OR EQUAL TO can be defined as <=

You also can impose multiple requirements on a condition by adding an AND, OR, or NOR between conditions, and you can impose reverse logic by adding a NOT to the conditional.

Samples Anyone?

Coming up now are examples of some login scripts, including what's programmed into the DEFAULT LOGIN SCRIPT in LOGIN.EXE.

DEFAULT LOGIN SCRIPT

This is from the *NetWare 3.11 Installation Manual*, Appendix A (Login Scripts). Changes might have been made in updates to the LOGIN.EXE as was originally shipped with NetWare 3.11.

```
WRITE "Good %GREETING_TIME, %LOGIN_NAME"
MAP DISPLAY OFF
MAP ERRORS OFF
Rem: Set 1st drive to most appropriate directory.
MAP *1:=SYS:;*1:=SYS:%LOGIN_NAME
IF "%1"="SUPERVISOR" THEN MAP *1:=SYS:SYSTEM
Rem: Set search drives (S2 machine-OS dependent).
MAP INS S1:=SYS:PUBLIC
MAP INS S2:=S1:%MACHINE/%OS/%OS_VERSION
Rem: Now display all the current drive settings.
MAP DISPLAY ON
MAP
```

SYSTEM LOGIN SCRIPT

The following is an example of a SYSTEM LOGIN SCRIPT:

```
MAP DISPLAY OFF
MAP F:=SYS:
MAP ROOT INS S1:=SYS:PUBLIC
MAP ROOT INS S2:=SYS:SYSTEM
MAP INS S3:=SYS:APPS\WP51
MAP ROOT INS S4:=SYS:PUBLIC\PCT71
MAP ROOT INS S5:=SYS:PUBLIC\TOOLS
MAP ROOT INS S6:=SYS:PUBLIC\STUFF
MAP ROOT INS S7:=SYS:PUBLIC\NORTON45
MAP ROOT INS S8:=SYS:PUBLIC\DOS\%OS\%OS_VERSION
MAP INS S9:=SYS:APPS\TEXTWARE
MAP ROOT INS S10:=SYS:APPS\CPAV
MAP INS S11:=E:
DOS SET NSE_DOWNLOAD="E:\DOWNLOAD"
MAP ROOT G:=SYS:DV
MAP ROOT H:=SYS:TAP53
MAP ROOT I:=SYS:TAPCAT
MAP ROOT J:=SYS:USERS\%LOGIN_NAME
DRIVE J:
SET PCTOOLS="J:\\"
MAP ROOT K:=SYS:TAP53\PREDOWN
```

USER LOGIN SCRIPT

The following is an example of a USER LOGIN SCRIPT:

```
DOS SET WPC="/u=mja"
FIRE PHASERS=5
EXIT "START.BAT"
```

Chapter 9, Short and Sweet

So, now that you've survived learning about login scripts, what you do with them and why, let's review. Unlike many of the other chapters in this book, it's hard to just specifically recap each item learned—there are a lot of different details in one main area. Instead, suffice it to say, you learned about the following:

1. What kinds of scripts there are, System, User, and Default.

2. The order in which they execute, including the conditions that would prevent one or more from executing.

3. How to bypass the login scripts from the command line.

4. How to run a special login script on a one-time basis from the command line.

5. What the script commands are and why you would use them.

6. What the operators are that can be used to modify the script commands.

7. What the identifier variables are and how to use them to modify or test the environment.

8. What the default login script is, and when it executes.

Chapter 10

Key Terms to Look for:

➔ menu hierarchy

➔ compile

➔ source file

➔ data file

➔ parameters

Menus

(Or, Everything from Creating to Ordering to Using Them)

Novell includes a utility program that lets you create menus for your network users in a fairly straightforward fashion. Under NetWare 3.11, this is the MENU utility; under NetWare 3.12 this utility has been replaced by a newer menu program called NMENU.

In this chapter, you'll learn about the following:

➔ Planning menus

➔ Using the MENU program in NetWare

➔ Using the NMENU program in NetWare

NMENU has several advantages over the older MENU program, chiefly surrounding the amount of memory it consumes in the workstations that use it. NMENU consumes no memory if configured that way (you'll learn how to do this), while the older MENU takes up about 50K of RAM, even when you're running a program that you started with it.

Using either program, you can even create different menus for different groups of people, customizing the menu they use with the work they do.

So, for example, you could create a menu for the executives that had only one choice (Turn off this stupid computer, I can't figure it out), one for the office assistant (Do Real Work, Do More Real Work, Do Even More Real Work), one for managers (Schedule Lunch, Make Other People Do Work, Spend Lots of Money) and so on.

This chapter will first discuss the MENU utility found in Netware 3.11 and then NMENU from Netware 3.12.

Planning Your Menus

Before creating a menu, it is important that you write down the structure that your menu or menus will have. During this process, keep these tips in mind:

→   Try not to make the menu structure too shallow. Try to group related functions under a sub-menu rather than putting them on the main menu. For example, if your organization uses three different word processing programs, you would probably want to create a sub-menu with these three choices, and just have an entry on the top menu called "Word Processors" or "Word Processing" which takes them to the menu of the different word processing programs available.

→   Try not to make the menu structure too deep. In other words, try to reduce the number of steps and menu choices that people have to go through to get to the menu option that they want.

→   Think about how your users will see the menu organization. For example, it would make more sense to most people to put the WordPerfect Printer utility next to the WordPerfect program than to put in a generic Printer Utilities menu. How you group your menus logically depends on what sorts of things you'll be adding to your menus, and what sorts of things your users use their computers for. Spend some time thinking about this particular subject as you arrange and rearrange the menus that you'll design.

Too shallow, too deep, how to group items: It requires some thought to come up with a menu hierarchy that gives the best of all worlds. One strategy for designing your menu is to draw it out in a chart format, much like an organization chart.

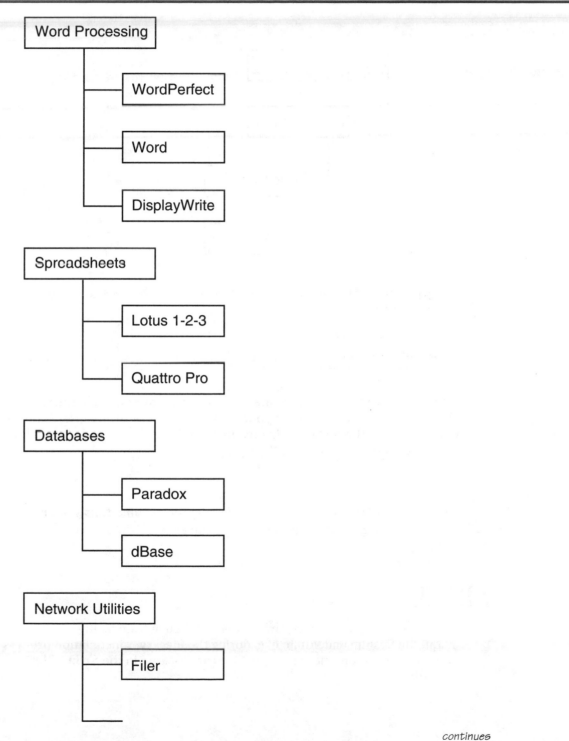

continues

continued

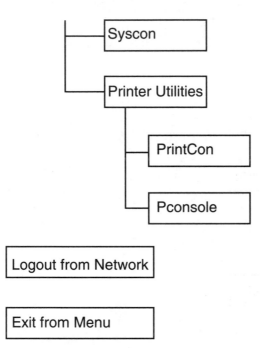

Logout from Network

Exit from Menu

Once you have your menu planned out, use the rest of this chapter to actually install and implement your menu. The rest of the chapter is divided into two parts, the first covering the menu utility in Netware 3.11, and the second covering the menu in Netware 3.12.

NOTE
All the set up steps in this chapter assume that you are logged into the fileserver as Supervisor.

MENU

The MENU program for Netware 3.11 is installed automatically when you install the System and Public files during the fileserver installation process. The MENU program and its support files are located in the SYS:PUBLIC directory.

Creating a MENU File

Creating a menu for the MENU program is as easy as typing in a text file that describes the menu. When MENU is run, you tell it which menu file to use, it reads the file, and then presents the menu.

To create a menu file, use a text editor, such as the EDIT program included in DOS 5 and DOS 6. You can also use many word processors that can save their files in a plain text, or ASCII, format. Make sure that you know how to do this in the word processor before you begin!

The following is a sample MENU file, based on the menu structure you saw previously.

```
%Main Menu
1.    Word Processing
      %WordProcessing
2.    SpreadSheets
      %Spreadsheets
3.    Databases
      %Databases
4.    Network Utilities
      %Network Utilities
5.    Logout From Network
      LOGOUT.EXE
%WordProcessing
WordPerfect
      WP.EXE
Word
      WORD.EXE
DisplayWrite
      DW.BAT
%Spreadsheets
Lotus 1-2-3
      1-2-3.EXE
Quattro Pro
      Q.EXE
%Databases,25,20
Paradox
```

```
        PDX.EXE
dBase
        DBASE.EXE
%Network Utilities
Filer
        FILER
Syscon
        SYSCON
Printer Utilities
        %PrinterUtilities
%PrinterUtilities
PrintCon
        PRINTCON.EXE
Pconsole
        PCONSOLE.EXE
```

What a bunch of gobbledegook! Amazingly, it ends up working, though. Let's examine how this menu file works, and how it is arranged.

First, at the beginning, you see the following lines that define the top menu:

```
%Main Menu
1.    Word Processing
        %WordProcessing
2.    SpreadSheets
        %Spreadsheets
3.    Databases
        %Databases
4.    Network Utilities
        %Network Utilities
5.    Logout From Network
        LOGOUT.EXE
```

The first line begins at the left-most position on the screen, and defines the name of the top menu (called, naturally enough, Main Menu).

The numbered lines show the actual entries on the menu. These entries will be sorted when you run the menu program before being displayed. For that reason, you may want to force the MENU program to display your options in a particular order by using numbers or letters at the beginning of each menu item, which has been done here.

The indented lines (%WordProcessing, %Spreadsheets, LOGOUT.EXE, etc.) are the actual commands that are executed if someone were to choose the menu item shown above them. In the case of the indented lines that begin with a percentage sign (%), it tells the MENU program to bring up a sub-menu. For example, the indented line %WordProcessing tells MENU to branch to the %WordProcessing section of the file when the user chooses that choice. When they do this, the MENU program goes to that section, shown below, and presents them the menu:

```
%WordProcessing
WordPerfect
        WP.EXE
Word
        WORD.EXE
DisplayWrite
        DW.BAT
```

Once a menu has been branched to, everything works just the same: The left-most items following the menu name are what the user sees and can choose. The indented items are the commands that get executed if they choose a particular item.

Changing Menu Positions

You can tell the MENU program where on the screen you want each menu to appear by adding two numbers after the menu entry. For example, consider this slightly different WordProcessing menu label:

```
%WordProcessing,5,20
```

The two numbers following the name of the menu define where the upper-left corner of that particular menu item will be positioned. The first number indicates the row (1-25) and the second number indicates the column (1-80). When you omit these numbers, as the earlier examples did, the MENU program automatically centers all menus.

Installing MENU for Users

After you have written your menu file, save it to a file in the SYS:PUBLIC directory. For example, assume that the sample menu above is saved as SAMPLE.MNU.

To bring up the menu, you would type the following command:

```
MENU SAMPLE.MNU
```

To set up a user so that the menu comes up automatically when they log in to the network, add this line to the very end of their individual login script:

```
EXIT "MENU SAMPLE.MNU"
```

On your network, substitute the name of the menu file you want to use for SAMPLE.MNU. Also, note that the quote marks are required for the login script command EXIT. Lastly, only one EXIT is allowed in a login script, and it should be at the very end of the login script; nothing after EXIT will be executed.

If you need to create different menus for various people, just create the different menu files, and then give each person the appropriate EXIT command to start up the menu file that you want them to see.

TIP

You can save lots of time by writing a master menu file that includes everything that everyone would possibly want. Then, when you want to customize a menu for a particular person or group of people, just delete the sections that don't pertain to them.

NMENU

The NMENU program is new to Netware 3.12, and adds some new features the older MENU program doesn't offer:

➜   NMENU can be set up so that it does not take away any memory from the applications the user launches.

→ NMENU gives you more control over how programs are run.

→ NMENU lets you design menu options that ask the user for input, and then use that input in the command that is finally executed by the menu.

Setting up NMENU

Setting up NMENU is a fairly easy task, following these steps:

1. Install the MENU program files onto your network.

2. Create a shared directory on the network for the menu files and temporary files that NMENU uses.

3. Use a text editor (like the EDIT program included in DOS 5 and DOS 6) to write the instructions for the NMENU program. Alternately, at this step you can upgrade the menu files used by the older Novell MENU program if you were using the older version on your system.

4. Compile the menu file that you created in step 3. Compile means that you take the text file that you wrote and then use a special program to reduce it to a more compact, faster structure that runs more quickly.

5. Set up the individual users' login scripts to integrate NMENU so that it comes up automatically when they log in.

The following sections will walk you through each of these steps.

Installing the Menu Program Files

The first thing you need to do is to install the NMENU program files onto your fileserver. To do this, follow these steps:

1. Locate the Netware disk labelled Menu.

2. Insert the disk into the disk drive on the workstation you are using. We'll assume that this is the A: drive on your computer, but obviously you can substitute B: if you need to.

3. The best place to install these programs is into your SYS:PUBLIC directory. To actually install them, type the following:

```
COPY A:\*.* F:\PUBLIC
```

Press Enter. That's it!

Creating the Shared Directory

NMENU creates lots of temporary files for each user as it is used. It needs a shared directory to store these files where everyone who uses the menu has full access.

The best place to put the shared menu directory is on your SYS: volume, which is normally your F: drive. To create the directory, you have to first create it and then assign rights to it for everyone:

1. Move to the SYS: volume.

    Type **F:** and press Enter. If your SYS: volume is a different drive letter on your system, go ahead and substitute that drive letter for F:.

2. Make sure you are in the root directory.

    Type **CD ** and press Enter.

3. Create the directory.

    Type **MD \MENU** and press Enter.

4. Move to the new directory.

    Type **CD \MENU** and press Enter.

5. Assign the EVERYONE group rights to this directory, giving them Read, Write, and Filescan rights.

    Type **ASSIGN R W F to EVERYONE** and press Enter.

Creating the Menu

Creating the menu is the most time-consuming task you have to do, and it's also the longest section in this chapter! You have to create a *source file* that contains all of the commands that will end up in your menu, and then compile that source file into the data file that NMENU actually uses. The hardest part (which isn't really very hard) is writing the source file.

You should locate your source and data files in the SYS:PUBLIC directory. This directory already gives your users Read and Filescan rights, but doesn't include Write rights. This is important because you don't want people messing with your menu files and screwing things up for you to fix later. Note that this is different from the shared directory where temporary files are stored; people will have full access to that directory.

Converting an Old Menu File

If you had a previous version of Netware (2.x or 3.11) and used the MENU utility, then you can quickly upgrade those menu files to the new format with the MENUCNVT utility included with the new NMENU program. To do this:

1. Move to the directory where the old menu files are located. For most systems, this will be SYS:PUBLIC.

    Type **F:** and press Enter.

    Type **CD \PUBLIC** and press Enter.

2. Run the MENUCNVT program for each of the old menu files that end in .MNU. If you need a list of them, use this command:

    DIR *.MNU and press Enter.

To actually perform the conversion, type this command:

MENUCNVT filename and press Enter, in which *filename* is substituted with the actual name of the menu file you're converting. For example, if you have a menu file called USER.MNU, you would type MENUCNVT USER.MNU and press Enter.

The MENUCNVT program will output a file with the same file name as the original, but with a .SRC file extension. This file can be edited and then compiled to become a usable menu file. Follow the remaining steps to learn how to edit it, compile it, and install it for your users.

Writing or Editing a Menu File

Once you have decided on the structure of your menu, you can begin writing the source file using the text editor of your choice. One good text editor is the EDIT program included in DOS 5 and DOS 6. Also, many word processing programs will work, but only if they have the capability to save the file into a pure text, or ASCII, format. Make sure it can (and that you know how to do it) before you start!

You write the menu source file using a number of different commands. Table 10.1 shows the commands:

Table 10.1
NMENU Commands

Command	Description
MENU	Indicates the main menu or sub-menu
ITEM	Indicates an actual menu entry
EXEC	Instructs NMENU to execute a DOS command
LOAD	Causes a menu to appear from a *different* menu file
SHOW	Causes a menu to appear from the *same* menu file
GETO	Short for GET Optional. Enables the menu program to prompt the user for some information that is optional.
GETP	Short for GET Parameter. This works very similarly to GETO and GETR, except that it stores the answer from the user in a variable that you can use elsewhere in the menu.
GETR	Short for GET Required. The user of the menu must answer the question before the menu program will proceed.

Let's now go through each of these commands in detail, with examples and the whole works.

MENU

Defines the following block of commands as being part of a single menu. The first MENU command in the file defines the top menu; other menus in the file are referenced by number.

Format

```
MENU menu_number,menu_name
```

Menu_number can be any number from 1 to 255, and each menu in the file must have a unique number. You can't have two menus with the same number.

Menu_name can be no longer than 40 characters.

Example

```
MENU 1,Main Menu
    (Menu commands appear here)
    . . .
    . . .
MENU 5,Network Utilities
    (More menu commands)
    . . .
    . . .
```

ITEM

Used to display an individual menu item. This command has a variety of *parameters* (sub-commands) that further define what it does.

Format

```
ITEM item_name {Option_1 Option_2 ...}
```

Item_name must not be longer than 40 characters.

The options are entirely optional; you do not need to specify any of them. If you do specify one or more options, however, you need to enclose them with the curly brace characters ('{'and '}').

Options

This command has four options that can control how it appears. See table 10.2 for a description of these options.

Table 10.2
ITEM *Options*

Option	Description
BATCH	Causes the NMENU program to remove itself from the computer's memory before executing the command. If you don't use the BATCH option, NMENU stays in memory, consuming about 32K of the

continues

Table 10.2
Continued

Option	Description
	user's RAM. With some programs, this might not leave enough memory for them to run.
CHDIR	Under the menu program, you still have default directories, just like when you type the CD command in DOS. If you have an ITEM command that ends up changing the default directory, when that ITEM is done, the user is still in the new directory. You can use the CHDIR option to tell the menu program to go back to the previous default directory once the ITEM is finished. In fact, you will want the CHDIR option in most cases.
PAUSE	One of the things you can use the NMENU program for is to execute DOS commands for the user. However, normally when the DOS command is finished, the menu instantly reappears, and doesn't give the user enough time to read any error messages or informational messages given by the DOS command. By using the PAUSE option, the menu will pause before returning. It leaves any messages from the DOS command on the screen until the user presses a key to return to the menu.
SHOW	Displays the DOS command being executed. This can be helpful if you want people to eventually learn what the commands are.

Example

```
MENU 5, WordProcessing
ITEM WordPerfect {BATCH CHDIR}
     EXEC WP.EXE
ITEM Word {BATCH CHDIR}
     EXEC WORD.EXE
ITEM DisplayWrite {BATCH CHDIR}
     EXEC DW.BAT
```

Above, each ITEM is using both the BATCH and CHDIR parameters. Additional parameters would be added in the same way. For example, if WordPerfect needed all of them, it would say:

```
ITEM WordPerfect {BATCH CHDIR PAUSE SHOW}
```

Notes

NMENU automatically assigns each menu option a letter, from A to Z. If you want to force it to assign specific letters instead of those (for example, the letter W for WordProcessing), put a caret in front of the letter in the name you want to use. For example, the following would force the letter W for WordPerfect, and the letter R for Word, instead of the default A and B.

```
ITEM ^WordPerfect {BATCH CHDIR}
     EXEC WP.EXE
ITEM Wo^rd {BATCH CHDIR}
     EXEC WORD.EXE
```

EXEC

This menu command causes the command following it to be executed when that menu option is chosen.

Format

```
EXEC command_or_option
```

Options

There are four forms of this command, shown in table 10.3:

Table 10.3
EXEC Options

Option	Description
EXEC	EXEC by itself simply executes the command following the EXEC word.
EXEC DOS	This option lets the user go into DOS without the menu. When they are done using DOS, they type the DOS command EXIT to return to the menu.

continues

Table 10.3
Continued

Option	Description
EXEC EXIT	This option exits NMENU. Under the old MENU program, any user could exit the menu simply by pressing the Escape key. Under NMENU, the user has to choose an option that specifically calls EXEC EXIT or they will not be able to exit the menu. This is useful in situations where security is critical.
EXEC LOGOUT	Exits the menu and logs the user off of the network in one step.

LOAD

The LOAD command enables you to call a *different* menu file. For example, you could have several menus for NMENU created, and link them together with the LOAD command.

Format

```
LOAD menu_filename
```

Examples

The following shows how you might link several menu files together using the LOAD command:

```
MENU 5, WordProcessing
ITEM WordPerfect
    LOAD WP_MENU.DAT
ITEM Word
    LOAD WD_MENU.DAT
```

In these cases, when users choose either WordPerfect or Word, they would then be shown either the WP_MENU.DAT menu or the WD_MENU.DAT menu. Instead, it is generally better to keep all of the menus in a single file and use the SHOW command, but there may be situations where this format makes more sense.

SHOW

The SHOW command displays another menu contained in the same menu file.

Format

```
SHOW menu_number
```

Examples

Using the sample menu structure shown at the beginning of this chapter, here is how the main menu would be defined:

```
MENU 1, Main Menu
ITEM Word Processing
     SHOW 5
ITEM SpreadSheets
     SHOW 10
ITEM Databases
     SHOW 15
ITEM Network Utilities
     SHOW 20
ITEM Logout From Network
     EXEC LOGOUT.EXE
ITEM Exit from Menu
     EXEC EXIT
```

GETx

There are three different GET commands: GETR, GETO, and GETP. Each command gets input from the menu user, and then builds a DOS command based on that input, which is eventually executed by the EXEC command. These commands are the most complicated commands in NMENU, but they are also the most powerful, and offer many opportunities to make your menu system as complete and flexible as possible.

GETR is for asking for *required* information. When you use GETR, the user must answer the prompt or the menu will not proceed.

GETO is for asking for *optional* information. The menu user can choose to enter or not enter information here.

GETP is much like GETO, except the user input is stored in DOS environment variables.

Concept

Many DOS commands need information before they can run. For example, the RENAME command requires a current file name and a new file name listed after the RENAME command. However, if you execute the command RENAME all by itself, it isn't smart enough to ask you for what it needs; you have to enter those pieces of information as part of the command (DOS is pretty stupid, after all). These pieces of information that some DOS commands need are called *parameters*.

So far, you've only seen how NMENU can execute simple commands. If you wanted to give your users a way to rename files using the menu, you would be out of luck because you can't just EXEC RENAME. Enter the GET commands to the rescue. They let you give the menu users a way to enter information that the command needs to proceed before the command is executed by NMENU.

You can have multiple GET commands before the EXEC. Each GET command takes the user's input and puts in into the EXEC command. This is best illustrated with an example:

```
ITEM Rename File { SHOW NOECHO PAUSE }
    GETR  Enter CURRENT file name: { } 30,, {}
    GETR  Enter NEW file name: { } 30,, {}
    EXEC RENAME
```

Here, when users choose the Rename File option from the menu, they are prompted for two pieces of information: the current file name and the new file name. Then, when the menu program has those pieces of information, it automatically tacks them onto the EXEC RENAME command, in the order the questions were asked.

Format

```
GETx {prepend} length,default, {append}
```

Table 10.4 shows you what each GET option means.

Table 10.4
GET Options

Option	Description
x	x is replaced with the letter R, O, or P, in which R means Required, O means Optional. GETP takes the user's input and puts it into DOS parameters.
{prepend}	This forces whatever is contained in the prepend brackets to be added to the front of the user's response.
length	The number you use for length is required, and specifies how long the user's answer can be.
default	When you specify a default, the user is shown the default and given an opportunity to accept it or change it. For example, you could ask the user "Enter the source drive" and use a default of A: to suggest that drive. They can accept it or change it before hitting the Enter key. If you don't want to give them a default answer, simply leave this option blank.
{append}	Whatever is contained in the append brackets is added onto the user's response before the command is executed.

Examples

Here are several useful examples of ways to use the GET commands, along with some comments on each one:

```
ITEM Change Default Disk Drive { }
    GETO  Enter new default disk drive: {} 01,, {:}
    EXEC
```

Here, the user enters the letter of the drive to switch to. The command then places a colon after the letter they enter, which results in a simple DOS command. For example, if the user entered the letter G, the command that EXEC would start would be the same as if you typed G: and pressed Enter.

```
ITEM Copy Diskette { SHOW PAUSE }
    GETR  Enter source disk drive: { } 01,A, {:}
    GETR  Enter target disk drive: { } 01,A, {:}
    GETO  Insert source diskette and press [Enter]: {} 00,, {}
    EXEC DISKCOPY
```

This command prompts the user for two pieces of information that the DISKCOPY command needs: the source drive and the destination drive. After both commands are entered, the user is prompted to insert the source disk and press the enter key, using a GETO command that doesn't do anything but pause for the Enter key.

Here's how the above example would look using the GETP command:

```
ITEM Copy Diskette { SHOW PAUSE }
    GETP  Enter source disk drive: { } 01,A, {:}
    GETP  Enter target disk drive: { } 01,A, {:}
    GETO  Insert source diskette and press [Enter]: {} 00,, {}
    EXEC DISKCOPY %1 %2
```

GETP takes the user's input and creates DOS variables, which are represented by the %1 and %2 parameters after the DISKCOPY command. You can create variables up to %9. With a complex series of options, using these parameters can help you keep straight what command will actually get executed by the menu program.

```
ITEM Show Directory { SHOW PAUSE }
    GETO Enter File Specification: { } 13,*.*, {/P}
    EXEC DIR
```

Finally, this example shows how you might set up a menu option to let the user do a directory listing. It prompts the user for the file name mask that they want to use, and suggests *.* (which would list all files). This example also uses the append field to add the /P parameter, which makes the DIR command pause after each screenful is displayed.

Complete Menu Example

At the beginning of this chapter, you were shown a sample menu structure. Here is that menu implemented with NMENU:

```
MENU 1, Main Menu
ITEM Word Processing
     SHOW 5
ITEM SpreadSheets
     SHOW 10
ITEM Databases
     SHOW 15
ITEM Network Utilities
     SHOW 20
ITEM Logout From Network
     EXEC LOGOUT.EXE
ITEM Exit from Menu
     EXEC EXIT
MENU 5, WordProcessing
ITEM WordPerfect {BATCH CHDIR}
     EXEC WP.EXE
ITEM Word {BATCH CHDIR}
     EXEC WORD.EXE
ITEM DisplayWrite {BATCH CHDIR}
     EXEC DW.BAT
MENU 10, Spreadsheets
ITEM Lotus 1-2-3 {BATCH CHDIR}
     EXEC 1-2-3.EXE
ITEM Quattro Pro {BATCH CHDIR}
     EXEC Q.EXE
MENU 15, Databases
ITEM Paradox {BATCH CHDIR}
     EXEC PDX.EXE
ITEM dBase {BATCH CHDIR}
     EXEC DBASE.EXE
```

```
MENU 20, Network Utilities
ITEM Filer {BATCH CHDIR}
     EXEC FILER.EXE
ITEM Syscon {BATCH}
     EXEC SYSCON.EXE
ITEM Printer Utilities
     SHOW 25
MENU 25, PrinterUtilities
ITEM PrintCon {BATCH}
     EXEC PRINTCON.EXE
ITEM Pconsole {BATCH}
     EXEC PCONSOLE.EXE
```

Compiling Menu Files

Before actually running the menu files that you create, you must compile them with the MENUMAKE command. To do this:

1. Move to the directory that contains your NMENU program files and the menu source files (usually F:\PUBLIC).

2. Enter the command MENUMAKE *filename*, where file name is replaced with the actual file name of the menu file you want to compile. For example, if your menu file was called MENU.SRC, you would enter the command MENUMAKE MENU.SRC and press the Enter key. The MENUMAKE command will read in the .SRC file and will output a compiled version that has the same name, but ends with the extension .DAT.

3. To run the menu, enter the command:

NMENU *menufile*.DAT and press Enter. Menufile should be replaced with the actual name of the menu file you are using.

Incorporating NMENU into Login Scripts

The final step in installing NMENU, after you write the menu files, is integrating it with your users' login scripts. To do this, add these commands in the login script:

```
SET S_FILEDIR="F;\MENU\"
SET S_STATION="%STATION"
EXIT "NMENU menu_file"
```

The first command sets the location for the temporary menu files. Earlier, you were shown how to create this as F:\MENU. However, if you used a different location, substitute the path name there.

The S_STATION command sets each workstation to a unique number. This number is used by NMENU to keep everyone's menu temporary files separate.

The final command exits the login script and passes control to NMENU. In the quote marks after the EXIT command, insert the actual name of the menu file.

NMENU: The Real Story

Previous versions of Novell's MENU program were actually written by Novell. However, in Netware 3.12 Novell instead licensed the new NMENU program from a company called Saber Software Corporation. Saber has long provided network menu programs through software dealers, and their menu products are among the most popular on the market, primarily due to the fact that they understand how to make menus work under Netware better than anyone else (even better than Novell, presumably!).

The big point here is that if you find the NMENU provided with Netware to run out of steam for you, and require more features for your network, you can easily upgrade to the more complete Saber products.

Saber Menu System for DOS

Saber Menu System for DOS includes these additional capabilities:

→   Login Processor, which gives your users a "prettier" network login and integrates with the menu system seamlessly.

→   Better security. You can configure the full Saber product to restrict certain menu selections with individual passwords.

→   Easier management. Under the NMENU utility, you have to create separate menu files for different groups of people (if you want them to have different choices, anyway). Under the full product, you can have a single menu file but indicate in the file who should be able to see and access different menu items.

➜ Better help screens. The full Saber product enables you to create an unlimited number of custom help screens for the menu selections.

While this chapter only covers the NMENU utility included with NetWare, it's important that you be aware that more powerful choices are available should you need to upgrade in the future. For most installations, the included NMENU program will be more than adequate.

Saber Menu System for Windows

Saber Software Corporation also has a Windows-based menuing program, which has no equivalent as part of NetWare. This product offers you these capabilities:

➜ Central management of the Windows control files: menu groups and INI files, primarily.

➜ Automatic PIF file creation for DOS programs run under Windows.

➜ Better security, as in the DOS product discussed in the previous section.

➜ Personalized menus for individual users on the network, letting them just drag and drop their own personal menu entries.

Chapter 10, Short and Sweet

Let's face it: computers can be scary to many people, particularly if they have to deal with the ugly DOS command prompt and learn all of the nerdy DOS commands. By providing an easy-to-use menu for your users, you will make them more comfortable with the network that you set up. It's also far easier for a person to choose one choice from many, as opposed to having to remember some cryptic command.

This chapter showed you how to implement a menu system for your users under either Netware 3.11 or Netware 3.12, using the tools that are included with NetWare. You learned:

1.   Rules for planning a menu.

2.   A sample menu structure.

3.   About the two Novell menu programs: MENU and NMENU.

Further, in the sub-section on MENU, you learned:

4.   How the menu file is created.

5.   How the file is structured.

6.   How to arrange sub-menus and execute commands.

7.   How to have the menu started from each user's login script.

8.   How to provide each user with their own individual menu.

In the section on NMENU, you learned:

9.   What a source file was, and what a compiled data file was.

10.   How to compile your source files into menu data files.

11.   How to use all of the NMENU commands in your menu files, including the tricky GET commands.

12.   How to add NMENU to your user's login scripts.

13.   About upgrading to the more advanced Saber Software products, if necessary.

PART FOUR

Now THIS Is Managing a NetWare LAN!

Sensing that his newfound NetWare training had opened up a wealth of career options, Joe heads off to greener pastures and a higher tax bracket.

Disaster Planning and Tape Backups

(Or, What To Do When, Not If, Disaster Strikes)

It is important that you prepare for disaster on your network —and be prepared with a plan to recover with the least amount of disruption. It's not a matter of *if* disaster strikes— it's a matter of *when*.

This chapter covers the following topic areas:

→ Figuring out what a LAN disaster could cost you

→ Preparing for trouble

→ What to do when trouble arrives

→ How to back up data

How Much Is It Worth?

Many factors are involved in determining just how much money it costs a company when its computers fail, and an in-depth study is beyond the scope of this book. But we will explore some of the major factors to consider when determining the cost of downtime.

Mission critical tends to be an overused term in the networking world, and few applications are truly mission critical. That term is applied to cases in which a computer disaster—even for a few minutes—causes the loss of millions of dollars, or in the case of NORAD (North American Aerospace Defense) Command, is merely unthinkable. A reservation system for an airline, for instance, is mission critical, as would some banking applications in which even a few minutes of downtime costs millions in lost interest.

Although your network being up and running might not be mission critical in the true sense of the term, it is critical to the operations of your department or company. Some of the costs are tangible and can be calculated with hard numbers, others—such as goodwill generated by quickly responding to customer needs—are intangible.

Some of the factors to consider include:

→   Salaries and lost benefits of the people who cannot accomplish their work

→   Additional time incurred because of the disruption; for example, having to "find your place" again in the work that was being done

→   Cost of generating ill will with established customers when orders can't be taken, processed, or delivered on time

→   Interest lost on the money that otherwise would have been collected or collected on time

→   Cost of losing potential new business because another company's computers are up and yours aren't

→   The cost of overtime needed to work to meet schedules and deadlines

The actual cost depends on your business and the applications running on your network, but no matter how you look at it, downtime is costly.

NOTE
The cost of a backup tape varies, but figure on about $30 for a ballpark figure. That's pretty cheap compared to the value of your data.

Preparing for Downtime

It might sound pessimistic, but the best network administrators make detailed plans for disaster and how they to recover. Some installations even have periodic "fire drills," so they can test the validity of their plans. They simulate a worst-case disaster (pretending a fire wiped out the main head-quarters building, for instance), and then follow the procedures they have written down to make sure that all bases are covered and a quick recovery can be made.

You don't have to take it to unnecessary extremes, but it is best to sit down and think about a few "what if" scenarios. As the network administrator, it is your responsibility to think about contingency planning and discuss it with the management. Possible "what if" problems and solutions might include:

1. The fan in the fileserver goes out and the computer overheats, including the disk drive, corrupting the contents of your drive. What would you do to get the machine replaced or repaired, and recover the data that was lost?

    Have a workstation computer on hand that could stand-in for the file server machine. (Other components might have been affected by the heat, so swapping drives in this case would not be a good idea until the machine can be looked over.) Restore from tapes.

2. Someone in Accounts Receivable accidentally hits the Delete key. All the files for the month are lost. Can you put your hands on the correct backup tape quickly?

    Make daily backups, make sure the backups are indexed, and know how to restore from the backups.

3. Your offices are broken into and your fileserver and several worksta-tions are stolen, along with the backup tapes in your drawer. Do you know where you can get a replacement machine quickly and get your data recovered from your backup tapes? What about the worksta-tions?

This is a case where relationships count—your dealer or the manu-facturer might be able to ship you machines quickly. How about reciprocal agreements with other NetWare administrators in your company? Your critical data could be restored to someone else's file- server and accessed by your users, perhaps by modem. Good relationships with your internal MIS department help in scrounging up other equipment. Of course, using other equipment will only work if you store backups off-site in this case. Some companies make this type of situation their business, and you can use their computers to run on until your machines are replaced.

4. The president's workstation computer gets a power surge and the machine gets fried. Do you have a source for another workstation?

    Another case in which good relationships with your internal peers, dealer, or vendor just might save your job. Make sure your users perform regular backups on their workstations—or are willing to risk the consequences.

5. There is an earthquake, and you cannot get to your site. Who is your backup?

    Identify backups for people as well as equipment. Train someone to act in your absence.

Notice one recurring theme in all of these scenarios—backups. All systems need backups, both tapes and personnel.

Another factor in making sure that you are up and running as quickly as possible is careful records. The types described in the chapter on trouble-shooting are what you need.

What To Do When Disaster Strikes!

Above all, *DON'T PANIC*! Here's what to do:

➡   Take three deep breaths.

➡   If the people around you are in panic, anger, or excitable mode, calm them down or clear them out of your office. This is a case where you really need to take charge. Rudeness isn't necessary, but calm, cool, collected heads are. When someone runs into your office like

Chicken Little, make him sit down, take a deep breath, and tell you about the problem.

➜ Determine what the problem really is. Write it down, if necessary. (Writing a problem down helps to clarify and state the situation clearly.) If it's a panicked user who suddenly finds that all his files are gone, have him tell you what he did before he came to that conclusion. Write down all the steps he took. This helps get the situation sorted out clearly for all concerned. (They might be looking for their files in the wrong directory—it happens.)

➜ After you know the *real* problem, investigate if necessary. In any event, make a list of possible solutions and alternative courses of action.

➜ Review your list. Have you looked at the consequences of each action? Does it involve money? How much? Call your vendor or supplier and find out. What about expedited shipping and related charges? Investigate all possible avenues.

➜ Communicate. Take your complete list to management, and review it. Even if they are not technical, the situation can be described in general terms (for example, the computer is down and can't get up) and your list containing resolutions (and prices where necessary) can be reviewed. If the solution involves money or alternate equipment, make sure management is apprised of the situation, costs, time involved in shipping, and so forth. Management can probably help to expedite matters internally, but at the very least they should know what is going on.

➜ Carry out your plan. Put the pressure of the moment out of your mind. Panicked or hurried people make mistakes and can exacerbate the problem. Take control of the situation—don't let it take control of you—and proceed calmly.

Those All-Important Backups

Making backups of your network is an integral part of your job—probably the most important thing you do as the network administrator. Not making backups is a good way to get fired.

TIP

It is worth noting that you should practice restoring both complete directories of information and a single file or two. It is important that you familiarize yourself with the restore software when there is no crisis, so you know what to do when you have to restore in a pressure situation.

What To Look For

The type of backup system you get depends on your company and its operations. Remember that the purpose of making backups is to restore your data in a timely manner.

Bindery

The Bindery is the special database that stores the information about users, rights, and passwords on a NetWare fileserver. Make sure your tape backup software can back up the Bindery. Some cannot. Novell tested and certified backup software certainly can. 'Nuff said?

Open Files

Carefully check the way your backup software handles open files. Make sure your software can either back them up or skip over them without stopping the backup process completely. This is especially critical with some database files. If a user has a database file open at the time the backup is done, the file might not be backed up properly or at all.

TIP

This is where login time restrictions (mentioned in Chapter 6) come in handy. If you restrict all users so that they cannot log in between 3 a.m. and 5 a.m., everyone will be off the system and all files will be closed for a 3:15 backup run.

Speed

Some LANs are in use 24 hours a day, or nearly so. In that case, you need to consider carefully the speed of the backup system under consideration. If you have a large disk drive on your fileserver (3 or 4GB), speed is an issue because a backup of that much data might take longer than 12 hours.

If your backup does need to overlap with working hours, consider the drag on the network. The backup is trying to work to keep the data pumping through the wire at a steady pace, and it will slow down the users.

Another speed consideration is verification. To verify, the tape typically backs up a chunk of data on the tape. Then it rewinds that part of the tape and makes sure it can read it again. Other systems rewind the tape and compare what it just backed up to what is on the disk. Either way, verification adds considerable time to the backup, but a backup is no good if the information cannot be restored.

Media Failure

Some tape backups come to a screeching halt when there is a bad spot on the disk or tape. In some cases, the backup might go well, but during the restore process a bad spot on the tape can halt restoration. Make sure your tape backup unit can handle these and skip over them with ease. Better to lose one file than the rest of the data on the tape that comes after the bad spot.

Empty Directories

Make sure your tape backup software backs up directories that are empty. Some backup software skips backing up the entire directory entry if there are no files. This could wreak havoc on your system if you restored and all your print queues and empty mailboxes had to be redefined. You might have to reinstall some software.

Logs

Most backup software programs produce logs of the files backed up and any errors that were encountered. Because most backups are unattended, make sure your system makes a log (and that you check it).

Server versus Workstation

Some tape backups attach directly to the fileserver. This eliminates the need of having it attached to one of the workstations and having that workstation log in and do the backup and log out. It eliminates extra traffic going over the wire, which is a consideration if your backup has to overlap your work hours. But it also requires that in the event of a complete failure, both the NetWare OS and the backup software be completely restored, usually from floppy disks. By the time that is finished, significantly more time could be lost than if the backup software and equipment were attached to a workstation.

Another thing to consider with a server-based tape backup is if there is a fire in the same room as the fileserver, the tape backup unit likely will get damaged or burned.

Unattended

Don't babysit your tape backup. Many come with software that enables you to set it for unattended backups. An *unattended backup* starts at a preset time and doesn't need to be looked after. Use unattended backups with login time restrictions as mentioned earlier in this chapter.

Of course, unattended backups only work if you don't have to change tapes. Buy a tape system that can put all your server files on the same tape. Actually, buy one that enables you to double your storage and still fit on a single tape.

Extended Attributes and Name Spaces

Operating Systems, including DOS and OS/2, store file attributes with each file. A file attribute is a way of giving more information about the file (rather than just its location on disk) to the operating system and to programs. You may be familiar with these DOS file attributes:

→ **System.** Files with the system attribute are used by the operating system, which cannot run without it.

→ **Hidden.** Some programs, as well as operating systems, use the hidden attribute to conceal files from normal viewing (such as when performing a DOS DIR command) so that it cannot be easily accessed or erased. These files are usually critical to the running of said program or operating system.

→ **Archive.** When the archive attribute is turned on, it means the file has been written over since the last backup was made. (That's how backup programs know which files have been changed since the last backup.)

→   **Read Only.** A read-only attribute means the file can be read, but not written to. In DOS, a read-only flag keeps a file from being erased.

NetWare has the capability of adding a few attributes to files. With NetWare, flags are more commonly called attributes. You probably will slip back and forth between attribute and flag in your use of terminology. NetWare file flags can be set up with the FILER utility. In addition to the attributes mentioned for DOS, some of the little extras that NetWare includes are:

→   **Copy Inhibit.** This attribute prevents Macintosh users from copying a file, and overrides the read and file scan rights.

→   **Delete Inhibit.** This attribute overrides the erase right, and prevents users from erasing directories or files.

→   **Execute Only.** Use of this flag is not recommended unless copies of the programs where this flag is set (EXE or COM) are kept handy on disk. Files flagged as execute only cannot be copies and the flag *cannot* be removed.

→   **Purge.** Purges a file as soon as it is deleted, and the file *cannot* be recovered with SALVAGE.

These are not all of the flags. Your documentation should be checked for a complete list. At any rate, you want to make sure your backup software can handle NetWare's Extended Attributes when backing up the files so that they can be restored with the correct attributes.

Name Spaces refers to the special naming conventions used by Macintosh and allowed by OS/2. If either of those types of files are stored on your file-server, make sure the backup software backs them up properly.

Setting Up Nightly Backups

Naturally, you'll want to babysit your first backup or two to make sure the backup works as you think it should. After you know it runs properly, you can make unattended backups regularly.

TIP

To make sure that your unattended backups make proper backups of your fileserver, set up an unattended backup on a weekend or evening when you can watch it run. This activity is not exactly thrilling, but some people have found blank tapes or incorrectly made backups because they didn't follow this simple step.

Security Is Your Watchword

Most workstation tape backups require that you log in as Supervisor or a Supervisor equivalent. Otherwise, files such as the Bindery cannot be backed up. Naturally, if you want your tape backup to run at midnight, it is a security risk to have a workstation logged in all night with Supervisor privileges. That is why it is important to have the workstation that does the backup behind locked doors.

What Are TSRs?

You can do a few things to lessen the security risk. One is to load a simple TSR (terminate-and-stay-resident) program into that workstation that prohibits someone from coming along and trying to hit a Ctrl+C key sequence. Normally, this key sequence breaks a program out of proper operation and returns to the DOS command line. You don't want this to happen on the workstation, so utilize this simple utility. One can be found in the NOVUSER section of NetWire (see Chapter 14, "Help at Hand," for information about NetWire).

NOTE

A TSR is one that is loaded into the computer's memory and sits there until it is invoked. This is unlike a regular application program that is run to solve a particular application when you invoke it. The NetWare shell programs are TSRs.

Keyboard Locks and Stuffers

Make use of computers that have keyboard locks when possible, and don't leave the key in an obvious place, such as the desk drawer where the computer sits. Keep the key someplace secure.

Utilities also are available that are keyboard stuffers. They aren't nearly as fun as stocking stuffers, but they are far more functional. With one of these programs, the workstation does not need to remain logged in as Supervisor (or equivalent) all night.

These automated programs work so that you can program events. An *event* is any type of task that you want it to be—it can even call another event. Type all the keystrokes that you normally type while sitting at your computer, including key functions such as pressing Enter, function keys (F1 through F10 or F12), and the words you normally type. Then tell the program to begin at a certain time of the day or night.

These programs run as TSRs on your workstation and "wake up" when they are programmed to do so, much like an alarm clock. Running one of these types of programs eliminates the need to have a workstation logged in as Supervisor all night. Notice, though, that these programs also can run an event that can logout of the network when the backup has completed.

Off-Site Storage

Off-site storage of your backup tapes is critical to your operation. Tapes in your office can be:

➡ Magnetized (and as a consequence, ruined), both accidentally and from carelessness

➡ Stolen

➡ Destroyed by Coke or coffee spills

➡ Crushed, burned, or flooded

➡ Misplaced

Backup tapes are about half the size of a paperback book and can be stored easily in some trusted employee's closet in a cardboard box at his home (away from dust and dampness, of course). Offices with more than one location in a city can act as storage locations for each others' offices.

An off-site storage service is even better. You should be able to find a firm in your area that will pick up your tapes, store them in a climate-controlled vault, and return them on request. Whether the cost is justified depends on the value you place on your LAN's data.

No matter how you do it, just *do it*.

Backup Schemes and Rotations

There are plenty of rotation schemes that you can use for backing up your fileserver, including the Grandfather Method, 10-Tape Rotation Method, Tower of Hanoi Method, and probably even a Full Moon Method, for all I know. The most commonly used method is the Grandfather Method (discussed in Chapter 4 complete with a diagram). The Grandfather Method usually is the method of choice; most sites I'm aware of use it. Backup tapes are cheap and small enough to store easily. Don't be cheap, and don't use an overly complex method. Remember, KISS (Keep It Simple, Stupid)!

Some NetWare administrators strongly believe in *incremental backups*, in which only the files that have been changed since the last backup are backed up. They like to use this method because it saves tape. As mentioned in the first section of this chapter, the cost of a tape is exceedingly cheap compared to the value of your data.

I prefer using a fresh tape every night and backing up everything every night, because the whole point in backing up is to restore easily and quickly. That is difficult to do if you have to apply four or five tapes to make sure all the files have been restored properly as you would have to do with incremental backups.

NOTE

Even with all your precautions in scheduling backups, sometimes the backup workstation loses its connection with the network or fileserver (or workstation), or loses power, and the backup ABENDs (Abnormal Ending). Some problems aren't discovered until the morning, when it might be too late to try to make a backup of the previous day's work. This is one of the reasons why complete backups every day are not necessarily a waste of tape.

Incremental Backups

Incremental backups have a place in two situations:

→   If it takes longer to back up your complete server than you can schedule for your nightly shutdown (some users don't want to go home), you have three choices:

Buy a faster tape unit

Buy a second tape unit

Back up only part of your files each night

→   Your server has too many files to fit on a single tape. (You were warned!) Then you need to back up a portion of the server each night along with any other files that have changed.

The *Tower of Hanoi* Method is a compromise between full and incremental backups. Remember the puzzle that has three spikes and a pile of ten different-sized disks arranged on one spike in a cone? The goal is to move all of the disks to another spike by moving one disk at a time and never placing a larger disk on a smaller one. If you try it, you'll see how some disks move around faster than others. (Somewhere, legend says, Buddhist monks are working on a tower puzzle with sixty-four disks. When they move the last disk, the world will end. Fortunately, that will take a long, long time.)

The Tower of Hanoi backup approach uses several sets of tapes (seven is typical) and rotates them through the backup schedule in a complex schedule. If you try the puzzle, you know just how complex the schedule is. Try writing down all of your moves!

The goal for using such a complex approach is to reduce the number of files that are backed up each night while ensuring that every file is backed up several times. Properly implemented, several things happen when using the Tower of Hanoi Method:

→   Stable files are backed up a few times (usually three) and are never backed up again. That saves time.

→   Changed files are backed up every time they change. Records go far back, and it is possible to restore a constantly changing file to its original status on any night.

→   Properly managed, each file is stored on-site and off-site for safety and convenience.

The trick is that the Tower of Hanoi Method is so complex that you don't want to do it without help. A program that automates the Tower of Hanoi schedule is Palindrome's Network Archivist. It's not cheap, but Network Archivist is an effective way to reduce the time it takes to back up your LAN server each night.

A Note about SBACKUP

Novell provides a tape backup utility with NetWare called SBACKUP. This utility is not recommended for use; instead it is important that you get a good tape backup hardware and software package. SBACKUP has some severe limitations, including:

→   **No verification.** What good is a tape backup if the backup cannot be occasionally verified?

→   **Limited hardware support.** The actual hardware that is supported by the SBACKUP software is very limited, and if you already have a tape backup unit in your office, it might not be able to be used with SBACKUP.

→   **No way to schedule unattended backups.** Do you want to stay late every night to run the backup, or seriously degrade the performance of your network during the day when your users are trying to get their work done? Probably not.

Invest in good tape backup hardware and software. Your company's business relies on it.

Chapter 11, Short and Sweet

It is important to make like a scout and be prepared for disaster when running a network. This chapter covered some of the things that can (and do) happen, and what to look for when shopping for tape backup systems, such as:

1. It is not a matter of if, it is a matter of *when* disaster will strike your network.

2. The smart NetWare administrator plans for disaster and plans what to do when it happens.

3. Network downtime can be substantially more costly than the price of repair or replacement. It can mean lost (sometimes irrecoverably) business, and don't forget to figure in salaries, benefits, and over-time.

4. When disaster strikes, take a firm grip on yourself and the situation. Breaking down the problem or situation into small pieces helps to understand and clarify the exact problem.

5. Write down all the possible solutions. If repair or replacement equipment is on the list, then call the appropriate person to obtain prices.

6. Don't work in a black hole. Consult with management, and let them know the overall problem, possible solutions, and your recommendations.

7. When looking at backup systems consider things such as flexibility in restoring, file attributes, and special files associated with backing up a NetWare fileserver, verification, and automatic scheduling.

8. Don't wait for a crisis to hit before you practice backing up and restoring single files and directories.

9. Sit down and watch your system go through a backup a couple of times before you rely on unattended backups. Make sure you have what you think you are getting.

10. SBACKUP is a minimally functional utility. It does not have verification, automatic scheduling, and supports limited hardware.

11. Many types of rotation schemes are available, but the Grandfather Method is probably the best. Don't be cheap when buying tapes. After all, they are economical compared to the price of your data.

12. Be sure to store tapes off-site frequently.

Key Terms to Look for:

→ "surprise inspections"

→ "housecleaning"

→ restructuring files

→ NetWare security program

→ MONITOR console utility

→ dirty cache buffers

→ current disk requests

→ resource utilization

→ Hot Fix table

Regular Duties

(Or, So That's What the SysOp Is Always Up To)

There are few hard and fast rules about the regular duties of administering a NetWare network. This chapter covers some of the things you should do to keep your system healthy and happy and purring along like a well-fed cat. Some of them you should do daily, some as-needed, and others periodically:

→ Regular (daily) backups

→ Configuration maintenance—adding and deleting users and groups as necessary

→ Adding users and groups

→ Installing (and updating) software applications

→ User support

→ Troubleshooting

→ Installing and changing hardware

→ Configuration and maintenance of your directories and files

→ Periodic housekeeping duties (including running security checks)

→ Performance monitoring

Naturally, a large chunk of time is spent getting familiar with NetWare in general and your unique setup in particular when you first become the NetWare administrator. It's important that you relax, take your time, and be thorough. That is the best way to be prepared for the things you encounter in your new role as (ta da!) Super Administrator!

Daily Activities

The first item on your list for daily duties is *backups*! Check Chapter 11 to find out the things you should know when you make your daily backups.

Always check the integrity of your backups by performing periodic "surprise inspections" and restoring a few stray files now and then. After all, you don't want to be surprised when you need to restore a file or files and you find they didn't quite get backed up properly. That is really the only thing you must do on a daily basis when you administer a network!

As Needed

You often cannot precisely predict when the duties of a NetWare Administrator will call. Some days you might spend only a few minutes to make sure the network is up and running, while other days your time might be completely devoted to various network tasks.

Adding Users and Groups

You need to add users and groups as a part of your regular duties. Always keep track of what you do on your network with proper log sheets, covered thoroughly in Chapter 13, "Troubleshooting." Even if you don't encounter trouble in the traditional sense of your network being down, you do sometimes have to quickly pinpoint who has access to what.

Application Software Installation

As the "keeper of the keys," it is your job to install and test new software programs as they come along. Unfortunately, some NetWare software installations can be very complex, and you need to devote some study to the documentation and some thought to how you want to structure things for your particular site.

NetWork Operating System Software Updates and Changes (Optional)

As you learn more about NetWare and your system in particular, you might feel comfortable installing the various patches and fixes that are periodically released to update your system and keep it humming smoothly. Novell distributes all patches and fixes on NetWire (see Chapter 14 for full information on NetWire). If you are more comfortable with your vendor or consultant applying these changes, don't sweat it.

If adding a new hardware or software component to your server gives you NetWare heartburn, check NetWire for a patch for your particular problem. Today NetWare 3.11 has little uncharted territory, and someone has probably gotten to your problem before you.

NOTE

If you upgrade from NetWare 3.11 to 3.12, or buy version 3.12, all the current patches are factory installed. Don't worry, though, more patches are more than likely on the way. Every complex program has holes in it, and users occasionally find new combinations of hardware and software that reveal a hole in NetWare. You might still get your chance to patch NetWare 3.12.

User Support

As a NetWare administrator, you are now in the Customer Support business and Diplomatic Corps. Treat all users with respect and patience.

There's a difference sometimes between what people say and what they really mean. This is often the case when getting feedback from users. It's important to be able to "read between the lines" of their comments to get to a deeper truth about how your system is perceived by its users. If many users have the same questions or problems, maybe it's time to adjust or change the network. Things like an easy-to-use and understand menu can slash the questions and support time. Consider making up and passing out cheat sheets. Even make up and pass out an evaluation form from time to time and ask for feedback on ease of use, suggestions, and ideas that might help to expedite work on the network. (A good "report card" from your users might also be "ammo" at your next review, too.)

Troubleshooting

Naturally, your NetWare-related life is not complete until you encounter trouble on your network. You can do several things to minimize problems and be prepared. Observe the following advice:

→ **Log.** Knowing how your network is configured can help you find problems, as well as report them.

→ **Read.** Check out the various available publications. In addition to the ones offered on the newsstand, several publications are mentioned throughout this book, including:

The NetWare Connection. Available free from NetWare Users International.

NetWare Application Notes. Available from Novell Research.

Various publications available on a complimentary basis. Check with your friends and MIS folks.

→ **NetWire.** Read about problems others experience and how they are solved to learn how you can prevent problems before they happen.

Add and Change Hardware (Optional)

If you feel comfortable with a screwdriver in your hand and the innards of a PC strewn over a desk, dive in. However, your position as network administrator does not require you to set up additional workstations or to change or add to the configuration of your fileserver.

Periodically

Some things need to be done, but not necessarily on a set schedule. The frequency with which you perform these operations depends on your installation: the number of users you have, the activity on your network, and so on.

Clean Up

Be sure to do periodic housecleaning on your network. Some of the things you want to do include the following:

→   **Delete users and groups.** As employees leave or change departments, your user list is not always current. Delete the names of users you can to minimize security risk. It also helps to keep a handle on your basic configuration.

→   **Restructure.** Sometimes when certain users or groups are gone, or projects are in the past, you no longer need certain file structures. You can move some files, and delete others completely.

→   **Purge files.** Either move them to tape or disk, but get rid of old files that no one accesses. Also, periodically purge the files that you delete, but are not really gone because of the salvage capabilities of NetWare 386.

Purging and Salvaging Files

Deleting a file does not delete the file entry immediately. NetWare removes the file entry from the directories and makes the space available for new files. However, the space is not reused until the file system fills up. Then NetWare reuses the space used by the files that have been deleted the longest.

You can use the SALVAGE utility to recover deleted files until they have been purged. SALVAGE is a DOS utility. To use it, change to the directory that contained the files you deleted. Then enter the SALVAGE command to bring up the SALVAGE main menu, as shown in figure 12.1.

Figure 12.1

The SALVAGE main menu.

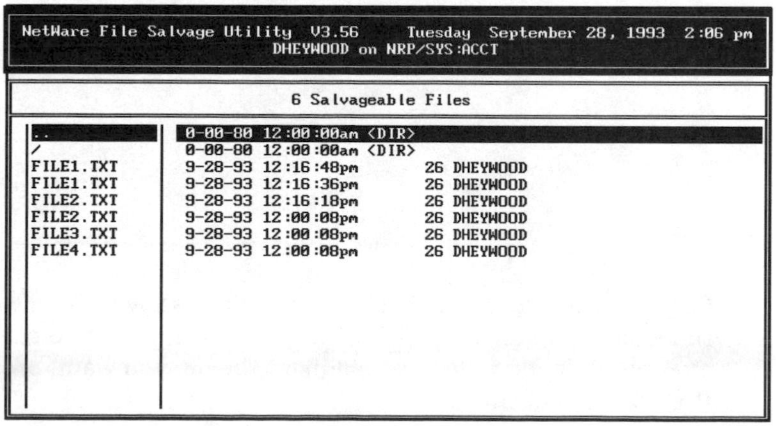

```
NetWare File Salvage Utility  V3.56     Tuesday  September 28, 1993  2:06 pm
                        DHEYWOOD on NRP/SYS:ACCT

                              6 Salvageable Files

  . .            0-00-80  12:00:00am <DIR>
  /              0-00-80  12:00:00am <DIR>
  FILE1.TXT      9-28-93  12:16:48pm      26 DHEYWOOD
  FILE1.TXT      9-28-93  12:16:36pm      26 DHEYWOOD
  FILE2.TXT      9-28-93  12:16:18pm      26 DHEYWOOD
  FILE2.TXT      9-28-93  12:00:00pm      26 DHEYWOOD
  FILE3.TXT      9-28-93  12:00:00pm      26 DHEYWOOD
  FILE4.TXT      9-28-93  12:00:00pm      26 DHEYWOOD
```

You can use Select Current Directory to set a directory. In this case you changed to the directory you wanted before starting SALVAGE. The option you want now is View/Recover Deleted Files. After you select View/Recover Deleted Files, a box appears that asks you for the Erased File Pattern to Match, as shown in figure 12.2. Usually you use an asterisk (*) to display all the deleted files, much like the one shown in figure 12.3.

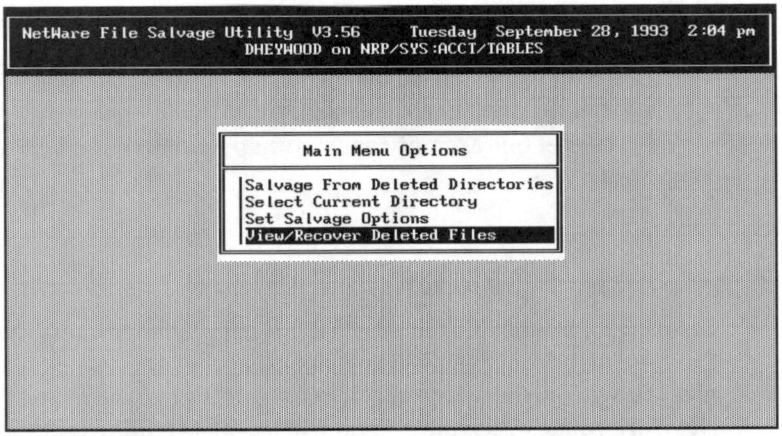

Figure 12.2

Using the View/Recover Deleted Files option.

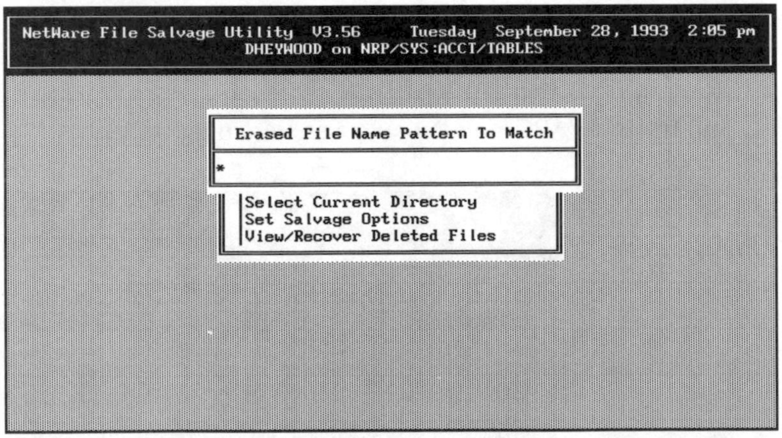

```
NetWare File Salvage Utility  V3.56      Tuesday  September 28, 1993  2:04 pm
                    DHEYWOOD on NRP/SYS:ACCT/TABLES


                         ┌─────────────────────────────┐
                         │       Main Menu Options      │
                         ├─────────────────────────────┤
                         │ Salvage From Deleted Directories │
                         │ Select Current Directory     │
                         │ Set Salvage Options          │
                         │ View/Recover Deleted Files   │
                         └─────────────────────────────┘
```

Figure 12.3

*Using * to display deleted files.*

```
NetWare File Salvage Utility  V3.56      Tuesday  September 28, 1993  2:05 pm
                    DHEYWOOD on NRP/SYS:ACCT/TABLES


                    ┌──────────────────────────────────┐
                    │  Erased File Name Pattern To Match │
                    ├──────────────────────────────────┤
                    │ *                                  │
                    ├──────────────────────────────────┤
                    │ Select Current Directory           │
                    │ Set Salvage Options                │
                    │ View/Recover Deleted Files         │
                    └──────────────────────────────────┘
```

Examine the list of files. Each deleted file is shown along with the data and timestamp. Notice that FILE1.TXT has two entries. You can salvage whichever version you want. Just highlight the file you want, press Enter, and Presto! the files are back.

If you keep your salvageable files around, the combination of undeleted and deleted files eventually fills up. Then NetWare has to purge a deleted file every time you need space to store new files. Deleting files takes some processing power, and you might prefer to purge all deleted files to improve performance.

If you use the PURGE command, NetWare purges deleted files in the current directory. PURGE ALL deleted files in the current directory and in all the current directory's subdirectories. To purge an entire volume, change to the root directory and enter PURGE ALL.

Secure the Premises

Once every couple of months, you should run the SECURITY program to check on the security of your system.

Monitoring

Many books and articles include the phrase "and tuning" at the end of monitoring. Don't worry about tuning your network to run faster or more efficiently at this point. You have enough on your plate learning NetWare and your networking administrative duties to keep you occupied for a while. Tuning comes with time and experience.

As far as monitoring your network, you want to keep an eye out for some of the statistics found in the MONITOR console utility. Start the monitor by typing **LOAD MONITOR** at the console. A typical MONITOR display is shown in figure 12.4.

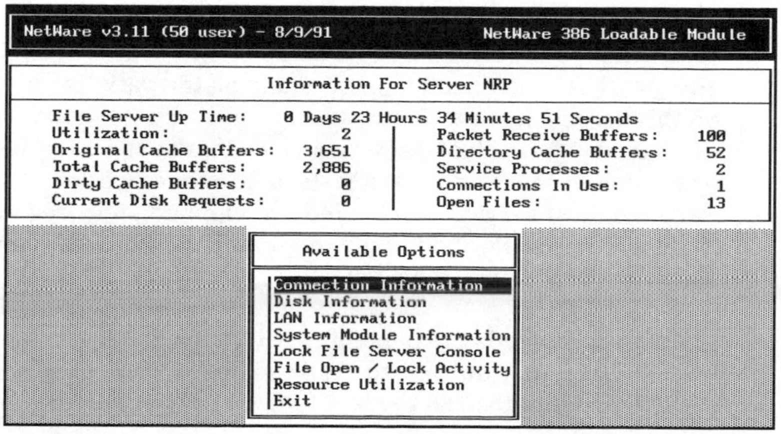

Figure 12.4

A typical MONITOR display screen.

```
NetWare v3.11 (50 user) - 8/9/91            NetWare 386 Loadable Module

                          Information For Server NRP

    File Server Up Time:    0 Days 23 Hours 34 Minutes 51 Seconds
    Utilization:                   2  │ Packet Receive Buffers:    100
    Original Cache Buffers:    3,651  │ Directory Cache Buffers:    52
    Total Cache Buffers:      2,886  │ Service Processes:           2
    Dirty Cache Buffers:          0  │ Connections In Use:          1
    Current Disk Requests:        0  │ Open Files:                 13

                          Available Options
                       ┌──────────────────────────┐
                       │ Connection Information    │
                       │ Disk Information          │
                       │ LAN Information           │
                       │ System Module Information │
                       │ Lock File Server Console  │
                       │ File Open / Lock Activity │
                       │ Resource Utilization      │
                       │ Exit                      │
                       └──────────────────────────┘
```

The main screen in the console MONITOR utility shows a number of vital statistics. Here are some you should pay particular attention to:

➔   **Utilization.** This statistic is an indication of the percentage of time the server's processor is working. Don't be alarmed if this figure peaks at high values. If it reaches a high value, such as more than 70 percent and stays there, your server is close to its maximum performance level. Expect users to start complaining about performance soon.

➔   **Dirty Cache Buffers.** This value represents the number of file blocks in memory waiting to be written to disk. NetWare does not necessarily write to the disk immediately because that strains performance. NetWare maximizes efficiency by queuing requests and servicing them as processing power becomes available. Unless a server is overloaded, NetWare is more idle some times than others, and the queued requests are serviced then.

   If the dirty cache buffers value goes high and stays high, then the disk channel is not capable of fullfilling all the disk requests efficiently. This is a clear indication that your disk system is a bottleneck in your server. You might need a faster disk controller, faster disks, or both. Busy servers cannot run well with hard disk systems that are intended for use in a single-user PC.

➔   **Current Disk Requests.** This statistic indicates the number of disk requests, reading and writing, that are waiting in line to be serviced. If this number goes high and stays high, it might be because your disk channel is not fast enough to clear the disk writes out of RAM, or the NIC card is not fast enough to clear disk reads off the network.

If you choose the Resource Utilization option, a screen similar to figure 12.5 appears. You don't need to understand all the various memory pools listed on this screen. Instead, focus your attention on the entry for Cache Buffers. NetWare owes much of its performance to an efficient system of caching (queueing up) file service requests. If no cache buffers are available, NetWare must service new file requests immediately, regardless of whether it is a good time. If a load of file requests flood in at the same time, the server's performance plummets.

Novell recommends the percentage of RAM available for Cache Buffers be at least 50 percent. However, the experts on NetWire suggest that it should really be no less than 65 percent for best performance.

Figure 12.5

The Resource Utilization screen in MONITOR.

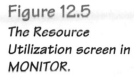

```
NetWare v3.11 (50 user) - 8/9/91          NetWare 386 Loadable Module

                       Server Memory Statistics

     Permanent Memory Pool:        872,248 Bytes   6%    871,152 In Use
     Alloc Memory Pool:             73,732 Bytes   8%     65,236 In Use
     Cache Buffers:             12,174,700 Bytes  79%
     Cache Movable Memory:       1,426,360 Bytes   9%
     Cache Non-Movable Memory:     957,940 Bytes   6%
     Total Server Work Memory:  15,504,980 Bytes

                                                       ons
              Tracked Resources                       ation
        AES Process Call-Backs
        Alloc Short Term Memory (Bytes)
        Alternate Debugger Handlers                   ormation
        C Library BSD Sockets                         Console
        Cache Memory Below 16 Meg (Bytes)             Activity
      ▼ Cache Movable Memory (Bytes)                  ion
```

So you have four statistics you should check periodically:

→   Utilization

→   Dirty Cache Buffers

→   Current Disk Requests

→   Cache Buffers

Examine these values periodically, several times a day at first. Learn what the numbers look like when your LAN is busy. If you develop a feel for these values, you can anticipate LAN problems. If the Cache Buffers percentage begins to fall, for example, you know your disk system is getting overworked.

TIP

You can improve the performance of a NetWare server in three primary ways:

→   *Add memory. Within reason, the more the better. Check the Cache Buffers percentage on the Resource Utilization screen to see if you need more memory.*

→   *Upgrade your file system. Don't be cheap here, and don't try to get by with a disk system that is intended for a single-user PC. If you duplex your disks (see Chapter 4) you can speed up disk-read operations quite a bit. NetWare fulfills a disk-read request from the drive that can get to the data fastest.*

➜ *Upgrade your network interface card. Or divide your network into several subnetworks, each with an NIC in the server. As explained in Chapter 4, adding NICs improves network performance. If you can, upgrade your cards and subdivide your network.*

Notice that these hints don't have much to do with everyone's favorite PC characteristic, the microprocessor. Surprisingly, the microprocessor is of less importance to NetWare performance than the preceding three items. The hottest 66MHz 80486 microprocessor performs somewhat better than a 33MHz 80386, but not as much as you might hope. Certainly not twice as well. And, if your system has a shortcoming in any of the preceding three items, getting a new, hot processor might not help at all.

NOTE

NetWare gets all the RAM that is used for all service requests out of the main RAM Pool—called the Cache Buffers pool. If Cache Buffers runs short, a high utilization process can cause the server to ABEND by running all the buffers out before NetWare can recover.

One more thing you should check is the Hot Fix table for each of your server hard drives. The main menu in MONITOR also has a Disk Information option.

Chapter 12, Short and Sweet

Nearly all of the topics covered in this chapter are explored more thoroughly in other chapters of this book. Basically, a NetWare administrator needs to do, or keep in mind, the following:

1. Make and monitor daily backups.

2. Add and delete users and groups as needed.

3. Install and configure application software on your fileserver as needed.

4. Optional duties include installing hardware and operating system updates and fixes.

5. The more you read and learn about NetWare, the more comfortable you begin to feel and the better prepared you are to head off trouble before it starts.

6. Log, log, log. Write down everything about your system and track it. Keep it updated. You or the experts you call on will need it.

7. Periodically clean up your system by clearing out unnecessary users, groups, files, and directories. Back up to tape or disk information you don't need.

8. Make regular check-ups on your system security. Run SECURITY and be sure to do everything you can to secure your NetWare system against unauthorized and unwanted access.

9. Monitor your system on a regular basis by checking the vital statistics examined in this chapter. It can help head off trouble before it starts.

Troubleshooting

(Or, How to Be Part Detective, Part Diplomat)

Troubleshooting a network is not the easiest thing to do, because there are so many factors involved. You have to keep track of the NetWare operating system, the workstation operating system, wire, network interface cards, the fileserver and workstation computers; sometimes when trouble occurs you'll just be sure it's sunspot activity. This chapter cannot cover all possibilities (or predict sunspot activity), but it will cover some of the more common networking problems. Most important, it will cover the basic techniques that will enable you to be able to break a problem down and tackle it. Or at least solve it. Some of the additional topics covered will be:

→ How to be prepared for trouble on your network—how and why to keep a log book

→ How to deal with those pesky users

→ Where you are likely to encounter the most problems and the things they might be (hint: can you say "cable?")

→ Common problems that might crop up with the fileserver

→ What to look for at the workstations

This chapter (and this book) can give you the tools that enable you to keep calm in a potential networking crisis; that's a quality highly prized in network administrators. Rewards sometimes follow this.

Log Books

One of the most important things to do when running your network is to keep careful and meticulous log books. Borrrrring, right? Not very glamorous? Wrong. Good records will be your very best friend and more desirable than the sexiest lover at the first sign of problems on your network.

The first network I ever worked on was a Unix-based system, which is more complex than a NetWare network for several reasons (not important to this story). Because it was so complex, I kept a very careful log book containing configuration information, and tracked every problem I had: the symptoms, steps taken to troubleshoot each problem, the results, and actual resolution.

When I started working on a NetWare network, I was too lazy to continue this excellent practice. As problems arose, they got solved and put behind. Unfortunately, more than once, the same problem would crop up a year or two later. ("Oh yes, I remember we had that problem awhile back... now what was the solution?") Because I had no records of what the problem had turned out to be and how it was resolved, I had to begin the troubleshooting process completely over, wasting many valuable hours in the process. I reformed.

In talking with many NetWare administrators, I found that I was not alone in either not keeping records, or starting out gung ho at the beginning and then letting it slide. In every case, we all regretted this lapse. Taking the time to log events on your network as you go along, even the seemingly minor ones, will save you many valuable hours in the long run.

In the Beginning...

It doesn't matter if your NetWare has already been installed and you are taking over an existing network, or if you're just diving into a new installation; it's never too late to start your own log book.

An integral part of your book will be configuration information about your network. That will include both the hardware settings on your fileserver and workstations as well as the configuration information about NetWare and the software that is on your workstations.

TIP

Some administrators keep all their log and configuration information on their network or workstation hard drive. That's great—until the network or their workstation computer goes down, which is when you need the information the most. If you want to keep your records available electronically, great, but don't forget to print them out as you update them.

Fileserver Records

In the back of the installation manual that comes with your NetWare documentation are several worksheets that you can use to record information. The following lists the information that should be noted about the fileserver:

➡ Fileserver name:

➡ Installed by:

➡ Fileserver make/model:

➡ Memory: Base, Extended, Total

➡ Server boot method: (floppy/hard disk)

➡ Internal network number:

➡ Non-network board information:

➡ Network boards: (name, LAN driver, I/O port, Memory Address, Interrupt (IRQ), DMA channel, Station/Node Address, Slot number, Network number)

➡ Floppy disk drives: (size of disk and capacity)

➡ Internal hard drives: (make/model, size, DOS partition size, NetWare partition, controller type)

→   Disk co-processor boards: (name, disk driver, I/O port, Interrupt)

→   Disk subsystems: (total number of devices, number of mirrored drives, drive make/model, size, heads, cylinders, mirrored with #)

If you are hiring someone to install your network, then work with your vendor or consultant and insist that they write this information down for you.

If your network is humming along already, here's where you can find the information that you need:

→   Look in SYSCON under Fileserver Information for the serial number (which you will need if you ever have to call Novell technical support), server name, version, and address.

TIP

Although you need to have the NetWare serial number handy when calling Novell technical support, you do not need it when you ask a question on NetWire. As a matter of fact, never provide your serial number on NetWire because many people can see it and could possibly use it wrongfully.

→   At your fileserver console, start the MONITOR utility by typing **LOAD MONITOR** at the ":" prompt. Use the **LAN Information** and **Disk Information** options to look at information about these systems, and record the required information on your worksheet. Figure 13.1 shows a typical Disk Information screen. Figure 13.2 shows a LAN Information screen.

→   To find out what type of disk drives your fileserver has examine the documentation that came with your computer. This information may also be on the purchase order or other sales information. Or, you may need to go to DOS and just try reading both a high and low density disk to find out.

Figure 13.1

Example Disk Information display in MONITOR.

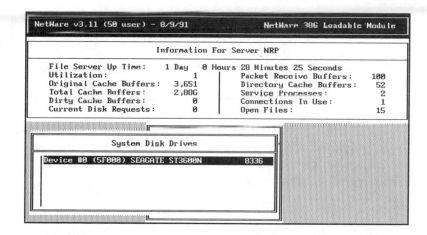

Figure 13.2

Example LAN Information display in MONITOR.

→ Much of the information about the optional hardware in your system can be obtained by using a system diagnostic/reporting tool. Microsoft Windows includes a program called MSD. An excellent independent program is QA Plus. Both programs will snoop around in your system and identify many of the components and settings, such as your video type, serial and parallel ports, memory, and so on.

What you can't get from a reporting program you need to obtain by physically examining the components. If you don't want to open up the box, remove the cards, and check all of the settings with the

manuals, you will need to check with the person who installed
your system, or get a little help from a hardware–knowledgeable
associate.

Configuration Records

In addition to the hardware configuration, you will want some NetWare
configuration information as suggested by the additional worksheets found
in the back of the installation manual. Here is a list of the information and
where it can be found:

→   System-wide parameter defaults for users are set in Supervisor
     Options in the SYSCON utility. This is where password parameters,
     time restrictions, intruder detection parameters, and all manner of
     important system information is found. Much of this information is
     used as a template when setting up new users. The fastest way to
     gather this information is to select each menu item and simply print
     the screen. (**CTRL-PRTSCRN.**) The user login script template is
     found in the utility USERDEF. Record this information also.

→   System AUTOEXEC File, System Login Script, Console, and
     Workgroup Manager information can also be found under Supervisor
     Options in the SYSCON utility.

TIP

*By utilizing the system-wide parameters, less individual
information will need to be kept on each user. Record the
system-wide parameters, and only make note in your log book
of any exceptions to these for the appropriate user instead
of recording each user's individual settings (since it would all
be the same).*

→   Group Information. Record the information found under Group
     Information in the SYSCON utility. Make sure you track the Trustee
     Assignments for each group, as well as the members of each group.

→   User Information. In the SYSCON utility, under User Information, find
     the Full Name, Username, Groups Belonged To, Access to Directo-
     ries, Station Restrictions, Managed by, and any information that is
     not a system-wide default already recorded.

→ File Information. If you have set any extended file attributes or Inherited Rights Masks in the FILER utility, record that information also.

→ The STARTUP.NCF and AUTOEXEC.NCF files can be looked at from the console with the INSTALL NLM loaded from the main Install menu.

TIP
Don't be afraid to peek around in your system. That's the only way you will become familiar with your installation and NetWare in general.

Workstation Records

The information you will need to collect on each workstation is fairly well covered on the worksheet in the back of the NetWare installation manual. Once again, if that isn't handy, the information is:

→ Current workstation owner:

→ Serial no.:

→ Network address for board A: (and B:)

→ Installed by:

→ Type of workstation:

→ Floppy disk size and capacity:

→ Memory: Base: Extended: Expanded: Total:

→ Internal hard disks: Size: Driver Type:

→ Network boards: (name, option number, I/O address, memory address, Interrupt (IRQ), DMA channel, station/node address, slot number)

→ LAN driver: (LAN A:, LAN B:)

→ Boot information: (hard disk, floppy, remote reset)

➔ Remote reset checklist: (Network board set to configuration option 0, remote reset PROM(s) installed on LAN board; remote reset enabled on network board; remote boot file name:)

➔ DOS version:

➔ Files needed to connect to the network: (IPX.COM, NETX.COM or EMSNETX.EXE or XMSNETX.EXE; NETBIOS.EXE and INT2F.COM; others; SHELL.CFG options:)

In addition to the information listed previously suggested by Novell, you should print out each AUTOEXEC.BAT and CONFIG.SYS file. Those are found in the root directory of the C: drive, or if the workstation is booted from floppy, in the root directory of the A: drive. If you run Windows on these workstations, then a printout of the WIN.INI file wouldn't hurt a bit.

Sometimes workstation information is hard to keep current, because things tend to change on a workstation more often than on a fileserver. It is often a good idea to tape a small piece of paper on the side of a workstation or its monitor that lists some minimal information such as operating system version, NIC information, and information on any additional boards installed. That way it's always handy in case you don't have your complete log book with you when you go troubleshooting.

TIP

As you go around and collect the preceding suggested information, you won't regret taking a few extra minutes to work with the user and find out what software applications they are running from their local disk drive(s). Note the revision number of the software by invoking each application and looking for the number on the startup screen or the main screen. If it is a Windows or OS/2 application, look in the "About" box (found under the Help or File menu).

Software applications and their revision numbers will be valuable in troubleshooting certain types of problems on the users' workstations. You'll need that information handy when making problem reports with the software vendor or the folks on NetWire (or Novell).

Problem Reports

Prepare blank worksheets for your "Operation Readiness" and put them in your log book for recording the information. You will want to customize the sheet according to the way you like to do and organize things, but some of the basic information you need to note on the worksheet will be:

→   Time and date problem reported

→   Person reporting problem

→   Hardware and/or software exhibiting problem

→   Version information of operating system and software

→   Statement of problem

→   Any error messages reported by software or hardware

→   Steps taken to solve problem

→   Results of each change made

→   Log dates and times of any telephone calls to vendors (when applicable) and note names and telephone numbers or extensions of the people you talk to

→   Final solution

Some companies institute a formal procedure for users to report problems, others do not. Many find that an electronic system is much easier for the users to utilize than a paper system, and cuts down on telephone calls to the administrator that are so disrupting. For non-critical problems and questions, electronic mail will usually get the job done just as well as a specially prepared electronic form, if you have passed out reporting guidelines to your users. Ask them to include such information as version numbers (when it's a software problem), error messages, specific keystrokes, and so on.

TIP

Make up a guideline sheet for problem reporting and give it to your users. Be sure to include approximate turnaround time that they can expect for you to investigate (and hopefully

resolve) their problems. If you let them know that your goal is to get with them within the hour or two hours (or whatever is reasonable for you), they will be far more patient than if you don't let them know what they can expect.

Separating Network and Applications Support

The network administrator often becomes the general PC and application support person by default. This happens simply because they are often the most knowledgeable and PC-literate person in the company or office. The users tend to call the administrator when they want to know how to make a macro in WordPerfect or create a spreadsheet in Excel, as well as when they have NetWare-specific problems or questions.

Support is a matter that needs to be planned and discussed with management. As the NetWare administrator, should you also take on software application support in your company? If you don't, who will be the designated person? If you do become the general PC support person in your company, the management needs to be made aware that this can easily become a full-time job.

As a full-time support person, your job would not only include supporting your users, but keeping up on what is happening in the industry so that you can move your system towards products and procedures that will help your company in the future. Your job would also include acquiring promising application programs and testing them out for suitability on your network and for your system's needs. In other words, you would be moving into a different career path than just running a small- or medium-sized NetWare network.

Some companies spread around the support duties by designating different people as specialists in different applications, leaving the NetWare administrator as the network support specialist only.

Support can become a "creeper," something that can creep up on you and consume more and more time as the users come to rely on your excellent and growing expertise. I strongly suggest that you address this issue with management at the very beginning of your budding NetWare administration career.

Troubleshooting Techniques

Unless a problem is so obvious it nearly bops you in the nose, you will have to perform some troubleshooting to find out just what the problem is and how you might go about solving it. This section contains some basic techniques that you will need to follow for just about any type of problem you might encounter.

Baby Steps

No matter what you are working on, *NEVER make more than one change at a time*. Changing more than one element at a time can end up causing you more problems than you'll believe possible. It can even make the original problem itself worse.

Two words: BE PATIENT. If the problem happens at 4:30 on Friday afternoon (of course), you have two choices. The first is to take a deep breath and resign yourself to staying late. The second is to tackle the problem on Monday morning. Trying to make a whole bunch of changes at one time and crossing your fingers won't work. People in a hurry make mistakes.

By only changing one thing at a time and testing, you will:

➡   Be able to find the problem and fix it faster.

➡   Recognize the culprit and the fix and be able to log the information so you know what to do in the future.

➡   Learn much more about your computers and NetWare and the way things work. It will help you to avoid future problem areas.

Trying to change too many things at the same time is the biggest mistake that people make when troubleshooting. Don't fall into that trap.

Peat and Repeat

The first thing you need to do when you encounter an anomaly is to duplicate or repeat the problem. If a problem is not repeatable, it's not solvable.

Start by asking "What's changed?" Even changes that "can't possibly cause the problem" can be the culprits.

> I once installed an application and had it working fine. Several days later it broke. Completely. But no one had touched the application.
>
> The problem was traced to a deleted disk volume that had been used for testing purposes. The application wasn't on the volume, so it never occurred to me that this change could affect the app in any way.
>
> However, when the application was installed it examined the server and built a list of every volume on the server, whether the application used that volume or not. After that, the application expected each volume to be there.
>
> To fix the problem, I had to re-create a new test volume. The application was then happy.

Then try to remember the sequence of events leading up to the problem. Sometimes it's a matter of a combination of programs that were running at the time, and even other traffic on the network.

Don't be discouraged if the problem is not immediately repeatable and don't summarily dismiss it as pilot error, either. Some problems take hours, days, or even weeks to show themselves again as the right circumstances converge, as illustrated by the following story:

> A reasonably experienced PC user came to me one time to report a problem with an application she had been running from the network. She reported that when the application was run from the local hard drive, there was no problem, but she had experienced intermittent problems when running on the network. The application would "freeze" the PC, forcing her to reboot the machine and losing all her data in the process.
>
> This problem began to occur frequently and eventually required the expertise of the company communications engineers. They analyzed the network traffic, and eventually found the culprit: a utility that came with a new brand of network cards sent out "bad" information over the network. This was a unique convergence of different programs and factors that was very difficult to repeat, let alone solve.

Baseline

The next step is to get the computer to a certain *baseline* state where no problems are encountered. Work backwards. If the machine has a complicated hardware or software setup, begin by simplifying the environment. Save the AUTOEXEC.BAT and CONFIG.SYS files to a different name and start out with a "bare-bones" system. Take out cards that are not germane to the problem (if you suspect a hardware conflict). Conflicts and problems can show up in funny ways.

Isolate

Once the problem is duplicated or can be repeated, it's time to try to begin to separate the problem into its logical components: software, hardware, or NOS.

Once again, this isn't always an easy thing to do, but practice will help you hone this skill.

First try loading and running the application from the local computer's hard drive (if possible) without even loading the network shells. Next, load the shells, but don't connect. Next, connect (login) to the network, and so on. Try running the problem application with the SUPERVISOR userid, it could be a matter of the correct access to files or directories.

Other things to try include duplicating the problem on another workstation. This can help to isolate problems to the hardware. If it works fine on one workstation and not on another, begin swapping out components one at a time.

By adding back *one at a time* each component (hardware or software) that you took out when trying to get to a baseline, you will soon find the culprit or at least be able to make a coherent call for technical support.

Those Pesky Users

The way you deal with the users on your network is one of the critical components in your network administration duties. Your attitude can make or break your success as an administrator.

When users report problems, they are not always likely to volunteer the entire story. They are sometimes afraid of looking dumb; very often they simply don't know what the entire story is, or what information is important to provide that will help you solve the problem.

No matter how nicely or diplomatically your questions are phrased, few users admit that something changed. The fact is, if things were working right this morning (or last month) and they aren't now, *something* is liable to be different. (Don't forget to take into account the changes you may have made on the system, no matter how innocuous they might have been.)

How to Win Friends and Influence Users

Once your system has been humming along for a while, problem reports are increasingly likely to be pilot error of some type. Non-computer-literate folks have a difficult time describing problems verbally. The fastest way to get problems resolved is usually to just visit the user at their workstation. When you do, here are a few tips:

→ Make sure that your attitude is comfortable and friendly. Never act impatient or in a hurry (even if you are). That can be very intimidating and it is difficult to get concise information from an intimidated user. Take this a step further and make a real effort to put the person at ease.

→ Speak English. Minimize the technobabble as much as possible. Computer jargon is intimidating to those who don't know it. Explain what you are doing as you go along in terms the neophyte can understand.

→ Never be condescending. Don't speak down to someone or display impatience of any type, even if they ask the same question for the 18th gazillion time. As the NetWare administrator, people need to be able to come to you with their questions and problems freely. Their productivity is affected if they waste time working with something when they should call you.

→ Share your know-how. Explain a little bit of what you are doing as you go along. People who just go in and make changes and walk away are intimidating, and by not explaining anything are in effect saying "This is too complicated for you, you won't understand."

→ Never make accusations. Even if it is obvious that the user made a change to something (and it is now failing as a result), don't be accusatory.

➡ Relate with the user. Even if you encounter the most simple and basic error, look the user straight in the eye, chuckle, and say "Oh, don't worry about it! I've done that myself!" This simple phrase (even if it's sometimes a white lie) will do more to ease your users' fears and intimidation than anything else you could do.

A good NetWare administrator is a consummate actor. Users who are at ease with you will be able to report problems and know they can get the answers and resolutions that they need. As you chat with them, explaining what you are doing and what you think the problem might be, *they will learn.* When they do report a problem:

➡ Ask them to repeat what they were doing when the problem exhibited itself

➡ Next, try to duplicate the problem yourself

➡ Begin troubleshooting, utilizing the techniques outline here

Remember: The network is a tool. It is the job of the administrator to help make it a productive and useful tool.

Common Problems and Helpful Hints

There is an excellent troubleshooting guide in the NetWare system administration manual that comes with your documentation. It covers a multitude of possible problems you might encounter and provides a number of reasons for those problems and where to look to solve them.

If you have NetWare 3.11, you received a complete set of manuals with the software. Starting with NetWare 3.12 and 4.0, however, Novell is no longer including printed manuals with the product. Instead the documentation is stored in files on your server. You can examine these on-line documents using a Windows NetWare Help facility. NetWare Help is very versatile, and you can search all of the manuals quickly for information. You will probably find it useful to purchase one set of printed documents, however. Often it's helpful to spread out a few volumes and ponder all the information that pertains to your problem. A combination of online and printed documentation is useful to have.

The areas covered in the manuals will not be repeated here; rather we will add to them and focus on a few of the tools that come with NetWare that might help you out.

Really Common Problems

What follows are some of the most common problems encountered when working with computers and on networks. They may seem simple, obvious, or basic (or all three), but you would be amazed at how many times you will encounter them.

1. **"My computer won't start!"** Check the power plug. Check to make sure the computer is turned on. Check to see that the case is on tight. Cleaning people move things, equipment gets jiggled and moved and becomes unplugged. Some computers don't operate properly unless the case is on and fastened securely.

2. **"My monitor is blank!"** Check the power plug. Check to make sure the monitor is turned on. Check the contrast and brightness controls.

3. **"I can't type anything!"** Some computers have keyboard locks.

4. **"I can't connect to the fileserver!"** Check to see that the connector is still connected to the NIC. Sometimes the NIC itself is loose. Make sure the fileserver is up and running. Make sure the workstation shells are loaded.

TIP

Don't get your exercise by jumping to conclusions. Sure, equipment will fail, but it is very much worth your while to check for the obvious. Hard equipment failure is easiest to detect by swapping out components with a system that you are sure does work.

Wiring Mysteries Revealed

Cabling can be a difficult thing to troubleshoot. Cable problems can be physical or will make themselves known with connection and communication problems to the network. If you suspect bad cable, here's what you can do before you call in the experts:

➡ Check the connections and connectors. Bad or faulty connections will comprise the majority of wire problems. Some of them are detectable by looking. Many faults, however, are hidden. The best way to isolate them is to start swapping components or cables.

➡ Run the COMCHECK utility that comes with NetWare. It will tell you if the workstation and fileserver can talk to each other. (If they can, it's not a cable problem.)

➡ Swap out the cable segment. Swap the questionable one with a known good one from a workstation that is working (where possible).

Look to the NIC and connections as your first step. NICs can and do go bad, often before cable does.

Fileserver Problems (Oh No!)

Unfortunately, the error messages that NetWare generates are not always as verbose or descriptive as we would all like them to be. Supplement the information that is in your Novell manuals with an Application Note that can be found on NetWire (NOVLIB, Library 11, AN010B.ZIP). (Please refer to Chapter 14, "Help at Hand," for more information on NetWire). All (or nearly all) of the error messages generated by NetWare 386 are documented, along with English explanations of what the problem might be and where to look.

TIP

Application Notes are in-depth reports on many aspects of NetWare; they cover everything from backing up your NetWare server to some really complex topics such as internetworking with your NetWare server. The Application Notes are a monthly publication written by a special department at Novell called Novell Research. These are top notch papers that can't be found anyplace else. There is no marketing hype, just pure information. They are well worth the annual subscription rate: currently $95 U.S. For more information, call 1-800-377-4136 or 303-297-2725. A complete information sheet, including an up-to-date index of articles that have appeared to date, can be found on NetWire in NOVLIB, Library 11, file name APPNOT.LST.

Some of the utilities that come with NetWare can help you troubleshoot problems at the server, including:

→   MONITOR, VOLUMES, CONFIG, INSTALL — all Console Commands.

→   SET—a Console Command—check the documentation for the many different parameters that can be called and checked.

→   Check address conflicts with workstations (if you are using Token Ring or ARCnet).

WARNING
Two additional utilities that are available for different types of problems are VREPAIR and BINDFIX. VREPAIR works on your NetWare volume in roughly the same manner that CHKDSK works on a DOS disk. But there's a difference in that a NetWare volume stores a lot more information than a DOS disk does, and by its nature is a lot more complex. Run under the wrong conditions, VREPAIR can cause damage to your NetWare server. Check with the experts on NetWire before you run this.

BINDFIX is a utility that works with the Bindery files. The Bindery files are a special database where all your user and file information is stored. It is also a complex part of your NetWare system. Once again, check with the experts before using this. Make sure you know what you're doing.

Hardware failures can and do happen on your fileserver computer. Memory chips can go bad, cables can wriggle loose or fail, boards can go bad. Follow the basic troubleshooting techniques, utilize the troubleshooting guide in your system administration manual and obtain the information suggested previously.

Workstation

In addition to the common problems already mentioned, here are some other things to check for:

➜   The network shells should be checked for proper configuration and integrity. Reload and reconfigure if you suspect they might be corrupted.

➜   Check the NIC and connections to the wire. Sometimes things can wriggle loose.

➜   Check for conflicts with the CONFIG.SYS and SHELL.CFG parameters. (Check the Novell documentation for complete information on SHELL.CFG.)

➜   Check for conflicts with other boards that may be installed in the workstation.

The Experts

If your own troubleshooting efforts are not successful, utilize the expertise of the folks on NetWire, 24 hours a day, 7 days a week. (No additional charge for the 24-hour access.) See Chapter 14, "Help at Hand," for complete information.

Chapter 13, Short and Sweet

This chapter covered the techniques for troubleshooting that the experts use. It also covered other important information, such as:

1.   Know your NetWare system and setup. Log everything about your hardware, software, and NetWare setup that you can find. A complete log will:

➜   Familiarize you with your system

➜   Help you to troubleshoot by being able to review the same or similar problems encountered in the past (last week or last year)

➜   Help you to troubleshoot and report problems by having the pertinent information close at hand

➜   Help you to rebuild your system quickly in case of catastrophic failure

2. The first and foremost rule in troubleshooting is to take baby steps. Never change and test more than one thing at a time.

3. Baseline your system. Try to get to a point where you do not encounter problems and then work up from there, adding one component at a time until the problem is encountered.

4. Baselining will also help you isolate the problem to help you determine the cause.

5. Always be patient when dealing with your users. Don't be condescending or in any way convey to them that you are not concerned about their problems. As a NetWare administrator, you are in the customer service field. Unhappy or intimidated users have a difficult time communicating their problems and frustrations.

6. Don't jump to conclusions about problems. KISS (Keep It Simple, Stupid) and start by looking for obvious things such as unplugged equipment, check the "on" switches, and check for keyboard locks.

7. The system administration manual has some excellent information about troubleshooting steps to follow and the utilities that come with NetWare that will help you out. Utilize this valuable resource.

8. Loose connections are a common source of problems. Use your eyeballs to check for wiring problems.

9. After you have performed the troubleshooting that you can, remember there is always help on NetWire. Check Chapter 14, "Help at Hand," to find out more about this invaluable resource.

PART FIVE

Zen Secrets, E-mail, and Installing Apps

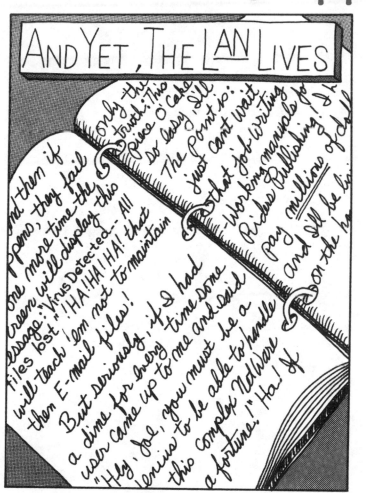

Joe, despite his absence, made his presence known daily, mainly through his system documentation and racy login scripts.

Help at Hand

(Or, Realizing You're Not Alone)

The real secret to being successful in any endeavor like administering a network is in knowing where you *can* get answers when you need them. Beating your head against the wall trying to learn everything on your own only gets you a bruised head and blurry eyesight. There are excellent sources available for you to do your own networking. This chapter will explore some of them and the types of information you can expect, such as:

→ Internal company resources—the people behind the scenes

→ Vendor resources—they really are human beings

→ CompuServe's business-related forums

→ NetWire: the best NetWare technical resource on the planet

→ User groups—use them wisely

→ Networking publications

→ Making full use of trade shows and conventions

Computer networking is simply not a job that can be done in a black hole. After all, people aren't born experts, they're developed. A growing number of LAN administrators have mastered networking, not by going to school, but by soliciting the help of knowledgeable others.

NOTE

Never preface your question with "I know this might be a dumb question, but... " Remember:

The only dumb question is the one that isn't asked!

Internal Resources

If you are administering a network in a department of a good-sized corporation, chances are pretty high that there is an MIS (Management Information Systems) department of some type that oversees all sorts of computer stuff in your company. If you work in a really large company, then chances are pretty high that you might even have a group separate from the MIS department whose job is to take care of communications—things like the network wiring, computer communications between different physical locations, and so on.

Check around and find the real communications engineers. Note that these are people with real engineering degrees, not the Certified NetWare Engineer (CNE) type designation. Almost anyone can earn a CNE in six to twelve months. An engineering degree requires four to five years of hard work. Who do you think knows more about your network cabling and hardware?

You will probably find that many of the more technically inclined people in your organization are thrilled to share their knowledge with you and answer your questions. Being the types that lean toward the technical—instead of the political—means they generally have less of a "stay out of my rice-bowl" mentality and are happy to share their knowledge with you. You have only to ask.

When you ask, do be cognizant of their time; prefacing your initial question or two with "I know you're swamped, but I could sure use some help... " won't hurt.

Just remember that most people knowledgeable in a certain field really enjoy it and therefore like sharing their knowledge with others.

Vendor Resources

Vendors are actually real people underneath all that smooth sales hype. But it's the techies in those companies who can become your most valuable contacts.

Vendors and Consultant Types

Some computer dealers understand that excellent technical support is a key factor in doing business, and will spend the money needed to hire very talented people. Get acquainted with the techies in the company, and let them know how much you appreciate the great job they are doing for you. You don't have to kiss up to these people (or anyone else) to let them know you appreciate their efforts. Just exercising a little common courtesy will do the trick. Keep in mind that the people who get the most attention at a dealer are those who are the star sellers. Techies tend to get ignored and treated as second-class citizens sometimes. After all, don't you like a little recognition when you've done a good job on a project?

Techies that work for dealers are no different than techies anywhere else— they like what they're doing and love sharing their knowledge. The only thing here is that you are walking a fine line. They know they have to bill for technical support (after all, that's how they get paid), but they rarely mind answering a short question here and there. Don't take advantage of them, but they can make a valuable resource in a pinch.

Product Vendors

Most hardware and software manufacturers charge for technical support these days, although there are a few notable exceptions. If you are already paying for a tech support call, then maximize it. When the question or problem you are calling about has been solved, this is the opportunity to ask the question that has been keeping you awake at night. Preface your question with something like "I know this is off topic, but say, I was wondering about... ." Most tech support people will be happy to help you or direct you to a book or whatever that has the answer you are looking for.

Online Help: CompuServe Business-related Forums

To say that CompuServe Information Service (CompuServe or just CIS) is an online information service is like saying the Pacific Ocean is a body of water. Neither description gives you any idea of the vast scope of the thing being described. If you can think of something and it's not against the law, you can probably find it somewhere on CompuServe.

Of particular interest to us, however, is NetWire, the CompuServe forum that is sponsored by Novell. NetWire is the place to ask questions, read about other people's solutions to problems, shoot the... uh... stuff, and get useful patches and shareware. No one should even think of being a NetWare administrator without having a CompuServe account and a modem at hand. (Well, that is the title of this chapter!)

In addition to NetWire, there are many forums relating to computers, both hardware and software. Many vendors have their own forums—or group of forums—relating to different products. The vendors have found that having a forum on CIS is a great way to provide technical support. The main reason is that this provides a way for them to support far more people than the usual one-on-one venue of telephone support. Instead of their answer on how to solve a particular problem being heard by only one person, it can be read by many people on the forum.

It is also a chance for non-employees to display their expertise, and they gladly do so, even though they don't get paid for helping others. These knowledgeable folks do this for the same reason I've been saying all along—people with an interest in what they are doing love to share that information with others.

NOTE

It is nearly impossible to receive an incorrect answer to any question on CIS. Because the messages on the forums are public, anyone giving an incorrect answer is immediately corrected by others.

Online Help: NetWire

NetWire is Novell's technical support forum on CompuServe Information Service (CIS). Here's why NetWire is the best resource for NetWare technical information on the planet:

→ **Knowledge base.** Instead of dealing with just one person, as you would by calling technical support, you are dealing with thousands of people whose combined skill level is staggering. Most of these people work in the "real world," and someone will know the answer to just about any question you might have, or any problem you are running into.

→ **Low cost.** Unlike calling Novell Technical Support, where the cost is $150 per "incident," there is no charge for this wealth of information over and above the normal charges incurred on CIS. (It is outside of Basic Services, if that is your billing option.)

NOTE

There are some areas on CIS that do have a surcharge associated with using them. Those areas are primarily databases of information. Whenever you see a dollar sign ($) next to a menu selection on CIS, that means there is a charge over and above the amount you are paying in your billing plan. If you choose the Basic Services billing plan, the areas that are not included in Basic Services are marked with a plus sign (+). NetWire is not included in Basic Services.

TIP

If you are not familiar with CompuServe or NetWire, there are a couple of things you need to know about first. This chapter contains the basic information you need to know about beginning to learn about and use NetWire. But if you would like to know more about the available resources on CompuServe, or just how to use CompuServe, you might want to pick up a copy of another New Riders Publishing book called Inside CompuServe.

NetWorking on NetWire

Like the businesses alluded to in a previous section, Novell is no exception when it comes to technical support; it too has found that having a forum on CIS is a great way to help a lot of people all at once. Having a problem with your tape backup on NetWare? Ask on NetWire. Have a question or a problem with your NICs? Ask on NetWire. Running into glitches with printing on NetWare? Ask on NetWire. Novell has found NetWire so successful and so heavily utilized that they have had to split from one forum into several and are still growing! Their libraries were so heavily used that they had to ask CIS for a completely different area that could handle that much traffic. In NetWire, rather than each forum having its own library area, there is one forum having only one message section and the rest of the area devoted to libraries. There is also a special section for the files that are downloaded the most. The updated list of those libraries and forums follows.

NOTE
The material that follows consists of the listing of the NetWire forums as of the date of publication and all the sections each contains. Because NetWire has to periodically make adjustments for growth, these listings may not be current at the time you connect to NetWire. A current list of forums can be downloaded from Library 1 of NOVLIB; file name is FRMORG.TXT.

NetWire Message Sections
Novell NetWare 2.X Forum (NETW2X)

1) Printing

2) Utilities (NetWare)

3) Disk Drives/Cntrls

4) LAN Cards/Drivers

14) 2.1x & Below/OS

15) Operating System

Novell NetWare 3.X Forum (NETW3X)

1) Printing

2) NetWare Utilities

3) Disk Drivers/Cntrls/CDs

4) LAN Cards/Drivers

5) Migration/Upgrade

13) SFT III

14) NLM/OS/Console Util

Novell NetWare 4.X Forum (NETW4X)

1) Printing

2) NetWare Utilities

3) Disk Drives/CDs/Cntrls

4) LAN Cards/Drivers

5) Migration/Upgrade

6) ElectroText/Documentation

7) Directory Services

14) NLM/OS/Console Util

Novell Desktop Forum (NOVDESKTOP)

1) DRDOS/Applications

2) DRDOS/Disk

3) DRDOS/Memory

4) DRDOS/Utilities

5) Customer Service

6) Programming ?'s

7) Dataclub

8) NetWare Lite

14) Netware NT Client

Novell Connectivity Forum (NCONNECT)

1) Access Services

2) NACS

3) NW for SAA

4) AS/400 Connectivity

5) Host Printing

6) SNA Links

7) LAN/LAN Links

8) NetWare Macintosh

9) NetWare VMS

10) Portable NetWare

11) NW NFS - TCP/IP

12) Email/MHS/FAX

13) LANWrkplce/Group

14) Other Conn. Issues

Novell Information Forum (NGENERAL)

1) Product Information

2) Suggestion Box

3) Application/Utils

4) User Groups/Train'g

5) CNE's

6) CNEPA

7) NSEPro

8) AppNotes

9) NASC Program

16) Other Information

17) The Lighter Side

Novell Vendors Forum A (NVENA)

1) Folio

2) LAN Suport Group

3) Computer Tyme

4) Infinite Tech.

5) Dell Computer

6) AST Research

7) Blue Lance

8) Best Power

9) Knowzall

10) Notework

11) RoseWare

12) Multi-User DOS

13) TriCord

15) Synoptics

Novell User Forum (NOVUSER)

1) General Q & A's

2) Help Wanted

3) Classifieds

Networking Hardware/Components Forum (NOVHW)

1) Power Monitoring

2) Token Ring

3) Ethernet

4) ARCnet

5) Backups

6) Cabling/Media

Novell Network Management (NOVMAN)

1) Network Management

2) NetWare Mgmnt. System

3) Lantern System Mgr.

4) Lanalyzer for Windows

5) NW for SAA Mngmnt.

Novell OS/2 Forum (NOVOS2)

1) OS/2 Printing

2) Client/Server

3) OS/2 Requester

4) NSM (OS/2)

5) NW 4.x for OS/2

6) GUI Tools

7) WINOS2/DOS

Novell Client Forum (NOVCLIENT)

1) IPX/ODI Issues

2) NETX Issues

3) VLM Issues

4) ODINSUP Issues

5) NetBios Issues

6) NetWare & Windows

Novell Developer Support Forum (NDEVSUPP)

1) General Business

2) Btrieve

3) NetWare SQL

4) NetWare Client SDK

5) NetWare Server SDK

6) Macintosh SDKs

7) Communication SDKs

8) To be assigned

9) Personal NetWare SDK

10) AppWare Foundation SDK

11) Lan Workplace SDK

12) Telephony SDK

13) Visual AppBuilder

Novell Library (NOVLIB)

1) LIB Questions Only

Novell Vendors Forum B (NVENB)

1) Ontrack

2) NetWorth

Novell UnixWare Forum (UNIXWARE)

1) General Info

2) Product Info

3) Developers

4) DOS Merge

5) Installation

6) X Windows

7) Networking

8) Device Drivers

9) Printing

10) Communications

11) Applications

12) Bug Watchers

13) Updates

NetWire Libraries

Libraries for NOVLIB

1) Novell New UPLOADS	Files Uploaded by Novell, Inc.
2) General Information	General Info, Education, Press Releases
3) NetWare 2.X Specific	Files Pertaining Only to NetWare 2.*X*
4) NetWare 3.X Specific	Files Pertaining Only to NetWare 3.*X*
5) Client/Shell Drivers	Workstation Shells, Drivers, Windows Files, etc.
6) NetWare Utilities	Utilities that Pertain to NetWare 2.*X* and 3.*X*
7) Btrieve/XQL	Novell Development Division Products Btrieve/XQL/Xtrieve
8) MAC/NFS/MHS/NMS/LWP	Files for Macintosh, NFS, MHS, Mgt. System, Lan Wkplace
9) Communications Product	Novell's Communications Products
10) NetWare Lite	NetWare Lite-Specific Files
11) Technical Information	Technical Documents
12) NDSG/DRDOS	Files for Novell's Desktop Systems Group and DR DOS
13) APPWARE	AppWare Files

14) Netware 4.X Specific   Files Pertaining Only to NetWare 4.*X*

Libraries for Novell Users Forum (NOVUSERS)

1) New Uploads

2) Disk Drvs/Patches

3) Lan Drivers/Patches

4) Comm Drvs/Patches

5) Host/UNIX/drvrs/ptch

6) Printer Utilities

7) Network (sys) Utils

8) Client WS Utils

9) Management Tools

10) Text Files/Help

11) Windows Utilities

12) Btrieve/Pgm Utilities

13) Virus Detectors

14) General Utilities

17) Classified/Jobs

Libraries for Novell UNIXWARE Forum (UNIXWARE)

1) General Library

2) Developer Tools

3) X Window Library

4) Network Utilities

5) Applications

6) Device Drivers

7) Updates

Libraries for Novell Vendor's Forum B (NVENB)

1) Ontrack

2) Networth

Libraries for Novell Vendor's Forum A (NVENA)

1) Folio

2) LAN Support Group

3) Computer Tyme

4) Infinite Tech.

5) Dell Computer Corp.

6) AST Research

7) Blue Lance

8) Best Power

9) Knowzall

10) Notework

11) RoseWare

12) Multi-User DOS

13) TriCord

15) Synoptics

Getting to NetWire

When you first log onto CompuServe, you will see the main menu as shown in figure 14.1:

Figure 14.1

Welcome to CompuServe.

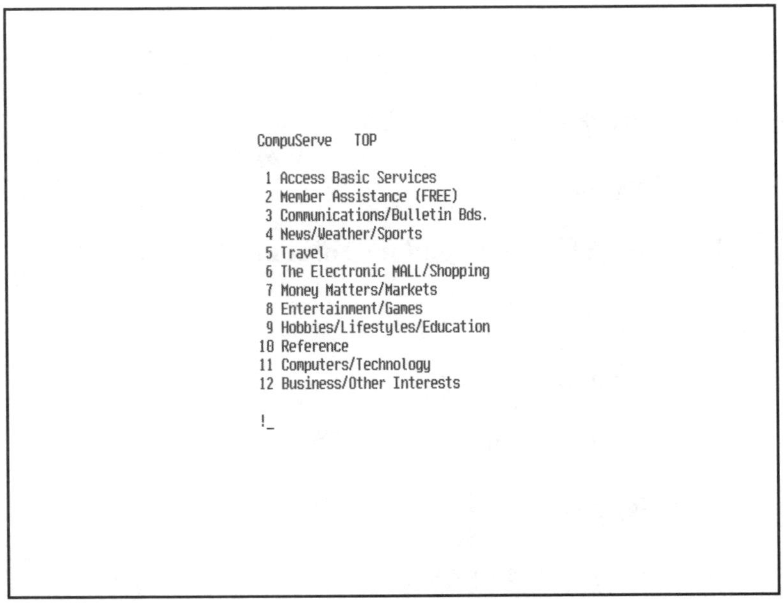

```
CompuServe   TOP

 1 Access Basic Services
 2 Member Assistance (FREE)
 3 Communications/Bulletin Bds.
 4 News/Weather/Sports
 5 Travel
 6 The Electronic MALL/Shopping
 7 Money Matters/Markets
 8 Entertainment/Games
 9 Hobbies/Lifestyles/Education
10 Reference
11 Computers/Technology
12 Business/Other Interests

!_
```

At the "!" prompt, type **GO NETWIRE**.

When you first enter the NetWire forums, you are greeted with the menu of options shown in figure 14.2.

Announcing...

You access the Announcements on NetWire from the NetWire main menu. (You also can type **ANN** at the ! prompt to see some announcements when you have entered a forum.) You can find Novell press releases (to get current product information), information on networking conventions and shows, information on NUI (the international NetWare users' group, discussed later in the chapter), as well as other information. One of the most useful areas is Service and Support, which is where you can find out about current patches, drivers, and fixes, and from which you can download them.

Figure 14.2

Welcome to NetWire.

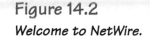

```
One moment please...

    You have left basic services

NetWire+   NOVELL

NETWIRE MAIN MENU

1 What's New
2 Service and Support
3 Sales and Marketing
4 Novell Programs
5 About the Network Support Encyclopedia
6 New User Information
7 Compuserve Information Service

!_
```

NOTE

There is one extremely popular feature in NetWire that draws everyday users and SysOps alike like a magnet. This "place" is called the Library. What is so popular about the Library? It's the fastest way that Novell can distribute patches, drivers, and informational files. For vendors who write their own drivers, it's a great way for them to distribute their products also. The alternative? Go to your vendor or order the patch, driver, or whatever from Novell. But in order to pay for distribution costs to individuals, your vendor and Novell have to charge a fee—a much heavier fee than what you would pay for the cost of downloading the file from CompuServe. Note that there is no additional charge for being on any of the NetWire forums or in the NetWire library over and above the usual CIS costs. (NetWire is not included in Basic Services.)

The area that will be one of the most useful will be finding out about current patches, drivers, and fixes (Service and Support) and where they can be found for downloading. Figure 14.3 shows the menu of options if you select Service and Support from the main NetWire menu:

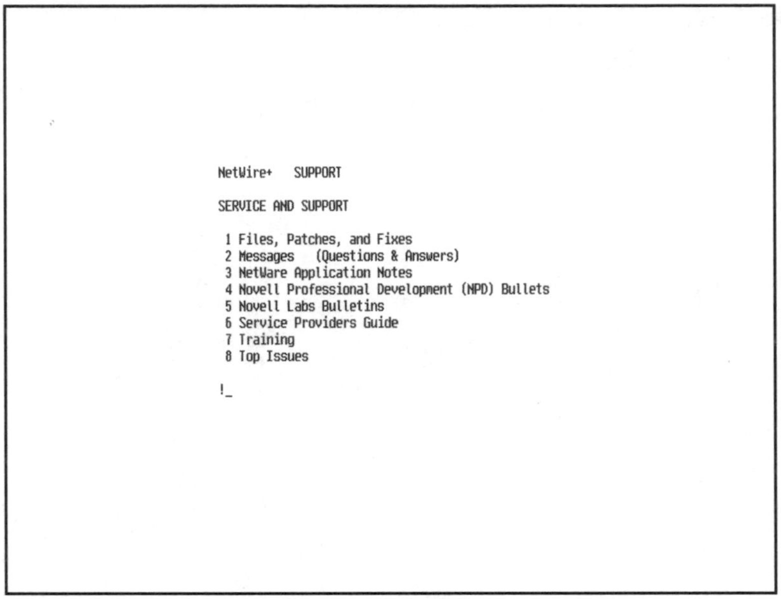

Figure 14.3

Service with a smile.

```
NetWire+  SUPPORT

SERVICE AND SUPPORT

1 Files, Patches, and Fixes
2 Messages   (Questions & Answers)
3 NetWare Application Notes
4 Novell Professional Development (NPD) Bullets
5 Novell Labs Bulletins
6 Service Providers Guide
7 Training
8 Top Issues

!_
```

A Message for You

The message areas are exceptionally valuable, and if you are the shy type, you may not even have to post your own message. Because these areas are open—for both reading and writing—to anyone with a CIS account, there is a lot to learn from reading the messages already on the board.

Every forum on CIS has a limited amount of space available for messages, and everytime a new message is posted, an old one "scrolls" off, or disappears into the bit bucket. (Which explains why you might see an answer to a question, but not the original question.) The rate at which a message stays on the forum before it scrolls off is called the "scroll rate." So if a forum has fewer active members, a message might stay on the forum for 30 days before it scrolls off. The NetWire forums are so busy that their scroll rate averages only about 3 days. If you do post a question there, you'd better check back well within the 3-day timeframe.

The target time for a question being answered on just about any forum on CIS is within 24 hours, and NetWire is no exception. However, it is not at all suprising to post a question on NetWire and receive an answer within 2 or 3 hours. The swiftness of the replies you receive is another reason why using NetWire is as good (or better) an option for tech support than calling Novell tech support.

Who Minds the Store?

Each forum on CIS is monitored by a *SysOp*, or *System Operator*. Some forums' SysOps are employees of the company that is the focus of the forum, and some SysOps are simply interested and enterprising individuals.

The Novell forum's SysOps are comprised of both Novell employees and non-employees who like what they do, like being online, and like sharing their knowledge.

NOTE

Online is the term for using a BBS or information system like CIS. A breakdown of the words shows that "on" means "on" and "line" refers to the telephone line. Online means that the person is on their telephone line, using it to connect and communicate with the service. In this case, CIS.

In most forums on CIS, the SysOp's job is to be a host to the forum. They help out newcomers who may have questions about using CIS, they put messages in their proper sections, and they check any files that are uploaded to their forums for viruses before making them available to everyone, and just generally help out and sometimes guide discussions.

Most SysOps are experts in the area of interest of their forum. There are lawyers who sysop the law forum, doctors who sysop the medical forum, veterinarians who sysop the pets forum, and so on. Most SysOps are rather diplomatic types and know how to keep a disagreement from escalating into a fist-fight (or "flamefest") and generally keep things going in an orderly, friendly manner.

NOTE

On those relatively rare occasions when a forum member posts a message that violates a CIS rule (no selling, no swearing, no personal attacks, and so on), the SysOp will move the message to the back room of the forum, which is an area out of the public view. The only ones who can see messages in the back room are the person to whom the message is addressed and the person who wrote it (and the SysOps, of course). SysOps very rarely delete messages in their forums; most of them like to foster an atmosphere of open communications and make their forums a comfortable place to be.

Be sure to follow "forum decorum," and conduct yourself appropriately. If someone offends you by calling you names or openly swearing, alert the SysOp. They are there to help you.

The SysOps on NetWire are a little different than the SysOps in most other areas on CIS in that their main focus is not diplomacy, but NetWare answers. The only way to get a job sysoping on NetWire is to be the best of the best, technically. These people are the cremé de la cremé. They have forgotten more about NetWare than most of us mere mortals will ever learn. One of the things that makes them so good is that they all (except the very few Novell employees) work at real jobs during the day, many of them as consultants. Among all of them there aren't too many problems or questions that have not been encountered.

You can also trust messages from people who are not SysOps. A lot of very knowledgeable people hang out there who simply don't have the time to commit to being a SysOp. Besides, as mentioned previously, if someone gives an incorrect answer you can bet that person will be corrected quickly.

The non-Novell SysOps on NetWire do not get paid for their services. They do, however, receive a "sponsored," or free, CIS account so that they do not incur any CIS charges while helping people out. To most of these folks, their hobby is also their work and many of them even have networks at home. But remember, they are giving up time to help you out, and they don't *have* to do that: always be polite.

The first few times I logged onto NetWire, I read through a number of messages. It was evident that several of the people online knew each other quite well. I did not realize at the time that many of these people rarely (if ever) saw each other in person; it was merely that they had been "hanging out" in the same forum for so long that they had developed online friendships. But they sure looked like they were having fun. I didn't know what my reception would be if I "butted in" with a message, but I got up the courage to do so in one of the sections that is put aside for idle chit-chat. Everyone greeted me warmly and quickly made me feel like one of the gang.

The moral of the story is that it is exceedingly rare to find any cliques online, or groups that will exclude someone or treat anyone like an intruder who ventures in to participate. If you don't want to be an active participant, you don't have to, but if you like the feel or atmosphere of a forum (and each one is different) and want to join in, your participation will be warmly welcomed.

Understanding Message Formats

When you do log onto NetWire or any forum on CIS, you will find that all messages have the same format. Figure 14.4 is a copy of a real message and reply and shows how to "read" the information given in a message.

Notice that in this figure, the "(X)" next to the name in the first message means that the person the message is addressed to has read the message. This does not mean that you will necessarily receive a response to the message immediately, because the message areas are not "real time" in the sense that a person has to be logged on to read and respond to message.

As a matter of fact, most people use programs (covered in the next section) that enable them to download copies of all the messages (that they want to) that are on CompuServe and read and respond to them off line on their own computer while they are not logged on. So although a message may be marked as being read, that only means that the person has downloaded it and will read and respond to it as soon as they can. When the person has finished their response, they reconnect to CompuServe and upload their response.

Figure 14.4

Reading a message.

1. Message Number

2. Section number

3. Section Name

4. Date and time (your time zone)

5. Subject name original poster used

6. Name and userid of person

7. Addresee

8. Note: Message number replying to is automatically added by CIS software

   1   2   3
\#: 294557 S3/Printing
   09-Sep-93 06:33:17 4
Sb: #printing postscript 5
Fm: adam morrison 100140,440 6
To: sysop (X) 7

We have an application that prints out two A4 sheets of graphics using the postscript language. This works fine on a local printer, but when printing via Netware 311 it will print out a few times and then stop printing altogether. It seems that the job is processed from the queue but then gets garbled, with the printer giving a postscript error.

This is despite using printcon print jobs and specifying No tabs, byte stream etc as recommended, the timeout setting does not seem to make any difference. What else can you suggest ?

Regards

Adam Morrison

There is 1 Reply.

\#: 294733 S3/Printing
   09-Sep-93 22:19:04
Sb: #294557-printing postscript 8
Fm: Mickey Applebaum(SysOp) 76704,71
To: adam morrison 100140,440

Put the commands on the CAPTURE line and don't use a print job...

CAPTURE NB NT NFF TI=45 Q=<queue_name> should work...

GO NOVFILES and get 311PTD.EXE and load at LEAST the SPX related patches...

GO NOVLIB and get STRTLI.EXE from DL 4 (NetWare 3.x Specific) and load those patches...

GO NOVFILES and get DOSUP7.EXE and use the latest ODI Drivers and shells..

GO NOVLIB and get PSERV4.EXE from DL 6 (NetWare Utilities) and load the latest Pserver and Rprinter...

You aren't trying to make Windows and Rprinter work on the same workstation are you??? They won't.... Get RPRNHE.ZIP from DL 10 (Text Files/Help) on NOVUSER and then ask in the Windows section (15) here on NOVB for more info....

You Don't Sew These Threads

Naturally, CIS would be of little use if you read the answers to questions before the questions themselves. That's why the CIS software takes care of making sure that responses to messages are all in the correct order by "threading" the messages. A message "thread" then, is a new subject topic where all the replies follow the original message in proper order. From what we have already discussed about forums and sections, it follows that there are several different message threads in each section. One thread can be 1, 2, or 120 messages long.

How to Figure Out Threading

We'll use an example for talking about message threads as follows: Sarah posts a question in Section 1/"General Q&A's," of the NOWSER forum. She tells folks that her boss has finally decided to part with a few dollars and buy a new fileserver computer. She is looking for recommendations on brands to consider.

What will happen is that Debbi might respond to Sarah by telling her that Compaq is the only way to go. But Dave responds (and before Debbi did) that he has had great luck with Zeniths. Carol posts a reply to Dave's message telling him her own experience has shown that Zeniths are real dogs to get working as fileservers, and she wouldn't recommend one to her worst enemy and that she recommends IBM. What we have so far are two responses to Sarah's original question and one response to Dave's message.

Since Dave's reply was posted before Debbi's, it will be the one to show up first. And since Carol posted a reply to Dave (not Sarah), her message comes next. And then we will read Debbi's message.

While you can see that one subject might go off on different tangents, each branch is followed to the end.

Another important thing to make note of here is that Sarah created a new message, but everyone else used the reply function of their software so that the message could stay threaded. If you post a reply to someone's message as a new message, even if it has the same subject heading, it creates a completely new thread. Always use the Reply function when responding to messages.

CIS Autonavigation Programs

The very best way to navigate around CIS and NetWire is to use an autonavigational program that does exactly what the name implies. It navigates CIS automatically. You simply mark the forums, sections, or specific message threads in different sections of forums that you want to read and the autonavigation program will automatically dial the local CIS node for you (details in a minute), go to the forums you have indicated, download the messages, and log off.

There are several reasons for using an autonavigational (autonav, for short) program:

1. **Cost savings**. Although in the U.S. CompuServe access is about $10 per hour, the time can add up quickly. Since you can grab the messages and download them (for reading and responding to them later) a lot faster than you can read them while connected, you will only be logged on for about two or three minutes in comparison to taking at least an hour to read the same number of messages while connected.

2. **Time savings**. Because your autonav program can keep many, many messages in the computer's memory at the same time, it is much faster to read messages offline. It is not only faster to go from one message to the next, it is also faster when you want to skip reading a message that you have no interest in. When I went from doing all my reading and responding online to using an autonav program, I found I could increase the number of messages I read and responded to by about 50 percent or more.

TIP

You don't have to increase the number of messages you read by using an autonav program, but most folks find that they do. You could always keep the number of messages the same and save even more time and money.

There are two main programs that folks use for autonav programs and those are TAPCIS and OzCIS. For the Macintosh platform, there is NAVIGATOR. These are shareware programs and well worth their registration fees. Since they are shareware, meaning "try before you buy," go ahead and try them out first and see which one you like best. They have documentation that comes with them, and the instructions for getting online are fairly straight-forward.

CIM and WINCIM

If you do not have a communications program and you don't know of anyone who can help you, then go to a computer store that carries a large selection of software. On the shelves you are likely to find a box labeled "CompuServe." This is a CIS starter kit and it contains not only the instructions, but the software that will enable you to log in for the first time and start getting online. The name of the software is CompuServe Information Manager (CIM), and the Windows version is WINCIM.

Use CIM or WINCIM to get online the first time. Immediately go to the TAPCIS forum and download TAP.EXE and TAP.DOC from Library 1. Or, if you prefer a CUA-type interface, go to OZCISDL and download the appropriate files from the menu. As soon as they are downloaded, log off. All of these files are self-extracting, which means you do not need PKUNZIP; you just type in the name of the file before the DOS extension.

TIP

TAPCIS may not be the most sparkly program around, but it is functional. To add some pizazz to your offline work, get a TAPCIS add-on (another shareware program) that makes reading and answering messages offline a real pleasure. RECON is highly recommended and is available in Library 2 of the TAPCIS forum.

If you prefer a GUI interface (Windows look and feel), then instead of TAPCIS, get OzCIS immediately. The OzCIS files can be found by typing GO OZCISDL at any "!" prompt.

TIP

Do NOT use CIM or WINCIM for regular access to CIS. These programs are written by CompuServe and are designed to keep you online, obviously making more money for CIS. While there is nothing wrong with H & R Block (owner of CIS) making money, there is no sense in you flushing your online money away when you can budget it wisely by using the autonavigational programs available to you.

It is important for you to know that you have many choices in not only autonavigational programs, but also programs that make reading and answering messages offline a pleasure instead of a chore. Do what the experts (SysOps) do and test drive one immediately.

Sounds Great but How Much Is It?

Access to CIS varies, and depends on these factors:

➜ **Country**. In the U.S., the hourly connect time charges can be around $10 per hour. Outside the U.S., charges vary greatly, depending on the country and the telephone system.

TIP

To find out about CompuServe's charges and different pricing plans, or to get an account, call CIS at 614-457-0802 or 1-800-848-8199. This is also the number to call to find out about local access numbers to call.

➜ **Pricing plan**. CompuServe has a few different pricing plans that you can choose from to suit your needs. Remember though, that you can change the plan you select anytime you want. Type **GO BILLING** to get information on costs if you are already online.

➜ **Access speed**. 1200/2400 bps (bps, or bits per second, is the measuring rate of data transfer) is cheaper than 9600 baud and 300 baud is the cheapest of all. For downloading and uploading messages, 9600 or 14,400 bps (if available in your area) is cheaper, even though the hourly rate costs more than the other speeds, because you can get on and off faster.

TIP

If you do not have a communications program so you can get online and download an autonavigation program to make things easier and cheaper in the future, you can still get online. You can call The Support Goup, the makers of TAPCIS, and they will send you their program with a start-up kit (CIS account number and initial password) if you want to take a chance and pay before you buy. Their number is 1-301-387-4500 or 1-800-872-4768. Call them for current pricing information.

Intangible Assets

Access to NetWire is essential to any NetWare administrator, particularly to the beginner. This chapter gives you all the basic information you need to know to get online and start utilizing NetWire right away. But how do you convince management of NetWire's utility to business?

Most companies today recognize, to some degree, the value of budgeting for a CIS account, and do so. Sometimes, negotiation with your boss can help the process. Although the first months' costs are bound to be higher because of initial exploration, you might try one or all of the following suggestions with a reluctant boss:

→   Get a CIS account under your own name and download some of the messages from the NetWire forum. Print them out and show them to your boss to show him or her the type of answers that can be had for a much lower cost than Novell technical support.

→   Negotiate for a cap on the account. Tell your boss you will pay any fees over x dollars a month. With an autonavigational program, costs can be controlled a lot easier than without. Start negotiating for a $100/month limit and go down from there.

→   With the help of some of the information in Chapter 11, "Tape Backups and Disaster Planning," estimate the dollar cost to the company in downtime on the network. Budgeting $100 to $200 per month ($300 per month for people who regularly visit several business-related forums is not unusual) for CIS access and usage is far cheaper. Prepare a simple cost comparison chart to show to your boss.

One of the reasons it is sometimes difficult to get the company to spring for an account is that it is difficult to show a "hard" costs savings. After all, how do you measure the cost beforehand of beating your head against a wall on a problem and troubleshooting versus browsing for general information and being prepared with answers before you need them?

While I have lost count of the number of times that posting or reading a question on NetWire has saved my administrative behind in running a network, there are other advantages to looking around and participating in other forums on CIS.

One of the topics I knew nothing about BC (Before CIS) was computer viruses and security. But by following others' conversations on the topic and jumping in with my own questions, I ended up getting acquainted with one of the better virus experts in this country, Ross M. Greenberg. Even though we have never met in person, over the years we have developed a friendship (a common happening on CIS). So, when it was time to write the chapter on viruses and security for this book, I was quite sure I had all the facts straight but sent it to Ross for another pair of eyes and a double check. He very kindly edited the section and returned it—at no charge.

This is by no means an uncommon example of the types of people that gather on CIS or the sense of "community" that develops or the willingness of people who are experts in their field to freely share their time and expertise.

User Groups

Okay, online is fine, but face-to-face has its place, you know? And finding a NetWare users group is the best way to get together in person with folks who are, probably more than less, your networking peers. User groups can be a very helpful place to:

→ **Network with other users**. It not only helps to know that you are not alone, but you can often find expert tips and advice.

→ **Attend vendor presentations**. Some user groups invite vendors in to make presentations, which can be very helpful in keeping up on new products and information.

Attendees at a user group can be a real mixed bag, and each group is run differently, taking on the personality of the people running it. Whether that is good or bad depends on the leaders.

Vendors and consultants attend user groups also, and a few of them have an agenda: they are trolling for new business. Most of them understand that a user group is not the place to do so, however, and are there for the same reason non-vendors are: to learn and share. Some vendors and consultants even run user groups, which is great, as long as they don't use them as a selling vehicle. Nevertheless, it is sometimes best to approach these vendor-run groups with some caution. If a vendor is ever pushy or obnoxious, let a leader of the user group know about it so that appropriate action can be taken as necessary.

If your first impression of the local group isn't favorable, attend at least one more meeting; these groups are run by people volunteering their time and resources, and they are just as harried as anyone else. A bad meeting here and there is not to be unexpected.

NetWare Users International

Novell helps to sponsor a national and international group called NetWare Users International (NUI). It is run by users, has a great deal of autonomy from Novell, and is worth checking out. Give the number a jingle and join up at 1-800-228-4NUI or call 1-801-429-7177. You can drop The Big Guy In Charge Of the Database, Brian Smith, a note at 76336,2107 to get on the list also. There is no cost or obligation when you join, and one of the benefits you will enjoy immediately is a copy of their bi-monthly publication, *The NetWare Connection.*

The NetWare Connection not only provides information about NUI activities and groups, but these people have some of the best technical talent on tap because they have an in with some of the Novell talent that other publications don't. It is what I term a "meaty" publication and well worth a browse. Each issue carries information about network management and also has at least one or two articles, many of them tutorials, targeted specifically at beginners. Another feature to be found is the Top 10 Questions and Answers received by Novell technical support. Debi Pearson, managing editor, does a superb job in pulling together a well-rounded publication. Since the publication is owned by NUI, it is not an advertising vehicle for Novell or any other vendor (although they are allowed to *purchase* advertising space).

Getting In Touch with NUI

NetWare Users International
P.O. Box 19007
Provo, UT 84605
Telephone: 1-800-228-4684
            1-801-429-7177
Fax: 801-429-3056

Searching for ...

If there is no NUI networking group near you, there are two alternatives:

➜   Check the newspaper or check with a really large local dealer for the name of the PC user group in your area. The PC User Group might have a networking Special Interest Group (SIG) that you could find out about.

➜   Start one. That's right, if you find yourself really liking this NetWare stuff, then call NUI (1-800-228-4NUI or 1-801-429-7177) and talk to them about starting a group. This organization doesn't have deep pockets, but they will be able to help you do some organization work and pay for your first meeting notice mailing. They can also help put you in touch with others in your area who have expressed an interest in an NUI group.

Don't think you have to be a NetWare wizard to run a user group or attend one. If you want to run one, it merely takes a consistent commitment of time on your part and good organizational skills. As a leader, your job is to bring the experts together, not necessarily to be one.

Leading

There are some benefits to leading, or helping to lead, a networking user group. It is a way to help you to increase your contacts with first-rate technical talent and vendors.

Let your boss know about your interest and efforts. Who knows, she might actually be impressed with the fact that you're further developing your technical and leadership skills on your own time. At least she might begin to understand that there is a trade-off between utilizing some work-time and resources with the added boost you get with the contacts and experience.

An Inside View

Another alternative to organizing or attending an outside group is to talk to the MIS department about a company-wide group. If the company you work for is really big, the network administrators can join together in enjoying not only the benefits of a regular user group, but share in company-specific problems and answers as well.

Your company may already have an internal user group in place. Check around.

Network Publications

Many top-notch publications are available at low or no cost. The "no cost" publications are available if you qualify. The exact qualification requirements are usually closely-held secrets, but it's no secret that a good way to make sure you get on the mailing list is to give yourself a promotion and ponder on the total number of PCs and networks a large company like yours really has.

There are networking publications that are not NetWare-specific, but because NetWare has the biggest market share, that is often the focus for many of the articles. Most have minitutorials on many different aspects of the networking industry and are well worth reading.

Finding the LAN Magazines

Check out the newsstand at your local book or computer store for some of the titles available. Ask your MIS department to see some of the publications they receive, check the company library (if you have one), check the local library, and ask other users at your local user group. Here are a few leading periodicals and their subscription information telephone numbers:

LAN Computing	215-957-4269
LAN Magazine	800-234-9573
LAN Technology	800-456-1654
LAN Times	415-513-6800

Network World　　　　　800-622-1108

The NetWare Connection　　　800-228-4684

In addition to vendors, publishers are also finding that it's good business to have a forum on CompuServe. They have their writers and editors online to chat with you and answer questions about stories that appear and what to expect in upcoming issues that can help guide you in making purchasing decisions. Tap into this terrific resource.

Networking Shows and Conventions

In addition to the large national networking shows such as NetWorld and Interop, call NUI to find out about regional shows that they help to organize. Some of the benefits of attending such shows are outlined in the following sections.

In a strange way it's too bad, but a lot of shows take place in Las Vegas. This is unfortunate because many bosses tend to look at conventions that take place in America's party-and-gambling capital as unproductive excuses to squander company money. However, the biggest reason that trade show organizers select Las Vegas is that the town always has adequate hotel and meeting space. The organizers of Interop, for instance, have selected Las Vegas as the site for one of the 1994 meetings over San Fransisco for that reason.

Seminars and Classes

The thing to remember about the seminars and courses offered at tradeshows is that, even though the organizers try to classify them by expertise level or area of interest, they cannot be all things to all people.

That's why it's wise to try to find a seat on the aisle. If, after the first 10 or 15 minutes, you find that the session is not addressing your expectations or needs for some reason, you can make a non-disruptive exit. This is not considered to be rude behavior in the least. It's merely an acknowledgement on your part that your time is important and can be better utilized at a different session or on the tradeshow floor.

Many people plan an alternate session to attend if the first one is not acceptable. Once again, it is not at all considered rude to be late for a session; as a matter of fact, people enter and exit freely.

Birds of a Feather

Many networking shows have what are termed "Birds of a Feather" sessions where folks interested in a specific topic can gather. Many of these tend to begin after the show floor is closed, or about 5:00 to 6:00 in the evening. These are usually more informal than a regular session or class and are more of a roundtable format with open participation encouraged. Sometimes these types of sessions are not necessarily "advertised" in the show brochure, but check at the NUI booth or with other users you might meet.

The Show Floor

Many of the national shows have *huge* show floors. It is impossible to make your way to every booth, so the best way to maximize your time is to organize yourself beforehand. List the top three or four hot spots in your current configuration. Maybe you need to select a menuing system, add a communications server, or you need a good network management tool. Whatever your needs are, here's what you do:

➜   Well before the show, leaf through technical magazines or other publications, selecting possible products and noting the product name as well as the vendor name.

TIP

Even if you do have an idea of potential vendors, do walk through the show floor looking for others. The whole point of prioritizing your needs before you attend is so that your attendance has a focus it might otherwise not have. It is very easy to get distracted (and even a little overwhelmed) when attending your first large show.

➜   When you arrive at the show, note the location of the vendor booths so that you can visit them at once.

➜   When visiting the vendor booth, take all the time you need to question the vendor, have them take you through a demonstration, and obtain business cards.

More often than not, you will find other attendees gathering around you so they, too, can hear your conversation with the vendor. Don't be embarrassed; you are more than likely asking the same questions that they have.

If a technical person or salesperson is in the middle of a demo, then sidle on up and listen to what is going on. You can pick up tips and hear the answers to the same questions that you have. Listening to other users ask questions is a terrific way to learn not only about the vendor's products, but to discern some of the important product features you might not have known about before.

After a demonstration, don't hesitate to corner another user and make further inquiries if you want to. Make it brief, but networking with other users at a networking show is what makes the entire show so valuable.

One on One

Attending a show is a great opportunity to meet the vendors you have been dealing with, especially their tech support people. Most vendors have sales-types, but they know that the only way they will sell the attendees their products is to have at least one person available to answer probing technical questions.

Take advantage of the show to meet these technical people and do your own schmoozing with them. Get them to answer all your nagging questions about their products. They are there to showcase their products anyway, so make use of their time.

If you happen to be having a bad time with a vendor's product because they won't fix a problem, you can't get through on their tech support lines, or for whatever reason, a trade show is the best time to buttonhole the vendor. Let them know what the problem with their product is, and I guarantee you, you will never be in a better position to get their ear—particularly if there are other users within earshot. Always be courteous and polite; the point is to get the problem resolved and to work through to a better relationship.

Turn the tables around and also take advantage to cement an already good relationship. If I think a vendor has really bent over backwards in working with me or my company, I do not hesitate to walk up when they are giving a demonstration to a nice-sized crowd and at the appropriate opening, let the other attendees know that I have been pleased with the product and service. You can pop out with a "That's right, they really *do* peform that well..." or "He's right, their tech support is great." After the crowd has dispersed, introduce yourself to the vendor, if they do not already know you by sight. Your vendor will love you for it and put you at the top of their "most favored customer" list. That and a buck might buy you a cup of coffee, but relationships, if you have not already guessed by now, are all important in the networking biz.

Creature Comforts

At a large national show, even if you attend plenty of sessions, you will be on your feet for long periods of time on the show floor. Wearing comfortable shoes is a *must*. Many wear tennis shoes, but at the very least, do yourself a favor and purchase an inside-the-shoe comfort sole or pad.

Most men seem to favor casual shirts (no tie) and slacks or even jeans. Women wear anything from a nice pair of slacks and a blouse to their best business suit. If combining a business suit and tennis shoes is not to your tastes, then at the very least make sure you wear flat shoes. Under no circumstances do women wear high-heels at these events.

Chapter 14, Short and Sweet

This chapter emphasized the importance of knowing where your resources are so you can get help when you need it. There is no substitute for sitting down in front of your computer and doing your own experimentation, but it is useless and wasteful to beat your head against the wall when you have problems or questions that are not in the Novell manuals or are difficult to understand.

Running a NetWare server involves far more software and hardware than just NetWare, as if that were not a complex enough topic by itself sometimes. No one is an instant expert on all aspects of running a network right away. Some of the important topics covered in this section include:

1. *No one* can run a network in a black hole. When you need help, there are many available resources.

2. People who really enjoy what they are doing like to share their knowledge. Don't hesitate to ask the experts. If a person talks too much tech, stop them and ask for further clarification. If you run into the occasional impatient-type person, then move on and find someone who will take the time to explain in terms you can understand. Everyone has to start learning somewhere.

3. Remember: ***The Only Dumb Question Is The One That Isn't Asked.***

4. Utilize your internal company resources, when and where available. The communications-type engineers have to deal with many aspects of NetWare and are great sources of information. Check with your MIS department gurus, also.

5. Maximize the conversations with technical support folks at your computer dealer, hardware, and software companies. Divert the conversation so that any nagging questions can be answered or further resources explored.

6. More and more vendors are finding that technical support forums on CompuServe are a great way to provide support for many more people than just one-on-one telephone technical support can reach. It is nearly always more cost-effective for their customers as well.

7. Novell is one of the major vendors who provide superb technical support on CompuServe. The *System Operators* (SysOps) are some of the most knowledgeable people on NetWare and related products and issues that you will ever find gathered together in one place.

8. The cost of resolving one "incident" on NetWire is approximately one tenth (conservative estimate) of the cost of resolving the same problem with Novell Technical Support.

9. The cost of regular access to the NetWire forums and other business forums on CompuServe need to be weighed with potential costs of wasted time spent troubleshooting or searching for answers in other less time-effective ways.

10. User groups can be an effective form of networking with other users who share your same questions and concerns about NetWare and administering a system.

11. NetWare Users International (NUI) has many resources, including *The NetWare Connection*, available at no charge.

12. Find one or more networking publications that suit your level of expertise and budget. Some of them sponsor forums on CompuServe where you can ask questions directly of the writers and editors and receive nearly immediate answers. Get more information on the products they review, as well as finding out more than just the information printed in the magazine.

13. Maximize your time when attending a trade show. Check out the sessions, but only stay in the ones that suit your needs. Plan your visits to product booths based on your priorities. Maximize the opportunity to make face-to-face contact with the vendors you already deal with to solidify relationships and resolve outstanding problems.

14. Wear comfortable shoes to a trade show.

E-Mail and Other Applications

(Or, Read this before Adding Stuff to Your LAN)

Electronic mail is a network application that has social and legal ramifications that go beyond the scope of a network administrator's control and authority. It doesn't matter what your position is in your company; electronic mail is an issue, as well as an application, and needs to involve the top management levels in making some basic decisions.

While electronic mail is an important application, it is not the only one, and even the most non-computer knowledgeable person can select applications by following good consumer practices.

This chapter will cover some of the highlights of electronic mail, as well as provide guidelines in evaluating, testing, and installing other applications. The topics in this chapter will include:

→ The role of electronic mail in your corporate culture

→ Some of the legal aspects of using electronic mail

→ Hints on some of the features to look for when evaluating your needs

→ Selection and testing processes you can utilize

→ Practicing good consumerism in making selections

→ Evaluating and testing products before releasing them on an unsuspecting office

Breaking Down Barriers

The key to widespread acceptance of a network in any corporation is to get the top bananas in the company hooked on electronic mail. It doesn't matter what type of business your company is in, it doesn't matter what their computer knowledge-level or background is; once they're hooked, there's no stopping the remainder of the company from following suit.

When a top executive at a company I was working at decided that he was going to use electronic mail as the main method of communication with his top level staff, I've never seen people scramble so fast to get a PC and get connected to the network. Even the most technophobic realized they needed to get connected if they were going to continue to be on "the inside track."

Within a couple of weeks, they were all using the e-mail like pros, and within a few short months, they were exploring ways to get their critical reports sent to them from other computers via the network; they otherwise began to view the network as a productivity tool as well as an excellent means to stay in touch.

In talking to hundreds of network administrators, I quickly found out that my own experience was in no way unique.

Maximizing Resources

People who utilize electronic mail (e-mail) quickly come to understand the advantages of doing so:

→   E-mail provides a non-disruptive method of communicating—no more standing around outside of people's offices while they finish up a telephone conversation or personal conversation with others to convey some quick thought.

→   E-mail's a good time-management tool. The first thing time-management courses teach is just how time-consuming those "Got a minute?" interruptions can be common in everyday corporate life. The sender and receiver can both take the time out for communication when it fits into their schedules.

→ Better communication. Because written memoranda tend to be more formal and require a little more thought to prepare, most people find that e-mail helps maintain better contact on all sorts of levels, from a status report of a project to an invitation for lunch.

→ Open communication. People tend to write e-mail the same way they speak in verbal conversation. While some situations call for careful and meticulous message composition, most people tend to be a little less formal and reserved than they are when using written memoranda. This can help foster a more open and relaxed atmosphere with company communications.

Privacy and Abuse

One of the most common issues concerning e-mail is the matter of privacy. A number of lawsuits are pending; probably one of the suits foremost in the public eye is that of Alana Shoars, who was an administrator of Epson America Inc.'s electronic mail system. Alana was assuring her users they had complete privacy, but alleges that she found out her bosses were reading messages regularly. She protested, and was fired.

On the one end of the spectrum are those who claim that since e-mail is housed on company-owned computers, the management has a right to look through the e-mail the same way they have the right to look through an employee's desk. On the other end of the spectrum are those who claim that e-mail is no different than the mail received through the U.S. Post Office, and is therefore covered under Federal privacy laws, and no one has the right to snoop.

Since no lawsuits have really been settled in this arena, it is difficult for companies to set policy. Many companies prefer to take a middle of the road approach and let their employees know that while they do not snoop at their employee's e-mail for no good reason, they do reserve the right to look at e-mail should the need arise. The e-mail does, after all, reside on corporate-owned resources and most of the business on the system is conducted during company time.

Most companies realize that if the employees feel like their every move is being watched, including their e-mail messages, productivity tends to plummet. In order to help foster an open corporate atmosphere, most management prefers to keep its nose out of e-mail unless a situation arises where it is in the best interests to do so. Some of those situations might include:

➔   Sexual harassment

➔   Threats

➔   Breaches of corporate security

➔   Abuses of e-mail

Abuse of an e-mail system might include anything from overuse for socialization purposes to utilizing the e-mail for want-ads. These types of abuses are really dependent on the size of your company and e-mail guidelines. Consider the consequences if everyone in a 4,000-person company considered want-ads a valid use of the mail system.

CYA

CYA is not a networking or computer term, but rather a commonly used acronym in most offices, meaning Cover Your A...ssets.

Part of the reason for the big flap in the Epson case is that the employees were supposedly not specifically made aware of any formal company policy concerning e-mail. Therefore, most experts agree that a policy should be formulated and included in any employee handbook or policy book that is commonly issued to employees. If there is no employee handbook, then a written letter or memorandum should be distributed.

At the very least, most experts agree that system administrators should display a brief, two- or three-line message for users to read when they first log in. Suggested wording (by the experts in the field) would include reminders that all the equipment, programs, and data on the computers belong to the company, and since they do, the company can peek at the data anytime it wants to without specific notification to anyone.

WARNING
Remember that I am a NetWare administrator, not a lawyer.
To be absolutely certain of the correct wording, your company
should consult with an attorney.

New net administrators also have a responsibility to let new e-mailers know about certain e-mail realities. Foremost among these: If you're on the net, you're in a glass house. *Never* write anything about someone you wouldn't want that person to see, because there's always a chance it'll get routed wrong, or somebody else will make a copy, or forward it, or you could space out and send it globally, or... . There are just too many ways for security to be compromised. All users on your network need to realize the importance of treating e-mail for what it is: a convenient, but very public, forum for communication.

Since a warning or reminder every time a person logs on to a system could be very stifling to open communications, and since most companies *do* like to encourage reasonably unfettered use of the e-mail system, many experts suggest that the two or three line message as mentioned in the preceding paragraph only be displayed infrequently, like once every three to six months.

Hopefully, it is clear now why electronic mail is not just a technical issue for the network administrator. In spite of some of the legal issues pending, most companies do find that electronic mail can be a terrific asset and an excellent way of providing open and free communications among employees.

To MHS or Not?

MHS stands for Message Handling Service and is a kind of messaging traffic cop that allows dissimilar mail systems to talk to each other. NetWare supports MHS. Many of the major vendors who provide e-mail programs have written their packages to work with MHS. If your company needs to communicate over dissimilar types of systems, then you will need an MHS compatible program.

A good example of using an MHS application would be the making of this book. New Riders Publishing has an MHS e-mail program. I was able to send them both electronic mail and chapters of the book over Compu-Serve because CompuServe has an MHS gateway. I only had to make a telephone call to my local CompuServe node, not a long-distance one, and dial directly into New Riders' e-mail system to send them messages and chapters. In other words, I don't know or care what type of e-mail program they have, except that it handles MHS mail. I was just using my normal CompuServe programs to compose, send, and read e-mail.

Some vendors don't use the MHS stuff in their programs, and it works just fine. Whether or not you need an MHS-compatible program is really up to your particular needs and applications.

Remember that MHS is not a stand-alone program that you actually run, it's a messaging engine.

NetWare 3.12 includes a new Basic Services MHS right in the core NetWare operating system. Unless you are running in a multi-server network, where you might need Global MHS, Basic MHS should do the trick for you.

Electronic Tidbits

Since e-mail can so quickly become an application in widespread use around your company (in some cases, the *only* application used), it is really important that your selection process is the most thorough and intensive of all your applications.

The reason you must be so careful in the selection process is because once in use, for even a short amount of time, the users on your system will soon find that their use is automatic and resistance to change will be great. Once users get comfortable with an application, it's tough to get them to accept an alternative, no matter how much better it is.

NOTE
Although NetWare 3.12 includes a basic mail program called First Mail, Novell claims that it is not meant to be a competitor to the providers of commercial e-mail applications. Therefore, if you are a first-time mail user, you may want to try it on for size, but only on a temporary basis to test-drive, and as an aid in deciding what you might want to look for in a heavy-duty application. If it meets all your messaging needs and you don't anticipate any growth, then by all means, stay with it. At the very least, however, you and your management might find it worth your while to look at a demonstration or three of third-party applications.

Electronic mail is not the simple application that it might sound like at first. There are a number of choices and options available and some of the features you may want to ask about include:

→ Does the e-mail program match the operating environment (or environments) you are using (DOS, OS/2, Windows, Macintosh, or a combination of several)?

→ Users have to be added to an e-mail database, there are usually mailing lists to be maintained, and users will need training. How much administrative attention does the e-mail package require?

→ What does it take to connect your local e-mail system to other systems, locally or in other cities? Can these connections be set up by mere mortals or will you need to hire an e-mail communications guru to get things working?

→ Does the program have the capability to exchange mail with other platforms, like Macintosh or Unix? If not, are there modules available that must be purchased at an additional cost?

→ Does the e-mail system require that a completely separate database of users, privileges, and access be created and administered; or, can it use the NetWare Bindery files?

→ Users frequently want to attach files to their messages. That makes it possible to send programs, graphics, and documents by e-mail. How about ease of use for sending attachments with e-mail messages? Are there any length limitations of the attachments? Are there any format-type limitations?

→ How about address books, both common and individual? How easy is it to create "mailing lists" for mass mailings?

→ What about when someone sends the exact same message to all the users? Are individual copies of the messages made and sent to each user's mail box (taking up tons of disk space) or is only one copy sent and each user receives a header only?

→ How about remote access capability? If you have lots of people on the road who need to check their e-mail frequently, then a remote access program can be a big asset.

These are only the tip of the iceberg, but a mail system really needs to be chosen based on each company's needs. If attachments (copies of other mail to forward, a WordPerfect letter, and so on), for instance, are only rarely used, then that is a feature you can put at the bottom of your priority list.

Testing 1, 2, 3...

Once you have found at least two, preferably three, e-mail applications that look good on paper, it's time to test each of them out. Most vendors understand that e-mail is a large, and fairly permanent, purchase, and if they don't allow you an evaluation copy to install on your network, then don't bother with them.

Allow plenty of time for installation and testing of each package. It is not uncommon for a corporation to take three or four months to make its final selection, testing and using each package for a month each. As a matter of fact, it is highly recommended. Test each package for ease of use, ease of administration, and other criteria as suggested earlier.

Some companies limit the access of the e-mail during the testing phase to a small, select group, but you may want to open up the testing to everyone in your department or company. Since one person cannot exercise all the options or put the program through its paces properly, at least four or five people should help with the evaluation process.

This also helps bring out what's called "The Beta Monkey Factor." Any system is usually more vulnerable to assaults that nitwits inadvertently bring upon that system. Let some e-mail idiots try to crash the program. If it's idiot-proof, you may have the e-mail that'll work for you. (Also called "Lowest Common Denominator administering.")

It's Final!

When it is time to open up use of the e-mail system to everyone in your department or company, don't just say "Okay, you all have e-mail now. Go for it!" No matter how short the manual is that is provided by the vendor, you can be guaranteed that your users will not read it. Most vendors do provide a "quick reference" type card, but that will not be complete enough for the beginning users to follow.

Users will look at a one-page summary sheet, not longer. Summarize the key features in a covering memo if you like, but write up a one-page instruction sheet. Organize it according to features, something like:

To Read Mail:

1. *Log into the network.*

2. *Select e-mail from the menu (or provide the appropriate command).*

3. *Press this key.*

4. *Make that selection.*

5. *If you want to save the message, do such and such.*

   Blah, blah.

To Reply to Mail:

1. *While the mail is on your screen, press "R" for reply.*

2. *You will see the editing screen; now you are ready to type your message.*

3. *When finished, press this or that key.*

   Blah, blah.

To Compose and Send Mail:

1. *Log onto the network.*

2. *Select e-mail from the menu (or provide the appropriate command).*

3. *Press this key to bring up the editing screen.*

4. *Compose your message. A brief list of editing commands is provided below.*

5. *To send to more than one user, do this and that.*

   Blah, blah.

Basic Editing Commands:

ERASE: *Backspace to erase characters. Blah, blah.*

MOVING: *First block word or phrase to move by
positioning cursor, blah, blah.*

Blah, blah.

You might be chuckling to yourself about the suggested instructions. Don't.
Remember that some of your users are very likely to be technologically
naive, and will need step-by-step instructions. Just because people are bright
in one area doesn't mean they understand something completely new to
them in a different area. Don't embarrass them by making them come to you
and ask questions because you haven't provided enough information. If you
do have "Quick Reference" cards to hand out, then attach them to your
instructions. Most people will put the quick reference cards in their desk
drawer and follow your instruction summary sheet.

Before you pass around your summary sheets and instructions, compose
and mail everyone a message so that they have one waiting in their mail box
when they log into the system for the first time. Tell them the vendor and
product name, let them know you have passed out instructions and extra
copies are available if they don't have one, and so on.

Other Applications

The time you spend selecting and testing other applications will depend on
the application and its complexity. A successful installation and introduction
of a product to your users will depend on how thorough your evaluation and
testing criteria is.

Making a List and Checking it Twice

Most companies follow a decision-making process similar to the one outlined
below:

Each product in the same category will have similar features, but you need
to find the one that best suits your needs. Reading reviews in computer
publications might be a good place to start, but never select a product
blindly from a magazine. Their selection criteria might be exactly opposite of
your own.

Several years ago, a leading computer publication carried an article on communications products, having tested and run each of them in their labs. The product that our group had chosen for our communication needs was the one that received the worst rating in the article. Why? Because that product didn't offer very many configuration choices— which was the exact reason we had selected it. Our users were not very sophisticated in some cases, and the simple configuration screen is what tipped the scales into making it the perfect product for our needs.

One of the things you will need to do is to follow a procedure similar to the following:

1. If you are not sure what features to look for in any particular class of application, begin by collecting sales brochures on each. Some companies have a demonstration disk that shows off the package's best features. Collect several brochures and demo disks from different companies.

2. After looking the sales material over, sit down and make a list of the features that you think should be considered in your selection criteria that apply to all the products offered.

3. Give each feature a number that signifies the importance of the feature. For instance, 1 would signify the feature is of little importance and 10 would indicate it is of high importance.

4. Now select the top four products that have the features you have decided are important.

5. Work with the vendors in obtaining evaluation copies of the software if possible, or work with your computer dealer or consultant.

6. Test each product against your list of desired features, noting how well it performs each task.

7. Invite others within your company to help finalize the decision between the top two contenders, if necessary or if possible.

Testing

Once you have chosen the product, it is not necessarily appropriate to install it on your server and make it available to everyone in the office all at once. Make sure that you understand the program thoroughly. The really important part is that you understand how it integrates with NetWare. What permissions do your users need to access the program and appropriate files? Remember, the fewer the rights, the more secure your server will be, but don't be unnecessarily stingy.

The best thing to do is to explore the NetWare rights your users will need by creating a make-believe user and giving it the permissions that you think will be needed. Log in as that user and exercise the application. More than one NetWare Supervisor has been surprised by not following this important step and then having hoards of angry users call when they cannot access the program the Supervisor said they could. Naturally, this has never happened to me (she said with a straight face).

Partial Release

Once you are sure that the application is ready for general use, it is not necessarily time to release it on an unsuspecting office. If possible, make it available to a small number of users (maybe half a dozen or so) and ask for their feedback. Make note of their questions or problems. Perhaps you need to limit or increase choices, access, or whatever. In other words, refine the installation.

Cheat Sheets

When you are ready to make an application available for widespread use from the NetWare server, take the time to make a cheat sheet for everyone. Base some of the items in your sheet on the feedback you received from those who have tested the application.

TIP

It is important that you remember that while your users might be very knowledgeable in their field of expertise, they might need a helping hand when it comes to utilizing the applications on the fileserver. By anticipating—and answering—the most basic questions on a cheat sheet, you will be able to minimize the support headaches inherent in introducing a new application on the network. Your users will really appreciate the extra care that you take.

Never let the cheat sheet get longer than one page. The cheat sheet is not meant to be a replacement for the manual, nor a supplement, but merely a quick reminder of the key steps and commands.

Ready for Release

Once you are thoroughly prepared, use your e-mail to announce the availability of the product. Name the product, brand, purpose, and include a very brief overview of its key features. Let everyone know you have the cheat sheets available. If your users are comfy with e-mail, attach the cheat sheets so they can have them available in their directories or print them as needed.

Conflicts

Never try installing more than one application on your server at one time. If problems arise, you will never be able to be quite sure which program is causing problems, or which one might be conflicting with NetWare, and chances are that you'll end up gray or bald or both within a very short time.

Let the application "settle down" for a few weeks before installing your next one. A month is not too long. If the program is heavily used, then two weeks might be adequate—but barely. With the complexity of applications these days, it often takes awhile before some little feature is used that might be the snag that reveals problems.

If you do experience any problems, follow the techniques outlined in Chapter 13, "Troubleshooting." Probably the most important concept in tracking down problems is that you never change more than one parameter at one time. You might be surprised at the number of times you change one small thing and shazam!—it works!—and you maybe aren't quite sure why. Patience is really the key here.

Chapter 15, Short and Sweet

This chapter should help you in understanding and using some of the keys to success in running a network. Some of the points in this chapter included:

1. Wide acceptance of the network in any department or company will happen the day the top executives discover electronic mail (e-mail).

2. E-mail is an excellent time-management tool. It saves the time of all parties and eliminates those pesky interruptions. "Got a minute?" should become words of the past in your office.

3. E-mail can help draw a company together with better—and maybe less formal—communications.

4. There are a few sticky legal issues involved in utilizing e-mail that need to be addressed. Namely: privacy. Make sure everyone understands the ground rules of utilizing this important resource.

5. Message Handling Service (MHS) is a messaging engine (not an application), supported by Novell's NetWare. If your company needs to communicate over diverse platforms, MHS might be a good thing to look for when looking at e-mail products.

6. Learn how to write a good cheat sheet. It will save you valuable time in supporting your users and they'll thank you for it. Be basic. Be brief.

7. No one needs to be a computer wizard to be a good consumer of computer products. Utilize the same techniques you do when making any other purchase:

   → Look to publications for ideas and leads—not selections

   → Look at your options from many vendors

   → Decide what features are important

   → Rate the features

   → Make your selection

8. Most vendors make evaluation copies available to their potential customers. After all, you wouldn't buy a car without a test-drive.

9. Test the application on your fileserver for functionality and also the rights the users will need to run it.

10. If possible, allow a small group of users access to the application before releasing it on an unsuspecting office. Make adjustments as needed.

11. Never try installing more than one application at a time on the server. Make sure that you allow plenty of settling in time to get all the kinks out.

Actually Installing Applications

(Or, Don't Panic! It's Only NetWare!)

"I'd rather go to the dentist and have a root canal without anesthetic than install [product x] on my LAN," are words that have been muttered by more than one NetWare administrator.

Not all products are that difficult to install on NetWare, but installing software on a LAN is not a walk in the park. This chapter will cover some of the common issues of installing applications on NetWare such as:

→ Preplanning your application installation

→ File permission considerations for data

→ How to test and release the application for general use

Installing an application on a NetWare fileserver is more complicated than installing on a stand-alone computer, but this chapter will give you some heads up tips to follow and look for when you do so.

Copyright Issues

Before you touch that dial, make sure you read and understand the license that comes with your software. Each one is different. While some NetWare application software takes care of monitoring the number of concurrent users, others do not. If you have some applications that do not monitor the number of concurrent users, you need to look into utilities that do. There are several commercial programs available that will do that for you.

NOTE

Remember that violating software licenses is stealing. You can place yourself and your company in serious jeopardy if the software license agreement that comes with your application is not followed correctly.

Why Is It More Complex?

Many new administrators don't stop to think twice about installing an application on a network—they are used to a 10- or 20-minute software installation on a stand-alone PC. After all, you just have to insert the installation disk(s) in Drive A:, type **A:INSTALL** and all the files install, your CONFIG.SYS and AUTOEXEC.BAT files are changed automatically, and you're set to jet.

The reason it is more complex on a fileserver is because the drive letter designations are not fixed (nor should they be), the installation program cannot make changes to the system login script, and the application can make no assumptions about where it resides on the hard disk drive, and where it might be able to find some of the files it depends on to run. It's up to the system administrator to pull all the pieces together to make it work and set things up for the users to run the programs easily.

Here's a little advice: don't sit down to install an application on your fileserver at noon on Friday. For all but the simplest utility, you should allow yourself the better part of a day and sometimes even a few days to install an application and get it up and running properly. The next section explains why.

Application Installation Preplanning

Installing an application involves more than just putting the installation disk in the disk drive and typing A:INSTALL. Before you even touch the first disk, you need to plan out the installation as follows:

1. Does the application support the hardware and software that you want to use? That includes things like the processing power and video displays of all the workstations it will run on; your printers or other peripheral equipment that may be applicable (modems, plotters, etc.); correct DOS versions, and so on.

WARNING

Two compatibility issues that you need to be absolutely sure about are the version of NetWare that you are using and the DOS brand and version(s) you are using. If the application uses the NetWare Bindery files, it could be version-specific. While Novell's DOS product is a fine DOS, most application developers use Microsoft's MS-DOS or IBM's PC-DOS to develop and test their applications. If there are any glitches in using another DOS product, they may just point fingers and not support another brand of DOS. Make sure you know before you install.

2. Have you planned the volume and directory locations for the new software so as to keep the security of your network intact? You want to make sure that you aren't planning on putting it on a volume or in a directory where you have limited access to general users and it just so happens the application will be in use by everyone. Conversely, you don't want to put the new payroll program in the same place you put the applications for use by the whole office, since the payroll program will be running sensitive data.

3. Have you read the installation instructions thoroughly? Make sure you understand what the instructions call for in terms of mapping search drives and drive mappings. How about what permissions users need to access directories where some of the files will reside? Do you need to set up any additional print queues? These are all questions you need to make sure you understand before you start.

4. Plan any changes to individual User and Group Trustee rights. Remember that if two or more people need the same permissions to the same directories, set up a Group in the SYSCON utility and grant permissions that way. The application may call for granting rights at the file level also.

5. Plan any changes to the Login Scripts. Hopefully, you won't need to make changes to existing commands in either the System Login Script or any individual User Login Scripts in order to provide proper search and drive mappings or any other settings required by the application.

   If you need to make changes to the System Login Script, don't forget the usage of the IF statement, i.e., "IF MEMBER OF *xxx* THEN ...," where *xxx* represents the name of the group. You can take actions such as mapping, displaying a special menu, and so on, for any particular group.

6. Changing menus or even restructuring needs to be taken into account. If you are using a menu system for your users, plan the menus for common groupings and ease of use. Sometimes an additional application may push you into a two-level menu because you have too many selections for one screen.

7. Anticipate other system changes. The application might be something where you want to think about making someone a Workgroup Manager or Queue Operator; giving someone else administrative authority for that directory or queue or whatever.

Installing

Now that you have planned ahead as much as possible, it's time to install the application. Nearly all application instructions require that you be logged in as the Supervisor because, as the installation proceeds, directories need to be made and sometimes access to the Bindery file is required.

Some application installations may try to change your System settings, such as the System Login Script or AUTOEXEC file. Before you blindly accept the changes, make a note of what is happening so that you can go back and make any adjustments that might need to be made.

It is always a good idea to watch the installation as it proceeds, with a pencil and paper handy so that you can make any quick notes that might be needed. There are those occasionally sneaky installation programs that might make changes that could cause problems with another application that you may be running. Pay attention.

Testing

Once the program is installed, it's time to give it some exercise. The first thing to watch out for are the file attributes. When new files are installed on NetWare, the default attributes are non-shareable and read/write. To change the file attributes, you can use either the command line FLAG utility or the FILER menu utility.

NOTE

All data files that will be shared by several simultaneous users must be marked shareable. This includes any files used by a database program that will be shared. Some data files are held open as long as a user is using an application. If a user opens a non-shareable data file it usually becomes unavailable to other users. (Some NetWare-aware applications will let additional users open the files for inspection but not to save them. You don't want someone else modifying a file while you're modifying it do you?)

If users will be modifying data files (word processing documents, spreadsheets, database files, etc.) be sure you don't accidentally flag the files as Read Only. Some programs automatically modify files behind the scenes. For example, Windows maintains several .INI files that contain users' Windows settings. Be sure these files aren't accidentally flagged as Read Only.

Program files don't usually need to be marked shareable. A program file (.COM or .EXE) is only open during the time it is initially run on the workstation (for example, in the moments after the user types the commands to start the application). It is then closed by NetWare and becomes available for other users.

However, program files should usually be marked Read Only. That way, if you goof and give a user Delete privileges in a program directory, the user won't be able to delete the file by accident (to be charitable). If you don't let users have the Modify right in the directory, they won't be able to change the flag to Read Write.

Because your users will not be logged in as Supervisor when running the application, create a temporary user with the same Trustee Assignments that the users will have and test. Allow plenty of time for this process so that you can exercise the major aspects of the application's functionality. You may want to ask the help of a coworker who is more familiar with the programs features than you are.

The next step is to log into two workstations as two separate test users simultaneously. Some problems that don't crop up with one user are likely to surface with two or more users. Once again, hit all the high points of the program.

Cheat Sheets

If applicable, don't forget to make up the cheat sheets as covered in Chapter 15. That type of preparedness is likely to save you many support headaches. To review, the successful cheat sheet will:

➡   Include step-by-step instructions

➡   Include an abbreviated command summary

➡   Be no longer than one page

Distribution

Once you are sure you know the application is functioning correctly, it is time to release it on an unsuspecting office. Make sure you allow extra time in your schedule for the inevitable slew of questions you will receive as the people in your office get acquainted with the new application. If your own work is pressing and you are running up against some serious deadlines, it is best to wait a day or so to make the application available to everyone until your time is freed up.

Database Applications

Database applications are a different animal than most software applications that you will run on your network. Entire books are devoted to that one subject, but when planning a database on your network, there is one major

consideration to be taken into account. That is whether you will go with a
fileserver-based or a database server-based application.

Fileserver Databases

Don't forget that the way programs run on a NetWare server is that the
fileserver itself is only the resting place for your applications and data. When
the application is run, the entire program is shipped to the workstation
along with the data file that is being worked with.

Consider what happens when a database with thousands of records is used
on a fileserver. The database application is shipped to the workstation along
with a humongous file, even if only one tiny record needs to be worked on or
used. Even one active database user can slow the performance for the other
network users down to a crawl, and if several people are using the database
application, it could bring the network to its knees. In network nerdy lingo,
that's called "choking."

Database Servers

Some databases are made to run on a database server. That means that you
can set up another computer devoted to nothing else except running the
database. In some cases, you can utilize your fileserver as the database
server, and combine the two functions into one PC-based computer.

A database server-based application is made so that the database functions
are performed on the server instead of the workstation. Instead of shipping
one humongous file over the wire, only the necessary record gets shipped.
Obviously, this prevents the entire network from getting choked because
there is considerably less traffic on the wire.

The type of database application you need is really determined by the
number of records and the activity in the database.

Other Database Considerations

A couple of other considerations when selecting a network database include
automated backout, recovery, and multiple user access.

Transaction Tracking

NetWare includes an installation option called TTS or Transaction Tracking Services. That means that if you are running a database application *that supports NetWare's Transaction Tracking Services*, and your system experiences a sudden power failure or other type of ungraceful crash, your database can recover from the disaster. In other words, a log is made of the transaction so that an incomplete transaction can be backed out and the integrity of your database will be intact when power is restored and the TTS has a chance to work.

Locking

When looking at database applications, it's important to consider multiple user access. Does it support record and file locking so that if one user has the database open and is making changes, another user cannot have the same file or record open and write over the first user's changes? You want to be sure to look at the features of database applications closely when running them on a network.

Chapter 16, Short and Sweet

This chapter touched on some of the things to consider when installing applications on a NetWare network. Every application and installation is different and it's impossible to cover them all, but it's important to follow some basic steps:

1. Installing an application on a network is not the same as installing on a stand-alone computer. On a stand-alone computer, it is easy for the installation program to make certain assumptions about location of files and make changes to the CONFIG.SYS and AUTOEXEC.BAT. That can't (or shouldn't) be done with a network installation.

2. It is important to read and understand the licensing agreement that comes with the applications you install anywhere, and especially on a network.

3. Even though NetWare doesn't care what brand or version of DOS your workstations are running, some application programs do. Make sure you find out if the application is picky before you install by checking with the manufacturer of the application.

4. Some of the pre-planning steps you need to take before installing your applications include:

→   Planning volume and/or directory location for security aspects.

→   Planning menu changes (if applicable).

→   Making sure you know about drive and search mappings that need to be modified and how they might affect the current settings.

→   Look for changes to Trustee Assignments. Plan additional Groups where appropriate.

→   Look for and plan other system changes that might be appropriate: Workgroup Managers, Queue Operators, and so on.

5.   Program files should usually be flagged as Read Only.

6.   Data files that users will share should usually be flagged as Share-able Read Write.

7.   Test the application before making it available to the rest of the users of the network:

    a. Run the application as Supervisor;

    b. Add a user for testing permissions with the same Trustee Assignments that the regular users will have;

    c. Test with two different userid's on two workstations simultaneously.

8.   Make cheat sheets for distribution to reduce your support load.

9.   Even with cheat sheets, you can anticipate plenty of questions and hand-holding requests from your users upon release. Make room in your schedule appropriately.

10.   Database applications are different animals on a network. Some things to look at are whether your application needs a database server or can be fileserver based.

11.   Make sure the database accounts for multiple users so that proper file and record locking (and even field locking) are done to maintain the integrity of your database.

12.   Some database applications support Novell's TTS, or Transaction Tracking Services.

Glossary

A

Address. A unique value identifying a location of a node, network, or position in memory.

Application layer. The seventh layer of the OSI Reference Model. It's at this level that software for messaging and the fileserver runs.

ARCnet. Attached Resource Computer NETwork. A network transport technology. Data is transferred at 2.5 megabits per second. See Ethernet.

ASCII (American Standard Code for Information Interchange). A standard data communications code defined by ANSI (American National Standards Institute). This code is used by most computer manufacturers to enable their devices to communicate with different brands of equipment.

B

Back-end. A system that provides services for another system. Often the same as a server.

Backbone. A network system used to interconnect a group of fileservers.

Balun. In wiring, an attachment that matches the electrical characteristics of two separate and different pieces of cable.

Baseband. A form of transmission in which the entire bandwidth of a channel is devoted to one signal.

Baseline. Measurements recorded to provide a point of reference. Generally baseline measurements are taken when a network is functioning well so that the figures can be compared when performance problems are encountered.

Baud. The signaling rate unit for analog communications. The measure of one baud is equal to one change of state per second.

Binary. A method of representing information in terms of two possible states. Binary numbering systems use digits with values of 1 and 0.

Bit. A binary digit having the value of either 1 or 0.

Bits/s. Bits per second.

Bottleneck. A point within communication where the data flow is at its weakest.

Bps. Bytes per second.

bps. Bits per second

Bridge. A device that functions at the data link level to connect multiple networks into an internetwork. Bridges usually interconnect networks that are similar with regard to topologies and access methods.

Broadband. A transmission medium that has capabilities of carrying multiple signals simultaneously.

Buffer. Memory allocated for the temporary storage of incoming and outgoing data.

Bus. A configuration that enables multiple devices to communicate through a common channel.

Byte. A group of eight bits addressed as a unit. Memory in most computers is organized in terms of bytes.

C

Carrier-Sense Multiple Access/Collision Detection (CSMA/CD). A transmission method used on networks that enables only one carrier on the line at a time.

Client-Server. The relationship between a service supplier (such as a dedicated fileserver) and a consumer (such as a network workstation) of that service in a network environment.

Coaxial cable. Cable consisting of a center conductor surrounded by a braided tubular conductor of uniform diameter.

Compact Disc Read-Only Memory (CD-ROM). A computer drive that stores large amounts of data in a format virtually the same as an audio CD.

Connectivity. Logical or physical connection between network workstations.

CPS (characters per second). The number of characters transmitted electronically per second.

CPU (central processing unit). The device in which data processing occurs within a computer system.

D

Daisy chain. Networking configuration, or topology, in which each workstation is joined on either side by two more workstations. This, of course, doesn't apply to computers on the end of a daisy chain. Also used as a verb to describe setting up this topology.

Data communications. The transmission of data from one network workstation to another.

Data link layer. The second layer of the OSI model. This layer compiles messages and manages their flow between computers.

Data packet. A logically assembled group of data.

Dedicated fileserver. A computer used solely for the purpose of managing workstation files on a network.

Demodulation. The conversion of analog to digital signal.

Disk caching. Where data is stored in memory, rather than on disk, to decrease access time.

Disk crash. Failure of the hard disk. Literally, failure of a hard disk drive when the read/write heads come into contact with, and damage, the disk media.

Disk server. A mass storage device capable of sharing its resources.

Duplexed drives. Twin hard disk drives, on which the contents are maintained in an identical state and are located on separate disk controllers.

E

EISA (Extended Industry Standard Architecture). A 32-bit PC bus architecture compatible with the ISA standard.

Electronic mail. Sending messages through a network of computers, primarily as a form of interpersonal communication.

Enterprise network. A network that brings all sites together through a communications medium.

Ethernet. A network transport technology that transfers data at 10 megabits per second and uses CSMA/CD access control. (See CSMA/CD.)

F

Fiber optics. Glass fibers through which light-signal data is passed. Also refers to the field embraced by this technology.

Fileserver. A computer system enabling the sharing of files from one source to many.

Flag. A bit commonly used for specifying a true or false condition.

Front-end. A system or client that uses the services of another system.

G

Gateway. A network node that operates as an interface between different network types, such as a NetWare LAN to an SNA (Systems Network Architecture) network.

Global network. A network extending between countries or even continents.

Groupware. Software used by many different users to facilitate group project coordination and communication.

GUI (graphical user interface). A computer screen display format that enables the user to carry out actions by electronically pointing at pictorial icons and menu lists.

H

Hub. A centralized point on a network through which all traffic flows.

I

IEEE (Institute of Electronic and Electrical Engineers). A committee creating standards for interfaces and LAN protocols.

Interface. A device that enables communications between multiple devices.

IPX (Internetwork Packet Exchange). Novell's datagram service.

ISA (Industry Standard Architecture). A widely used 16-bit PC bus architecture.

L

LAN (Local Area Network). Computers connected together through various types of media, sharing files, and peripherals. See WAN.

LANtastic. Artisoft's popular peer-to-peer network operating system.

Logical drive. A PC drive that is mapped to a device such as a hard disk.

Login name. The name a user enters that identifies the user to the system.

M

MAU (Media Access Unit). A device used as a center for wiring networks together. See Hub.

Message. An ordered collection of data in a form that can be processed by a receiver.

Message switching. A process in which messages are stored at one or more intermediate points between sender and receiver.

Middleware. Software that works between a client and a server.

Mirrored drives. Two hard drives with identically maintained contents, located on the same disk controller. See Duplexed drives.

Modem. From MOdulator/DEModulator. A DCE (data circuit terminating equipment) used to connect a DTE (data terminal equipment) to an analog communications circuit. This converts the DTE's digital signal to analog form for transmission and converts the received analog signals from analog circuit to digital.

N

NDS (NetWare Directory Services). The distributed directory service for Novell's NetWare 4.0.

NETBIOS. Network Basic Input/Output System. A standard for supporting network communications that is independent of the underlying network transport type.

NetWare. The popular fileserver network system created by Novell.

NetWare Lite. Novell's peer-to-peer network operating system.

Network adapter card. See next entry (NIC).

Network interface card (NIC). A computer board that enables computers to be connected to media for communication between stations.

Network layer. The third layer of the OSI Reference Model; the network layer controls message traffic.

Node. Any computer, modem, printer, and so on, that is connected to a network.

Non-dedicated server. A fileserver that also can be used as a workstation. See Dedicated fileserver.

O

Online. A description for an accessible, operational PC or fileserver.

OSI (Open System Interconnection) Reference Model. A reference to a model used for creating standards for today's computer communications. This model is an architecture that divides communications into seven structured layers.

P

Peer-to-peer network. A network system that enables computers to be both fileservers and workstation/clients.

Peripheral device. An attached device on a computer system for mass storage or for data output such as printing.

Physical layer. The first layer of the OSI Reference Model. This layer manages the transfer of individual bits of data over the interactive means (cabling, for instance) connecting the computers.

Point-to-point. Data-link supporting direct communication between the two devices.

Port. A point at which a device can be connected to a computer.

Presentation layer. The sixth layer of the OSI Reference Model. Data formatting and translating is performed here for the Application layer.

Proprietary. Something created under the impression that it will be used for only one specific purpose, with specific equipment.

Protocol. An agreement between parties on a format and sequence of control messages to be exchanged between the parties.

Protocol suite. Differing protocols based on a common architecture.

R

RAM (Random-Access Memory). The data storage area that holds data only while the PC's power is on.

Record. A fixed, defined block of data in a file.

Remote booting. Downloading to a PC the programs and data needed to initialize and execute the computer's operating system and network connection.

Remote workstation. A computer that is used to dial into a LAN, but is not connected to that LAN on a full-time basis.

Ring. A network topology that joins each computer to those on either side to form a closed circle.

ROM (Read-Only Memory). Memory that has data stored in it before it was placed in the computer. In most circumstances, the data contents of ROM cannot be changed.

RTFM (Read The F**** Manual).** A networking term most commonly used in technical support circles. Usually used as sarcastic response to questions whose answers are obvious (at least to one of the parties).

S

Session. A temporary logical connection between two network-addressable units.

Session layer. The fifth layer of the OSI Reference Model. This is responsible for the security and administrative tasks of communicating.

SFT (System Fault Tolerance). The capability of a system (particularly a Novell system) to avoid and correct errors. Novell systems have three levels of SFT in their operating systems.

Shell. A software module that intercepts requests from programs to access data and services and sends them to a network server, if required.

Shielded twisted pair. Twisted-pair cable surrounded by a special shielding, usually metallic or foil.

Signal splitting device. A device on the network that takes a signal and splits it to be sent to multiple destinations.

Star. A network topology that has all communicating computers interact through a central computer.

Street price. As compared to manufacturer's suggested retail price, the street price is the usually heavily discounted sale price that hardware and software retailers actually charge for products.

System 7. The operating system used for Apple's Macintosh computers. This includes built-in peer-to-peer networking for all models.

T

T-connector. A piece of hardware used to connect coaxial cable to a network interface card on a linear bus topology.

TCP/IP (Transmission Control Protocol/Internet Protocol). A protocol introduced in the early 1970s by the U.S. Department of Defense (DOD) for interconnection of DOD networks. Still widely used today on the Internet.

Terminator. A hardware device used for termination on both ends of a linear bus cable system.

Thick Ethernet. A cabling system for Ethernet that uses a heavyweight coaxial cable.

Thin Ethernet. A cabling system for Ethernet that uses a light coaxial cable.

Throughput. Productivity measurement for a network, computers, and their drives.

Time-sharing. The capability of multiple users to share computer resources from one common source.

Token. A special message that signifies that the possessor has the right to send messages on a network system.

Token Ring. A network transport technology that can transfer data at either 4 or 16 megabits per second. See ARCnet, Ethernet.

Token passing. A protocol used to coordinate network access.

Topology. The way a network can be configured or laid out.

Transport layer. The fourth layer of the OSI Reference Model, responsible for error checking and correction, and limited message flow control.

Tree. A network topology that enables computers to be attached to other computers in a branching structure.

Twisted pair. Cable consisting of one or more parallel sets of two insulated wires twisted together.

U

Upload. Client-initiated transfer of data to the server. What you do when you send a file from your PC to another. See Downloading.

V

VINES. Banyan's popular fileserver system. It stands for VIrtual NEtwork System.

Virtual machine. Having one computer work as if it were several computers.

W

WAN (Wide Area Network). A large network typically connecting multiple LANs and MANs (Metropolitan Area Networks) together. See LAN.

Workstation. A personal computer that has a network interface card and is connected to a network.

Worm. A form of computer virus that replicates itself insidiously.

Adding Workstations

There are two parts to adding a workstation to the network: physically connecting the machine and setting up the NetWare shell or redirector. The physical addition of the workstation is generic across the platform of clients that NetWare supports including PC–compatibles running MS or DR DOS with or without Windows, as well as OS/2, Macintosh, and Unix workstations.

Step-by-Step

When adding a computer to the network the first thing that needs to be done is to assemble the parts. Here is what you will need:

1. Your stand-alone PC that will function as the workstation.

2. The Network Interface Card (NIC).

3. The disk marked Client Workstation Drivers from your big, red Novell box.

To turn all these parts into a workstation, the basic steps will be:

1. Set the configuration on the NIC. Some are set by little jumpers or switches on the board, others with software, and others are a combination. If there are little jumpers or switches on your card, you will need to set those before installing the NIC in the workstation. All software settings are made after the card is installed.

2. Grasping screwdriver firmly in hand, take the cover off the PC (make sure it's unplugged!).

3. Most free slots will have a small plate over the back of the PC so that dust and dirt cannot get inside. Remove the cover plate.

4. Grasping the card firmly, insert it into the matching slot on the PC. Press down firmly. Nerdy types call it "seating" the card in the machine. Make sure you use the lock screw that held the cover plate in place to hold the NIC in place.

5. Slide the cover back on the machine, but wait to replace all the cover screws until you are sure the card works.

6. Next, plug in the network cable connector to the back of the NIC.

7. Make sure the power cord is back in the computer and that the monitor and keyboard are attached, then turn it on.

8. When you are sure all the hardware is running correctly you are ready to install the NetWare LAN Drivers and shell.

When adding an NIC to a PC workstation, the things you have to be concerned about are the interrupts used, the shared memory address the card may use, and the I/O Addresses the card may use. Before going much further, it's necessary to understand at some level what each of these are.

Interrupts

Interrupts are the signal lines that a computer uses to signal the CPU that it wants to do something or that it's ready to do something. Most, but not all, devices use an interrupt to operate in a PC.

Once an interface device has signaled the CPU that it wants to do something, it has to have some means of transferring data from the computer to the adapter or vice versa. The data transfer can be accomplished in one of several ways:

→   Shared Memory Transfer

→   Programmed I/O (PIO) Mode

→   Bus Mastering or DMA Direct Memory Transfer

Each method offers benefits and drawbacks as compared to any other method. While some methods function together, most often the adapter manufacturers configure the adapter to use one primary method of data transfer. So, as a slight overview of the technology, let's review how each works.

Shared Memory Transfer

In this method of data transfer, the adapter card overlays some area of the computer's Upper Memory Blocks (UMB), which is the BIOS/ROM memory area above the DOS 640K limit and below the 1M mark (Memory addresses A000:0 through FFFF:F). This is the same memory space that Video Adapters and Disk Controllers use to store their BIOS and memory addresses. Network Adapters using this memory area will use anywhere between 8K and 64K of address space. Examples are, at the low end, the 3Com Etherlink II Ethernet adapter, which uses an 8K shared memory space and, at the high end, the SMC PC 100 ARCnet Adapter, which uses a 64K shared memory space (frame).

What happens is that when the adapter card is ready to accept or send data to the PC, the adapter fills some or all of its buffer and then transfers that data as a single chunk to the PC's CPU so that it can move it to some RAM memory address space. This method of data transfer is very good for slower adapter cards since it can move large amounts of data at one time. However, it is a rather inefficient method of moving data if the amount of data to be transferred is consistantly less than the size of the shared memory space.

Programmed I/O

In this method of data transfer, the adapter card opens a small window to the PC's CPU and streams the data from the adapter to the PC in bursts of small chunks. The I/O Window is usually some space between 4 and 64 bytes in size. When the adapter card is ready to transfer data, it just opens the window and starts pushing data from its buffer into the PC.

This method of data transfer can be very fast for moving small amounts of data consistently, but can be inefficient when having to move large amounts of data for any extended period of time. This is because the adapter card's buffer may fill faster than the card can transfer data, in which case the card will stop accepting new data until the buffer frees.

In both of the above methods of data transfer, there is a two-step procedure for getting data from one end of the adapter to the other. First, data goes into the adapter card's buffer, and then the buffer is flushed to the computer's CPU for processing. This brings us to a method that does not use an intermediary stopping point in the transfer of data.

Bus Master and DMA Direct Transfer

In this method of data transfer, the adapter card has its own intelligent processor embedded on the card. This processor takes control of the computer's BUS from the main CPU and performs its own memory transfer. In this mode of operation, there is usually no explicit I/O Port address or shared memory address because the adapter can map itself into any RAM address that's required as needed.

This method of data transfer can be very efficient for moving large amounts of data for consistently long time frames. Unfortunately, for small data transfers, it is exceptionally inefficient due to the overhead imposed by having to have the CPU on the adapter setup and perform its own memory transfers.

Common Addresses Used by Various Devices

The settings used on your NIC must not conflict with the settings used by anything else in your computer (with few exceptions). The following tables list some of the most commonly used settings:

Table A.1
Commonly Used Interrupts by Device

IRQ level	Use by PC (8088/8086)	Use by AT and up (80x86)
0	System RAM	System RAM
1	Keyboard	Keyboard
2	Video	Cascade
3	COM 2/4	COM 2/4
4	COM 1/3	COM 1/3
5	Hard Disk	LPT 2
6	Floppy Controller	Floppy Controller
7	LPT 1	LPT 1/3
8	N/A	System (clock)
9	N/A	Video
A	N/A	Open
B	N/A	Open
C	N/A	Open
D	N/A	Open
E	N/A	ISA Disk
F	N/A	Open

Table A.2
Commonly Used Shared Memory Addresses

A000 - AFFF	64K	VGA Graphics
B000 - B7FF	32K	Unused
B800 - BFFF	32K	VGA Text
C000 - C7FF	32K	Video ROM
C800 - C9FF	8K	DISK ROM
CA00 - DFFF	88K	High RAM
E000 - EFFF	64K	EMS Memory Page Frame
F000 - FFFF	64K	System ROM

Commonly Used I/O Port Addresses

Although there aren't many conflicts that one would have to worry about normally, there are a couple that need to be defined.

378h - LPT 1

This can become a problem when using a LAN card that used PIO transfers through port address 360h. Many LAN cards use a 32 byte (20h) window, which will range from 360h to 380h and overlaps the LPT 1 port address at 378h. This can cause printers to malfunction, or LAN cards to lose the network when printing starts.

2E8h - VGA Video Reset

This can be a problem for any LAN card that is set to use I/O Address 2E0h. This is because the xE8h line is the RESET for the whole address window. This is a problem when using any application that is written to use hardware reset of the Video channel to clear or scroll the display.

Communication Drivers and Redirectors

After the workstation is assembled and functioning, it's time to make the connection to the fileserver itself. You do this by loading into the workstation's memory the LAN Card communication drivers, the Protocol drivers, and the Shell or Redirector. As with the hardware for Macintosh and Unix workstations, much of this is integrated into the workstation's operating system. This leaves DOS/Windows and OS/2 PCs that need to be properly configured to communicate with the fileservers.

Many of the concepts between DOS and OS/2 workstations are the same when loading the drivers and redirectors, with the major difference being where you load the drivers from. In OS/2 workstations, you would add the drivers to the CONFIG.SYS, while in DOS workstations, you load the drivers in the AUTOEXEC.BAT.

A basic DOS workstation's AUTOEXEC.BAT may look similar to this.

```
@ECHO OFF
LSL
NE2000
IPXODI
NETX
F:
PROMPT $P$G
LOGIN
```

This loads, in order, the Link Support Layer driver, the common interface between the computer and the LAN card specific drivers;

then the LAN card specific driver, also known as the MLID (Multi-Link Interface Driver), which enables the specific LAN card installed in the workstation;

then the Protocol Stack Driver, in this case IPXODI, which provides the IPX and SPX protocol stack;

then the Client Shell, which redirects network requests from the local operating system to the network's services.

The parameters and configuration options that the LAN Drivers and Shells are capable of using are defined in the NET.CFG file that is stored on the workstation's boot disk. The commands placed in this file control such things as the Frame Type the protocol driver will utilize, the maximum packet size the workstation will generate, the LAN card's physical configuration, as well as many other options. Following is a list of many of the more common NET.CFG parameters and what they do for your workstation

→   **CACHE BUFFERS=xx.** This controls the amount of RAM reserved at the workstation for caching Non-Shareable Read-Only files and files that are opened in Exclusive mode by applications on the network.

→   **FILE HANDLES=xxx.** This is the network equivalent of the FILES= line in the CONFIG.SYS. The only restraint on the number of file handles you can define is that the total number of FILES= and FILE HANDLES= can not exceed the DOS limitation of 254.

→   **DOS NAME=xxxxx.** This allows you to define the workstation's DOS name, up to five characters long, which gets used in the login scripts by the %OS variable identifier. Using this enables you to have many versions of DOS (both Microsoft and Digital Research/Novell) on your network. Currently the default is MSDOS.

→   **PRINT HEADER=xxx.** Defines the largest printer setup string you can send via Capture using PRINTCON print jobs.

→   **PRINT TAILER=xxx.** Defines the largest printer Reset string you can send via Capture using PRINTCON print jobs.

→   **SHORT MACHINE TYPE.** Allows you to set up a short name, up to four characters long, to identify your specific machine, or group of machines.

→   **LONG MACHINE TYPE.** Allows you to set up a long name, no less than five characters, to identify your specific machine, or groups of machines. This also gets used by the login script when using the %MACHINE variable identifier. The default for this is IBM_PC.

→   **FRAME xxxxx.** This allows you to set the communication type to match any of the available frames for the specific NIC you are using. This can allow you to have multiple data streams on a single network cable, or have specific devices talk to each other without anyone else being able to "see" the data.

As well as identifiers, you can set the LAN card's specific protocol and physical configuration options. Doing so is done through the use of Linking information to a driver or physical adapter. When a Link has multiple options, you would INDENT those options immediately below the LINK statement. Some examples are as follows:

```
LINK DRIVER NE2000
     PORT 300
     INT 5
     FRAME ETHERNET_802.3
PROTOCOL IPX
     Bind 0
```

The preceding example links an Eagle Technology NE2000 LAN card driver to the NIC itself at Interrupt 5 and I/O Address 300 while telling it to use the ETHERNET_802.3 frame type. It also binds, or attaches, the IPX protocol stack to the logical LAN driver assigned to board 0 (the first network driver loaded).

What might be considered a common NET.CFG follows:

```
LINK DRIVER NE2000
     PORT 300
     INT 5
     FRAME ETHERNET_802.3
CACHE BUFFERS=0
FILE HANDLES=45
DOS NAME=DRDOS
LONG MACHINE TYPE=HEWLETT
SHORT MACHINE TYPE=HP
```

Generating IPX Drivers

In NetWare 3.11 and older versions of NetWare the LAN Card Specific Drivers were linked into the Protocol Driver as a single executable program. This involved taking two specific OBJECT files (program code in its native format), IPX.OBJ and the LAN card's specific OBJ file, and linking them together to form one executable program: IPX.COM.

Besides having to link the parts together yourself, there were other differences between the current ODI Drivers and the linkable IPX drivers.

IPX linkable drivers support only one protocol stack at a time

IPX linkable drivers support a limited number of possible physical configurations

IPX linkable drivers do not always support loading in High Memory

IPX linkable drivers do not always support Enhanced Packet Drivers for large internet packet exchange

IPX linkable drivers do not support NetWare Directory Services

But, there are some reasons to continue to use the IPX linkable driver. The foremost reason is that not all LAN cards have ODI Drivers available. For those cases, using the linkable IPX driver is your only option. Taking this into consideration, we will guide you through using the Novell Utility for generating the linked IPX.COM from both floppy-based and hard disk- or network disk-based systems.

Getting Started

Floppy Disk Basics

1. Find the WSGEN and LAN_DRV_001 disks from your NetWare disk set.

2. If your LAN card came with its own driver disk, get it ready.

3. Make working copies of these disks using DISKCOPY. In most cases, these disks are high-density disks; make sure you use the same type to make the copies.

4. Put the WSGEN disk into the A: drive on your workstation.

5. Skip to the "Running WSGEN" section ahead.

Hard Disk Basics

1. Find the WSGEN and LAN_DRV_001 disks from your NetWare disk set.

2. If your LAN card came with its own driver disk, get it ready.

3. Make working copies of these disks using DISKCOPY. In most cases, these disks are high density disks; make sure you use the same type to make the copies.

4. Change to the hard disk of your choice; you can use a local hard disk or a network drive. For example, if you want to use the C: drive you would type C: at the prompt.

5. Make a NetWare directory on the hard disk.

```
MD NETWARE
```

6. Change to the NetWare directory.

```
CD NETWARE
```

7. Make directories to match the disk volume names for the disks you have copied, or to match the volume name the LAN driver manufacturer suggests in its documentation.

NOTE

If you do not have the documentation for a particular LAN Driver set, you can, in most cases, determine the necessary volume name by using the DOS TYPE command to print the LAN Driver Specification File (*.LAN) on the disk. You can issue the following command:

```
TYPE S3C503.LAN
```

You will get a response similar to the following:

```
 LAN_DRV_180)3Com 3c503 EtherLink II  V3.00EC
(900507)HA:S3C503(IRQ = 3, I/O Base = 300h, RAM = DC00,
BNC)IRQ = 2, I/O Base = 310h, RAM = D800, DIXIRQ = 4,
I/O Base = 330h, BNCIRQ = 3, I/O Base = 300h,
DIX&Driver Configurable by Jumpers Utility
```

The volume name/directory name is specified in the upper left corner by the specification:

```
LAN_DRV_180
```

You would either use the DOS LABEL command to set the disk name using the following command:

```
LABEL A:LAN_DRV_180
```

Or create a directory with this name using the following command:

```
MD LAN_DRV_.180
```

Make at least the following directories in the NETWARE subdirectory.

```
MD WSGEN
MD LAN_DRV_.001
```

8. Copy the WSGEN.EXE file from the WSGEN disk into the NETWARE directory. Use the following command:

```
COPY A:\WSGEN.EXE
```

9. Change into the WSGEN directory using the following command:

   ```
   CD WSGEN
   ```

10. Copy the entire WSGEN disk content into this directory. You would use the following command:

    ```
    COPY A:\*.* *.*
    ```

11. Change back up to the LAN_DRV_001 directory using the following command:

    ```
    CD ..\LAN_DRV_.001
    ```

12. Place the LAN_DRV_001 disk in the A: drive and copy the contents to this directory using the following command:

    ```
    COPY A:\*.* *.*
    ```

13. If you have a specific LAN Driver disk from the LAN card manufacturer, you would change directory back to that directory and copy the disk's contents to the directory using the previous commands.

14. Change Directory back to the NETWARE directory using the following command:

    ```
    CD ..
    ```

15. You are now ready to run the linker utility.

Running WSGEN

1. From either the A: drive when using disks, or from the NETWARE directory using a hard disk or network disks, issue the following command to start the generation utility:

   ```
   WSGEN
   ```

2. You see a menu explaining your options. Press F10 to take you to the next option. Press ESC to exit.

3. Select the LAN Driver that is specific to your NIC and press ENTER from the list of available drivers.

4. Select the LAN card physical configuration option from the list of driver options presented. This *must* match what the LAN card is physically configured for.

NOTE

Some LAN card drivers have an option that is listed as Driver Configurable by Jumpers Utility. This is an option that enables you to select any of the listed configuration options in any combination rather than using one of the preselected options. This offers some additional flexibility to the hardware options you can set your LAN card for. JUMPERS.EXF is a single menu, self-explanatory configuration utility used after generating the linked IPX.COM.

5. After selecting the LAN driver options, press F10 to continue. If you are running from floppy disk, it will ask you to insert the proper LAN_DRV_xxx disk. In a matter of moments, the generation process will be complete, and you will be prompted to press ENTER to continue.

6. Copy the generated IPX.COM from the WSGEN directory on the hard disk or network drive, or from the WSGEN disk to the workstation's boot drive. If you selected a Jumpers Configurable driver, you would now run the JUMPERS utility to configure the IPX.COM.

After copying the newly generated IPX.COM and Shell to the workstation boot disk, add the appropriate commands to load them into the workstation's memory at boot. To do this you would use a text editor to change your AUTOEXEC.BAT to look something like this:

```
@ECHO OFF
IPX
NETX
F:
LOGIN
```

Network Wire
and Wiring Options

The heart and soul of any network is the cabling plant that it runs on. This is the single most critical part of the network, outside of the fileserver, and the one which usually receives the least respect when the network is in the planning stages. What follows is a basic guide for some of the more popular network protocols and topologies for a Local Area Network. Included in this discussion will be:

→ Ethernet

→ Token Ring

→ ARCnet

Ethernet

For the Ethernet protocol, there are many options available for topology (physical layout) and cable type. One thing to keep in mind is that no matter what the physical topology, Ethernet is a linear bus system. This simply means that there is a single start and end point on the cable system, with each node attaching off a parallel connection, as shown in figure C.1.

Figure C.1

An Ethernet topology.

The preceding illustration can be used to illustrate any of the Ethernet options by describing it a little differently for each option.

For Thinnet (also called cheapernet) and Thicknet coax, the layout in the figure would be one network segment with 50 Ohm terminators at each side of the cable segment and nodes attached directly off the cable.

For 10BaseT, fiber optic, and multi-port coax installations, the horizontal line would represent the repeater or concentrator (hub) with nodes plugged into that.

The physical media, or type of cable that can be used for Ethernet, include the following:

➜ Thin coax, IEEE Thin Ethernet, RG-58C/U, or equivalent

➜ Thick coax, IEEE Thick Ethernet, Belden 9880, or equivalent

➜ 10BaseT, IBM Type 3 Grade (Category or Level) 3, or higher

➜ Fiber optic

Each type of media has its own distance and node limitations, but each passes the full network signal at full bandwidth. In other words, you don't go slower on 10BaseT than you do on fiber optic using Ethernet. It is possible to daisy chain the same media type, or mixed media type cable systems to extend the maximum distance limitations.

1. Thin Ethernet has a maximum distance limitation of 185 meters or 607 feet and 30 nodes per segment.

WARNING
You do not want to mix different types of coaxial cable on the same network segment. Ethernet requires a very specific signalling capability and electrical properties of the wire it travels on, and mixing different types of RG-58 together on a single segment could cause problems due to the slight differences in the signal and electrical properties of the cable. You should only use coax that is specifically marked IEEE Thin Ethernet on the jacket, or RG-58C/U, to maintain system communication integrity.

2. Thick Ethernet has a maximum distance limitation of 500 meters or 1640 feet and 100 nodes per segment.

3. 10BaseT has a maximum distance limitation of 100 meters or 325 feet with a single node per cable segment.

4. Fiber Optic has a maximum distance limitation of 2 kilometers, or 6,550 feet (just over 1 mile) with a single node per cable segment.

You can configure the topology of Ethernet in a physical bus using Thick or Thin coax; or a distributed star using Thin coax, 10BaseT, and fiber optic using a repeater (also known as a concentrator or hub).

One other option for Ethernet is known as Broadband. Broadband uses a different signaling method that allows much greater distances, up to 3,600 meters or 11,800 feet per segment. It also allows for multiple signal types on each cable, thus allowing closed circuit TV, voice and telephone, and other signals to be passed on the same cable as the Ethernet data. This makes Broadband a very good option for government agencies, education facilities, and large industry because they can make more efficient use of a single expensive cable system with it.

Token Ring

As the name implies, this protocol uses a topology that runs in circles. Although the cable does not have to physically appear as a circle, it must be a closed loop system with no open "start" or "end" points. Each node attaches to the network through a parallel connection off the main ring. The connection is made through a Multistation Access Unit (MAU) or Lobe Access Modual (LAM). See figure C.2.

Figure C.2

A Token Ring topology.

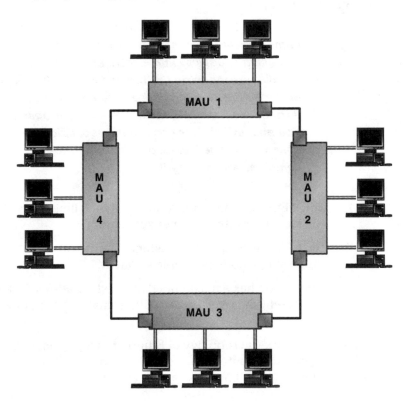

The distances you can run on a Token Ring network depend on a variety of things, including the type of cable media you use and the speed the ring is running on. You have two options for speed, 4 Megabits per second and 16 Megabits per second. There are several options for cabling, most of which are just different configurations of the same cables.

IBM Type 1   Shielded Twisted Pair (STP)

IBM Type 2   Shielded Twisted Pair w/2 UTP pairs

IBM Type 3	Unshielded Twisted Pair (UTP) Grade 3 for 4 Mb/s, grade 4 or 5 for 16 Mb/s
IBM Type 5	Fiber Optic

To determine maximum Node distances from the MAU, you need to determine the total ring length. This can be done using the following guidelines, but for exact calculations and recommendations you should consult the *IBM Token-Ring Network Introduction and Planning Guide*, IBM Part Number GA27-3677.

Add up the length of cable in the main ring (all the cable between MAUs). Add 25 feet for each MAU. Add the length of the longest lobe. For a 4Mb ring, that number has to be less than 1200ft.; for a 16Mb ring, 550ft.

The prior paragraph assumes type 1 or type 2 cable. If you're using type 3, multiply the physical length of each type 3 cable by 1.5.

Because the main ring path affects the maximum lobe length, you should never use anything but type 1 or 2 in the main ring. If you need to go further distances, there are always Token Ring repeaters (like the IBM 8220).

Any of the data grade cables (types 1, 2, and 3) may be freely mixed on the network, but you have to adjust the "effective" length of the type 3 media.

When using fiber optics in the main ring, you have the benefit of the cable imposing a 0 foot distance length on the total ring length. What this means is that you can have a 500-foot segment of fiber optic between MAUs on different floors, or in different buildings on your campus, and the length of the fiber itself does not have to be added into the total ring length calculations.

ARCnet

For ARCnet there are three basic options available for cable type, and two options available for topology. As with Ethernet, ARCnet is a linear bus, but it's been designed to be a *distributed* linear bus. What this means is that the bus is maintained for each cable segment in the hub, and you distribute the bus off the hub. You can also have parallel attachments off the bus in high impedance installations, or with UTP cable systems.

The physical media that ARCnet uses is either RG-62 coax, Unshielded Twisted Pair, or fiber optic. Each media type has its own limitations as to the distance you can run. You also have the ability to use RG-62 coax in either a STAR or BUS distribution pattern. An example of combining both is as follows (see fig. C.3):

Figure C.3
An ARCnet topology.

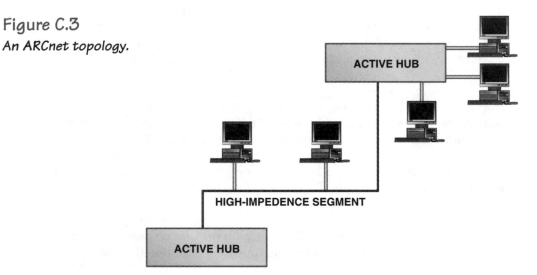

Each type of media has its own distance and node limitations, but each passes the full network signal at full bandwidth. In other words, you don't go slower on UTP than you do on Fiber Optic using ARCnet. It is possible to daisy chain the same media type, or mixed media type cable systems, to extend the maximum distance limitations.

1. RG-62 coax, in a STAR configuration, has a maximum distance limitation of 2000 feet and one node per segment. You can also daisy chain active hubs off ports, which would count as one node.

2. RG-62 coax, in a BUS configuration, has a maximum distance limitation of 1000 feet and can support up to 10 nodes per segment. Each end of the segment *must* be terminated by a 93 ohm ARCnet terminator. This can be either a Resistor Cap terminator, a STAR configuration LAN Adapter (which would also count as one of the connections on the segment), or an Active Hub port.

3. Type 3 UTP has a maximum distance limitation of 325 feet with up to 10 nodes per cable segment. Each end of the UTP ARCnet segment *must* be terminated by a 100 ohm ARCnet terminator. This can be internally mounted in an ARCnet Active UTP Hub.

NOTE

Thomas Conrad Corp. has its enhanced ARCnet TP+ product that has the capability to run on high quality Unshielded Twisted Pair for a distance of up to 800 feet. This is not the standard and the use of this adapter would impose a restriction to use this adapter and hubs throughout the network.

4. Fiber optic has a maximum distance limitation of more than 3000 feet with a single node per cable segment.

Don't Panic!
It's Only NetWare
REGISTRATION CARD

NRP

Fill out this card to receive information about future NetWare books and other New Riders titles!

Name _____ **Title** _____

Company _____

Address _____

City/State/ZIP _____

I bought this book because: _____

_____

I purchased this book from:

☐ A bookstore (Name _____)

☐ A software or electronics store (Name _____)

☐ A mail order (Name of catalog _____)

I purchase this many computer books each year:

☐ 1–5   ☐ 6 or more

I currently use these applications: _____

_____

_____

_____

I found these chapters to be the most informative: _____

_____

I found these chapters to be the least informative: _____

_____

Additional comments: _____

_____

☐ I would like to see my name in print! You may use my name and quote me in future New Riders products and promotions. My daytime phone number is: _____

New Riders Publishing 201 West 103rd Street • Indianapolis, Indiana 46290 USA

Fold Here

PLACE
STAMP
HERE

New Riders Publishing
201 West 103rd Street
Indianapolis, Indiana 46290
USA

WANT MORE
INFORMATION?

CHECK OUT THESE RELATED TITLES:

	QTY	PRICE	TOTAL

Inside Novell NetWare, Special Edition. This #1 selling tutorial/reference is perfect for beginning system administrators. Each network management task is thoroughly explained and potential trouble spots are noted. The book also includes a disk with an extremely easy to use workstation menu program, an MHS-capable E-Mail program, and workgroup management tools. ISBN: 1-56205-096-6.

QTY ____ PRICE $34.95 TOTAL ____

NetWare 4: Planning and Implementation. The ultimate guide to planning, installing, and managing a NetWare 4.0 network. This book explains how best to implement the new features of NetWare 4.0 and how to upgrade to NetWare 4.0 as easily and efficiently as possible. ISBN: 1-56205-159-8.

QTY ____ PRICE $27.95 TOTAL ____

Downsizing to NetWare. Get the real story on downsizing with *Downsizing to NetWare*. This book identifies applications that are suitable for use on LANs and shows how to implement downsizing projects. This book lists the strengths and weaknesses of NetWare—making it perfect for managers and system administrators. ISBN: 1-56205-071-0.

QTY ____ PRICE $39.95 TOTAL ____

LAN Operating Systems. Learn how to connect the most popular LAN operating systems. All major LAN operating systems are covered, including: NetWare 3.11, Appleshare 3.0, Banyan VINES 5.0, UNIX, LAN Manger 2.1, and popular peer-to-peer networks. The following client operating systems are covered as well: MS-DOS, Windows, OS/2, Macintosh System 7, and UNIX. This book clears up the confusion associated with managing large networks with diverse client workstations and multiple LAN operating systems. ISBN: 1-56205-054-0.

QTY ____ PRICE $39.95 TOTAL ____

Name _____

Company _____

Address _____

City _____ State ____ ZIP _____

Phone _____ Fax _____

☐ Check Enclosed   ☐ VISA   ☐ MasterCard

Card # _____ Exp. Date _____

Signature _____

Prices are subject to change. Call for availability and pricing information on latest editions.

Subtotal _____

Shipping _____

$4.00 for the first book and $1.75 for each additional book.

Total _____
Indiana residents add 5% sales tax.

New Riders Publishing 201 West 103rd Street • Indianapolis, Indiana 46290 USA

Orders/Customer Service: 1-800-541-6789
Fax: 1-800-448-3804

NetWare LAN Workstation Record Template

This form can be kept blank and copied; all subsequent changes or system additions can then be logged and kept at hand.

➜ Current workstation owner: _____

➜ Serial no.:_____

➜ Network address for board A: (and B:): _____

➜ Installed by: _____ _____ _____ _____

➜ Type of workstation: _____

➜ Floppy disk size and capacity: _____

➜ Memory: Base: _____
              Extended: _____
              Expanded: _____
              TOTAL: _____

➜ Internal hard disks: Size: _____   Driver type: _____

➜ Network boards: (name, option number, I/O address, memory address, Interrupt (IRQ), DMA channel, station/node address, slot number) _____
_____
_____
_____
_____
_____
_____

➜ LAN driver (LAN A: , LAN B:): _____

➜ Boot information: (hard disk, floppy, remote reset) _____

➜ Remote reset checklist: (Network board set to configuration option 0_____;
remote reset PROM(s) installed on LAN board_____; remote reset enabled on
network board _____; remote boot file name
_____

➜ DOS version: _____

➜ Files needed to connect to the network: (ipx.com, net4.com or net3.com,
or EMSNET or XMSNET; NETBIOS.EXE and INT2F.COM; others:; SHELL.CFG
options:) _____
_____
_____

This record should be kept with printouts of this workstation's AUTQEXEC.BAT, CONFIG.SYS, and WIN.INI files (usually found in either C: or A: drives).

NetWare v3.11 and v3.12 User Rights

Right	Description
Access control	Grants the right to modify trustee assignments and the Inherited Rights Mask for the file. Users having this right can grant rights that they themselves have not been given. Users cannot grant the supervisory right, however.
Create	Grants the right to salvage a file after it has been deleted.
Erase	Grants the right to delete the file.
File scan	Grants the right to see the file in a directory listing.
Modify	Grants the right to alter file attributes and to rename the file. To modify the contents of a file, the user must have the Write right.
Read	Grants the right to open the file and examine its contents.
Supervisory	Grants all rights to thedirectory, its files, and its subdirectories. Also grants all rights to individual files. Supervisory rights circumvent all restrictions, including the Inherited Rights Masks. Users having this right can grant Supervisory rights to users or groups. The Supervisory right can only be revoked from the directory to which it was granted, not from the files or subdirectories.
Write	Grants the right to open the file and modify its contents.